New Cultural Identitarian Political Movements in Developing Societies

I0130866

Applying an intercultural and comparative theoretical approach across Asia and Africa, this book analyses the rise and moderation of political movements in developing societies which mobilise popular support with references to conceptions of cultural identity. The author includes not only the Hindu nationalist movement but also many Islamist political movements in a single category – New Cultural Identitarian Political Movements (NCIPM). Demonstrating significant similarities in the pattern of evolution between these and European Christian Democracy, the book provides an instrument for the analysis of these movements outside the parameters of the fundamentalism debate.

The book looks at a number of key variables for understanding the evolution of NCIPM, and it goes on to analyse the transition of developing societies from rent-based political economies to capitalism and the (partial) failure of this transition process. It argues that there is a need to incorporate economic and class analysis in the study of political processes in developing societies against the continuing emphasis on cultural factors associated with the 'cultural turn' of social sciences. The book is an interesting contribution to studies in South Asian Politics, as well as Comparative Politics.

Sebastian Schwecke teaches South Asian Politics at the Centre for Modern Indian Studies (CeMIS), University of Göttingen, Germany.

Routledge advances in South Asian studies
Edited by Subrata K. Mitra
South Asia Institute, University of Heidelberg, Germany

South Asia, with its burgeoning, ethnically diverse population, soaring econo-mies, and nuclear weapons, is an increasingly important region in the global context. The series, which builds on this complex, dynamic and volatile area, features innovative and original research on the region as a whole or on the countries. Its scope extends to scholarly works drawing on history, politics, development studies, sociology and economics of individual countries from the region as well those that take an interdisciplinary and comparative approach to the area as a whole or to a comparison of two or more countries from this region. In terms of theory and method, rather than basing itself on any one orthodoxy, the series draws broadly on the insights germane to area studies, as well as the tool kit of the social sciences in general, emphasising comparison, the analysis of the structure and processes, and the application of qualitative and quantitative methods. The series welcomes submissions from established authors in the field as well as from young authors who have recently completed their doctoral dissertations.

New Cultural Identitarian Political Movements in Developing Societies

The Bharatiya Janata Party

Sebastian Schwecke

R Routledge
Taylor & Francis Group

LONDON AND NEW YORK

First published 2011
by Routledge
2 Park Square, Milton Park, Abingdon, Oxfordshire OX14 4RN

Simultaneously published in the USA and Canada
by Routledge
711 Third Avenue, New York, NY 10017

First issued in paperback 2015

Routledge is an imprint of the Taylor & Francis Group, an informa business

Typeset in Times by Wearset Ltd, Boldon, Tyne and Wear

British Library Cataloguing in Publication Data
A catalogue record for this book is available from the British Library

Library of Congress Cataloging in Publication Data
Schwecke, Sebastian.
New cultural identitarian political movements in developing societies: the
Bharatiya Janata Party/Sebastian Schwecke.
p. cm. – (Routledge advances in South Asian studies; 19)
Includes bibliographical references and index.
1. Bharatiya Janata Party. 2. Group identity–Political aspects–India.
3. India–Politics and government–1977– 4. India–Ethnic relations–
Political aspects. I. Title.
JQ298.B55S39 2011
324.254′083–dc22

2010027554

ISBN 13: 978-1-138-94815-0 (pbk)
ISBN 13: 978-0-415-59596-4 (hbk)

For Michaela

Contents

Illustrations

Foreword

New cultural identitarian political movements in a global perspective

Hartmut Elsenhans

The decline of secular nationalist forces creates apprehension in western countries. The decolonisation process has been considered as at least a partial success: The retreating colonial powers were able to negotiate the conditions of the transition to independence with forces which they considered as culturally close to them. Schwecke describes the decline of these typically secular forces as the result of their failure in delivering sufficient results concerning economic development on the basis of state-led industrialisation combined with the modernisation of the lower and more distant strata of society which were expected to be slowly absorbed by either the highly capital-intensive modern sector or by an increasingly market-oriented and modernising small-scale industry.

New cultural identitarian movements trace their origin back to the same period as the national liberation movements and are asserting that they form an important element as cultural nationalists, within a specific framework of the political economy in which this decline of the secular forces took place and which provides the tools the new cultural identitarian movements need for their political success. A central element of this political framework is formed by the persisting significance of rents for political mobilisation. The main goal of all rising forces is to participate in the allocation of these rents. If rents are declining in significance, the main goal of these forces is to keep the old forces from continuing to use the rent in order to maintain their political predominance via patronage and clientelism. The success of the old secular forces to monopolise rent allocation constitutes an important variable in the political strategy of rising movements. In the case of India, the political framework has been characterised by increasing rent scarcity since at least the 1970s. Schwecke argues that under these conditions the process of the replacement or partial replacement of the old secular nationalist forces by the newly rising cultural identitarian movements will largely tend to facilitate political moderation, provided that the established political culture of a society is sufficiently open to facilitate accommodation between established and rising social strata.

Within a pattern of possible configurations, the case of the BJP in India is presented as being highly conducive to accommodation and political moderation. The conflict between the colonial power and the local forces which gave rise to the national liberation movement in which the secular forces and the cultural nationalists to some extent found common ground is characterised in India by a low level of experience of deep wounds. Especially concerning foreign policy, Schwecke observes that the former colonial powers are treated with distance and distrust but not with hatred. This results in an image of the west in which curiosity and admiration still mix with the wish for distance and assertion of difference, in contrast to the relation between much of the Islamic world and the west, but probably very close to many cultural nationalist tendencies outside the Islamic world.

The various shifts within the Hindu nationalist movement can be linked to a multiplicity of interactive processes at various levels but ultimately do not only explain changes in the orientation of the movement, but allow to assess the probability of its stability. One major interactive process is formed by the participation in the organisational structure of Indian politics in which accommodative strategies become important, especially if one tries to maintain acquired positions of influences. The success of the BJP in expanding its social base shows that cultural identitarian issues matter in the long term if they are proposed in a non-divisive manner. Winning over social strata with cultural identitarian topics requires putting them in a way in which they do not appear as possible issues for rising civil war, which Indian public opinion desperately fears. In order to become attractive, the cultural identitarian programme has to be supplemented by other policies. The main champions of cultural identitarian values in India had originally been the small town petty bourgeoisie, especially traders. The party realised that apart from cultural identitarian issues, it had to accommodate the views of these social strata and develop a vaguely liberal economic policy, supplemented by elements of a moral economy which – in the Indian discourse – could be derived from Gandhian ideas. This forms a path-dependent process because in adopting these additional topics, the party had to accommodate various contradictory demands from its original cultural identitarian constituency. As a result, BJP economic policy became characterised by a pragmatic, vaguely liberal economic programme which at the same time tried to win over additional segments of public opinion by complementing it with select social policies.

'Shining India,' a party slogan the BJP had selected in 2004, reinforced traditionally held notions and hopes of India's new middle strata which had emerged as a result of state-led industrialisation efforts, but which did not find appropriate jobs in an ultimately too slowly growing modern sector. For these newly rising young generation the only way to open up new opportunities consisted in proposing new qualifications which the entrenched elites did not possess. The extension of education had touched more and more milieus outside the metropolises, characterised by a lower level of command of the colonisers' language and a greater identification with local values and the vernacular languages. Hindi therefore became a major issue for these strata. Cultural identitarian values emerged as distinct characteristics of a rising new middle class.

At the same time, increasing rent scarcity compromised the social and political predominance of the secular nationalist elites. Less people benefited from rent allocation processes and those who were ejected from the mechanisms of rent allocation tended to consider themselves as victims of an illicit practice. Even if originally committed to the rent-based state-led model of industrialisation, the rising middle strata of society increasingly began to perceive the state as a rapacious tax collector which used its resources in a corrupt manner. The BJP was able to reach out to the rising new strata which were obliged to enhance their status under conditions of competition by introducing a new requirement (the identification with national culture), to parts of the old middle strata which returned from their dependence on the state to a more traditional definition of moral economy and – if to a lesser degree – to the increasingly left out poor who wanted some minimum subsistence programmes by proposing a relatively conventional moral economy doctrine which essentially favours the market, complementing it with select social programmes and a cautious industrial policy in favour of maintaining the political and military power of India and consequently high technology sectors.

In order to rise, the BJP could not rely on assembling the pre-existing 'civil society' of India, since these strata and especially their political leadership were already allied to the Congress. Unable and in many cases also unwilling to become allied to the Congress, Hindu nationalism by necessity could only rise if it was able to create an alternative political organisation. As a consequence, the RSS emerged as the principal focus of the Hindu nationalist movement, imbibing the latter with a strong preference for cadre-based political organisation, coupled with a trenchant for strict organisational coherence. Within the cadre-based organisations of the Hindu nationalist movement, generational issues play a role. Entrenched cadres had entered the movement at a time when the cultural identitarian agenda had been prominent. Therefore, if the leadership of the BJP realised that for electoral purposes it needed to emphasise a different agenda, this new emphasis needed to be convincingly conveyed to the cadres. Over time, with the entry of new cadres in a changed political environment, changes in the party's direction may become established.

In opposition to preconceived ideas, Schwecke shows in his case study on the BJP in Aligarh that this enlargement of the agenda has been adopted by the cadres, especially because in a cultural identitarian movement the turn to economics does not imply a precise programme, but relatively imprecise notions and principles. Schwecke's work shows that the Hindu nationalist discourse at the centre, especially concerning its foundations in moral economy, is characterised by pragmatism within a larger framework of overriding principles which correspond to the value system of the cultural nationalists. The question therefore is not which programme to adopt, but to what extent the new issues can be privileged in relation to the core issues of cultural nationalism in India.

The agendas of cultural identitarian movements are relatively favourable for such strategies as they allow the combination of principled statements within a framework which is by and large imprecise. The BJP leadership in this way is able to protect the party's opening to the middle classes against possible resistance to the course correction by the cadres by a moral economy discourse with imprecise models of how to run the economy.

Schwecke's work makes a major contribution to the relation between a realist theory of action and a constructivist interpretation of action. Those who have to deal with the real challenges, e.g. the economy or foreign policy, have to create coalitions on the basis of relatively vague over-arching principles which enable them to bring the practical decisions to be taken into correspondence with the principles of possible support groups. It is the art of the politicians to try to present the issues in line with these world-views, to appeal to world-views which are compatible with these overall goals. In this endeavour, politicians will use the available ideas of a society like a quarry in order to locate elements for the political mobilisation of loosely interrelated views and emotions. Characteristic of these views is their imprecision, but imprecision has the disadvantage that commitment of any particular group centred on these issues is also limited. Accordingly, ideas have to be found which are, at the same time, sufficiently vague and sufficiently precise to generate commitment among the core sup-porters without facilitating polarisation within the movement.

The BJP did precisely this in turning towards the Ayodhya issue in the early 1990s in order to counter caste-based affirmative action policies, *mandir* versus Mandal. Its overall strategy of cultural nationalism would have required the BJP to go along with the Congress line on affirmative action policies. The necessity to maintain the class interest of its original support base required to undo any attempt to provide reservations for lower caste groups as the higher castes would have lost political influence. In order to keep lower classes and lower castes from identifying with the reservation policy, a competing idea of unity had to be found. This was the construction of the Hindu temple in the place of a Muslim mosque. It led to a polarisation between Hindus and Muslims on an issue where the 'Hindu' soul is really hurt, the Muslim occupation of India and the perceived second class status of the Hindu population.

The BJP strategy on the Mandal–*mandir* issue allows drawing one further important result from Schwecke's work: It shows that the radicalism of Hindu nationalism and its militancy are not specifically linked to cultural identitarian ideology. The ideology of the BJP in foreign policy relations is by and large accommodative. The secondary origin of the violence does not stem from any ideological inheritance, but from the necessity to find something emotionally sufficiently strong in order to assemble social support, so that the class-based conflict which became expressed in the reservations issue can be overcome.

Although Schwecke does not draw all the richness of the conclusions of his work, he is a major scientific witness for the fact that the clash of civilisations is an unscientific notion based on ignorance. Never Huntington was aware that inde-pendently of the contents he attributes to cultures, their tendency to violence is not derived from any such historical heritage, but simply from the fact that in a mod-ernisation process, the failure of developing mass employment through industriali-sation implies that – to the difference of the typical European party system – the class issue cannot be allowed to become the major cleavage in society because in contrast to the western historical experience it does not necessarily create large tendencies for co-operation based on the mutual interdependence of capital and labour, but may really be divisive since the material issue of the class conflict is not a distributional issue of the capitalist type but of a rentier type. In the capitalist type, the empowerment of labour leads to more consumption which leads to more investment and ultimately profit. The distributional issue in a not yet capitalist society is oriented to the distribution of rents. The struggle over the allocation of rents forms a zero-sum game. Hence, classes which compete over rent are pitted against each other much more strongly than the two classes of a capitalist society.

If a political party rises due to the fact that the secular, modernising forces failed, this party cannot ignore economics. The BJP had to introduce a moral discourse on economics and it was not able to rely only on its cultural identitarian core issues. Typically, the cadres think that the core issues are the most important aspect and economic policies form simply a subordinate issue which the party needs for a comprehensive political programme. In reality, in order to attract social strata to the core issues of cultural nationalism, the less committed cultural nationalists need to be convinced that they have an economic stake in cultural identitarian issues. This stake cannot be provided in a class-based programme. It has to be packed into something else, just as in the case of European cultural nationalists, e.g. the German nationalists in Brunschwig's analysis of the crisis of the Prussian state and romanticism. Cultural nationalists may use a society's traditions like a quarry, but many issues which can be used for the political mobilisation of identity are relatively vague and have only a limited reach which will normally inhibit strong mass support. In order to use this cultural sphere independently of its contents, the issues have to be presented as extremely important, as a sort of drama.

Here Schwecke's work nicely complements Brass' work which shows that communal riots in India correspond to a pseudo-dramatic structure behind which there may be a very simple everyday issue. Schwecke argues that the prospect of a non-violent character of the BJP will depend on whether the BJP is able to manage the daily problematic of economic and political development of India in a way which is satisfactory for a sufficient number of support groups. In this way the BJP can emerge as a conservative party, partially supplemented by 'social democratic' policies and packaged in a discourse on national self-respect and increasingly concerned with the external projection of Indian national identity. Globally, cultural identitarian movements in this way may facilitate the emergence of a relatively saturated system of major powers, of which India will be an important member. And the BJP will remain an important player as long as it is able to combine a cultural identitarian world view with pragmatic politics. The current crisis of the BJP is not due to the fact that cultural identitarian movements have lost their strength, but to the fact that the management of the modernisation processes and the resulting social conflicts is difficult to achieve in such a large country.

Acknowledgements

This research project on the BJP was funded by the Deutsche Forschungs-gemeinschaft (DFG). I wish to express my gratitude to all those who helped me – each in their own way – to carry out the research and work. First and foremost I wish to thank Hartmut Elsenhans, not only for his relentless guidance but – just as importantly – for all the excellent conversations we have had. In many ways, this is my *guru dakshina* to him. Furthermore, I wish to thank Rachid Ouaissa, now University of Marburg, for all his help in developing the details of the NCIPM concept, and for his friendship. I am highly grateful to Subrata Kumar Mitra whose knowledge of India *and* political science provided the early starting point for my engagement with Indian politics.

The support I received at the Department of International Relations at Leipzig University was more than anyone could hope for. I am especially thankful to Heidrun Zinecker who stepped in when my funding ran out after 2008 and con-tinued to provide a congenial atmosphere for work and related activities at the department. Dorit Thieme did all the tedious organisational work associated with my research; I wish to thank her particularly. Lastly, I wish to thank the team of research assistants, who helped with the BJP part of the project and who did more than was due: Bhaswati Chatterjee, Juliane Günther, Kalyani Unkule, Lukas Bauer, and Sarah Albrecht.

I am most thankful for the hospitality I received during my stays in India, especially in Aligarh. I am most grateful for the friendship and hospitality I received before, after, and during my stays in Delhi from Björn Rahm, Tejaswini Apte, Clemens Spiess, Michael Koeberlein, and Anila Chandy. Furthermore, I wish to thank the Centre for the Study of Developing Societies (CSDS), Delhi, and the Delhi office of the South Asia Institute of Heidelberg University for their co-operation. My research would not have been possible without the efforts of Ranbir Jain and Rajendra Sharma, both at Delhi. I would also wish to thank Klaus Voll for his help and hospitality in Delhi.

I am highly grateful for the hospitality shown by the local unit of the BJP in Aligarh city and the staff at the BJP national headquarters in Delhi. Most import-antly, I wish to thank Satyendra Sharma in Aligarh for all his help in arranging interview partners. At the BJP national headquarters, it was Sourabh Malviya who helped me to organise interviews. At the Shri Varshney College, Aligarh, I owe special thanks to S. D. Gupta without whom I could not have conducted the survey of BJP cadres. At the Aligarh Muslim University, I am most obliged to Noor Mohammad for his help with my research and his co-operation with the household survey in Aligarh.

My last 'thank you' is reserved for Michaela who was always the greatest help of all.

Abbreviations

ABVP	Akhil Bharatiya Vidyarthi Parishad
AIADMK	All India Anna Dravida Munnetra Kazhagam
AKP	Adalet ve Kalkinma Partisi
BJP	Bharatiya Janata Party
BJS	Bharatiya Jan Sangh
BLD	Bharatiya Lok Dal
BMS	Bharatiya Mazdoor Sangh
BSP	Bahujan Samaj Party
CBI	Central Bureau of Investigation
FIS	Front Islamique du Salut
HMS	All India Hindu Mahasabha
IAF	Islamic Action Front
IAS	Indian Administrative Service
INC	Indian National Congress
JD	Janata Dal
JD(U)	Janata Dal (United)
JI	Jama'at-i-Islami Pakistan
MB	Muslim Brotherhood
MSP	Mouvement de la Société pour la Paix
NCR	National Capital Region
NDA	National Democratic Alliance
NF	National Front
PAS	Parti Islam se Malaysia
PJD	Parti de la Justice et du Développement
PKS	Partai Keadilan Sejahtera
RJD	Rashtriya Janata Dal
RKP	Rashtriya Kranti Party
RLD	Rashtriya Lok Dal
RSS	Rashtriya Swayamsevak Sangh
SJM	Swadeshi Jagran Manch
SaP	Saaded Partisi
SP	Samajwadi Party
SVD	Samyukta Vidhayak Dal

TD	Telugu Desam
UF	United Front
UP	Uttar Pradesh
UPA	United Progressive Alliance
VHP	Vishwa Hindu Parishad

1 Introduction

The last decade has seen the emergence of movements which propagate cultur-ally or religiously defined conceptions of identity as significant political actors in a variety of developing countries. In India, the *Bharatiya Janata Party* (BJP) led two successive coalition governments between 1998 and 2004 and remained the single largest opposition party afterwards. The *Adalet ve Kalkinma Partisi* (AKP) has remained in power in Turkey since 2002. Across northern Africa, West Asia, and South and South East Asia many other movements have increased their popular support and political influence, among them the *Mouve-ment de la Société pour la Paix* (MSP) and *El Islah* in Algeria, the *Parti de la Justice et du Développement* (PJD) in Morocco, the Muslim Brotherhood and *Al Wasat* in Egypt, the Islamic Action Front (IAF) in Jordan, the *Parti Islam se Malaysia* (PAS) in Malaysia and the *Partai Keadilan Sejahtera* (PKS) in Indo-nesia. The Palestinian *Hamas* has won the parliamentary elections in the Pales-tinian territories in 2006, while the Lebanese *Hizbullah* has reinforced its political influence in recent years.

All these movements have in common that they and the respective ideologies they represent have, at times, been classified as forming part of the fundamental-ist spectrum of politics. While this classification is rejected here, unless being used in a highly vague sense which does not appear to contribute to our under-standing of the nature of the various movements subsumed under this category, the type of movements outlined above have other crucial commonalities. The most significant of these in order to understand the evolution of these move-ments is the role played by them vis-à-vis the potential transition of the societies they are operating in from at least to a significant degree rent-based to increas-ingly capitalist socio-economic and political orders. Where this transition is rela-tively successful, for example in India, it coincides with the emergence of increasingly influential, predominantly capitalist new middle classes in the respective developing countries.

The emergence and rise of the BJP and its predecessor has been linked by various observers to its support among the middle classes, the petty bourgeoisie in the initial stages of its evolution and the new middle classes since the late 1980s. Mostly, however, the party's evolution has been discussed in terms of its cultural identitarian agenda (and radical interpretations of the latter.) Critical studies have tended to highlight the threat Hindu nationalism is perceived to pose to the fabric of Indian society and India's polity, not only by the Hindu nationalist movement's propensity, at times, to employ violent means but also with respect to the unifying aims of the movement and its alleged proximity to authoritarianism which are seen to endanger the principle of 'unity in diversity' underlying the process of nation-building in India.

While it has rarely been doubted that the Hindu nationalist movement should be considered to be anchored in modernity itself, Hindu nationalism as a political and social force, at least in its initial phase, is often linked to a failure of some supportive social segments to adapt to modernity. In this, the debate on Hindu nationalism shows striking similarities with the discourse on movements outside India which also propagate alternative conceptions of identity, defined by religion or, rather, culture: especially Islamist movements. In contrast to the debate on Islamism, the discussion of Hindu nationalism lacks the pervasive sense of urgency, especially in western countries – the effects of the rise of Hindu nationalism in India are not generally perceived to threaten the stability of the western dominated international order to the same extent. This perception has contributed to a relatively low level of concern and, consequently, interest in the topic among the western academe outside the circle of scholars focussing on Indian or South Asian affairs. With some notable exceptions, the study of Hindu nationalism and Islamism (or other structurally similar movements) has remained separated. For the case of Hindu nationalism, this simultaneously results in a lack of broadly comparative perspectives in the analytical approaches employed.

Broadly speaking – and evidently as a rough generalisation – most approaches of studies on movements of recent origin (or prominence) which mobilise support via the propagation of culturally defined alternative conceptions of identity can be divided into three categories: Studies focussing on the origins and development of the ideological discourses of these movements; analyses of political processes, especially violence or processes perceived to threaten secularism, civil liberties, and in case of Islamism national and international stability; and analyses derived from area study approaches which focus on the emergence and evolution of these movements, their respective support bases, or specific policy contents. With reference to Islamist movements, area study approaches have increasingly tended to include comparative perspectives.

Analyses of the support bases of these movements have shown substantial differences, especially in class terms, among various Hindu nationalist and Islamist movements, and the importance of middle class support for some of these movements. However, since these are most often from area studies oriented disciplines, studies which include a theoretical framework based on the significance of political economy for the evolution of Islamist and Hindu nationalist parties remain rare. This is especially deplorable since political economy provides a link between the various movements which serves at least partially to transcend cultural and political contexts and thus facilitates comparison.

The present study of the BJP starts from an assumption of cross-cultural comparability, notwithstanding the fact that some aspects in the evolution of specific

Hindu nationalist and Islamist movements can only be understood within the distinct cultural and political contexts these movements are operating in. The rationale for the cross-cultural comparison of these movements rests with their operation in similar contexts of political economy, of which several sub-types are discernible in the areas in which many of these movements have emerged. The BJP is seen here as one of the most important representatives of a specific sub-group of movements encompassing some, though not all Hindu nationalist and Islamist movements which are classified here as New Cultural Identitarian Political Movements (NCIPM). Their evolution can primarily be understood by the interaction of a specific set of factors pertaining mostly, though not exclusively, to political economy.

The broad theoretical framework for this study was originally developed by Hartmut Elsenhans in the mid-1990s, and elaborated in a research project on the partially isomorphous evolution of the BJP in India and two of the successors of the *Front Islamique du Salut* (FIS) in Algeria, in co-operation with Elsenhans and Rachid Ouaissa who directed and conducted the research on the Algerian case.[1] The theoretical concept of NCIPM is outlined in Chapter 2.

This theoretical framework is based on an interpretation of politics in many developing countries which is influenced by the Elsenhansian understanding of (at least partially) rent-based economies and the possible transition of these societies to a capitalist mode of production (Elsenhans 2009). As these theoretical concepts are not well established in the Indian context, a concise outline of the concepts in the context of the evolution of modern Indian politics is provided in Chapter 3.

The case study of the BJP in India commences in Chapter 4 with an outline of the origins and development of the ideological discourse of the Hindu nationalist movement and its specific adaptation to the context of Indian politics. Chapter 5 traces the development of the BJP after its foundation to the present and the reasons for its emergence as a viable contender for political power in India. Chapter 6 discusses the evolution of the BJP at the regional and local level of Indian politics in two case studies: the North Indian state of Uttar Pradesh and the city of Aligarh. Chapter 7 analyses the process of transformation of the BJP under the impact of the changing context, defined mostly by factors of political economy, and the discursive framework in which this transformation is being established, at the national and the local level. For the latter, the analysis is based on a detailed local case study of the BJP local party unit in Aligarh city. Finally, the general hypotheses of this study are taken up again for the case study of the BJP and the general concept of NCIPM, respectively, in Chapter 8.

The general hypotheses of this study can be shortly summarised as follows: In a number of developing countries, among them India, the political system after de-colonisation depended to a significant degree on rent allocation processes to ensure the continued legitimacy of the established political elites. In the Indian case, socio-economic development and the relatively open political system resulted in increasing rent scarcity from the mid-1960s onwards, since demands for participation in the rent allocation process from rising social strata began to exceed the availability of rents for distribution. The political process, accordingly, resembled a contest between established and rising social strata, notwithstanding intermittent alliances between various strands belonging to the two respective groups. The moderate success of Indian development policy, apart from leading to rent scarcity, increasingly provided new avenues for the relatively prosperous sections of society for the maintenance and improvement of their socio-economic position.

This resulted in a paradigm shift in Indian politics: the advent of economic liberalisation policies and the corresponding emergence of new social coalitions. Economic liberalisation in India essentially constitutes a gradual and selective dismantling of the state's interventionist structure in the economy. It is selective because it tends to concentrate on economic sectors providing comparatively highly-paid employment especially for the new middle classes, a recently emergent conglomerate of the established middle classes and certain rising social strata. While the discursive framework of Indian politics had been characterised by the contest between a discourse based on 'social justice' – the preferred idiom of rising social strata – and a discourse based on 'merit' propagated by the established middle classes, the two discourses increasingly began to co-exist as two separate idioms targeting distinct social strata.

In this context, political parties tend to propagate a combination of the two separate discourses as outlined above, depending on the parties' respective composition of social support. The BJP – as the principal NCIPM in India – strongly benefited from the paradigm shift since some of its core ideological conceptions were highly conducive to its emergence as one of the main representatives of the interests of the new middle classes while, at the same time, augmenting the party's capacity to reach out to select lower class groups. The unifying agenda of Hindu nationalism (if interpreted pragmatically) and its pre-occupation with a culturally defined concept of nationalism as opposed to its only vaguely defined body of economic thought served as a potent (and flexible) tool for political mobilisation.

To establish its presence as a major political force in India encompassing various strata and diverse interests but dominated by its core support from the new middle classes, the BJP turned towards political moderation in the mid-1990s. Notwithstanding the impact of institutional and ideological features pertaining to this course correction, the most important reason for it derived from political economy:

- an increasing realisation on the part of the party's leadership of the need to maintain its presence among the new middle classes by propagating these sections' interests which had to be balanced to some extent by addressing the interests of select lower class sections;
- and an implicit (though often denied) awareness that identity politics serves to facilitate political mobilisation but cannot serve as a substitute for the articulation of sectional (and primarily economic) interests, at least not in the long-term.

In contrast to the institutional and ideological factors pertaining to the party's turn towards political moderation, the factors arising from political economy to a significant degree facilitate path-dependency in the gradual evolution of the BJP to an increasingly moderate centre-right political party. While the turn towards moderation has been challenged within the party and within the larger Hindu nationalist movement, its opponents lack political issues and strategies which could form viable alternatives to the direction of the party's evolution. Essentially, opposition to the turn towards moderation is taking place in a discursive framework which, notwithstanding occasional setbacks, favours the proponents of political moderation as long as the context, especially regarding political economy, remains as defined above.

In its rise and subsequent evolution, the BJP represents a specific sub-category of NCIPM, distinct from other sub-categories by the contextual framework of political economy the various NCIPM are operating in. Hence, in this sub-category, it can be assumed that various NCIPM distinguished by their respective ideological origins and the political and cultural contexts they are operating in, will tend to follow a similar path of development, unless secondary factors gain overarching importance – exemplified by the presence of violent conflict in which an NCIPM is operating as a resistance movement.

2 The theoretical framework

The concept of new cultural identitarian political movements (NCIPM)

> Religion, a central component of culture, becomes an important factor in the struggle for political democracy when it contributes to either concentration or dispersion of social, economic, and political resources.
>
> Abootalebi (2000: 1)

Hindu nationalism and fundamentalism

Discussions on the topic of Hindu nationalism have often conceived this ideology and the Hindu nationalist movement in India within the bounds of the theoretical discourse on right-wing political movements in developing, non-western societies. According to the respective observers' positioning within this discourse – specifically the emphasis placed on either religion as a source of political ideology or authoritarian tendencies within the movement – Hindu nationalism has variously been classified in proximity to either the concepts of fundamentalism[1] or fascism.[2] Since both these classifications appear problematic, other scholars working on Hindu nationalism have tended to situate the ideology in a category of its own, a specifically Indian political phenomenon. These attempts have resulted in a discourse devoid of the trappings associated with the fundamentalism debate and the leftist or liberal rejection of fascism. At the same time, they have tended to isolate the debate on Hindu nationalism from the discourse on related phenomena in other parts of the world: the almost coterminous emergence and rise of political movements in large parts of the developing world which derive ideological sustenance largely from indigenous cultural tradition and, therefore, have tended to reject secular conceptions of politics at least partially.

It is argued here that many of these movements can be subsumed under a single category, irrespective of the cultural content of their respective ideologies and the various political contexts they are operating in, as New Cultural Identitarian Political Movements (NCIPM) – following Elsenhans' attempt to classify certain Islamist and the major strands of the Hindu nationalist movement in the mid-1990s (Elsenhans 1994). Before proceeding to discuss the concept of NCIPM (and its applicability in the case of the BJP) it is necessary to trace the ambiguities that arise from the approximation of these movements with fundamentalism.

The concept of fundamentalism originates from the literature on Christian religious political movements in North America, especially the United States, in the early twentieth century which indicated a revival of political values and sentiments which were perceived to be opposed to modernity and the rational foundation of modern politics (Riesebrodt 1990; 2000). The term fundamentalism later became associated with certain religious revival movements belonging to the spectrum of Semitic religions, most notably Islam, and was then extended to non-Semitic religions and even political ideologies unrelated to religion.[3] The discourse on fundamentalism comprises a significant disconnect between the original narrow definition of the concept and the manifold uses of the term that followed the various extensions of the concept to an increasingly wide range of political phenomena.

Fundamentalism has an ambiguous relationship to religious orthodoxy: While the recourse to religious scriptures supports the orientation towards orthodoxy, the lay character of most fundamentalist movements[4] and its strong emphasis on political action contribute to their emergence as religious reform movements with a tendency to emphasise a simplified version of the respective religion's moral ideas. This, in turn, has in some cases led to the estrangement of traditionally organised religious functionaries, especially those representing historically grown 'folk' traditions.[5]

Fundamentalism's opposition to established political systems is primarily based on their opposition to secularism, not on a socio-economic agenda. Secularism is perceived as the root cause for social ills in that it allegedly distances society and political leaders from the tenets of ethical conduct. Fundamentalism, hence, is about moral and ethical restoration. Often, fundamentalist movements will point to a mythological or superficially interpreted historical past as a role model or reference for a utopian ideal state and society. This affects the fundamentalist perspective on modernity and the perception of fundamentalists by outside observers.

The tendency to refer to a mythical or distant past for political legitimacy or ideological demonstration in itself does not set fundamentalism, even defined narrowly, apart from other political movements in a significant way. The interpretation of a distant past is turned into a point of reference for 'the good society' in the distant future. The 'anti-modern' character of fundamentalism originates neither from a clear opposition to technological progress nor from a reactionary programme to return to a previously established political order. The distance in time to the imagined historical point of reference is too large to allow the latter interpretation, while with regard to the former, technological progress is not generally opposed as such. Instead, the uses of modern technology are opposed if perceived as obstacles in the way of the restoration of morality and ethical behaviour. To illustrate this stance from among the Indian tradition of political thought, the fundamentalist treatment of technological progress in many ways resembles Gandhian political ideas.[6]

The primary focus of fundamentalist movements being the ethical behaviour of individuals and political leaders, other social, economic or political issues are in general not treated as relevant unless they impinge on this focus or are of strategic importance for the movement. This lack of clear and distinct ideological positions on many political issues and, most importantly, on issues of political economy enables fundamentalist movements to pragmatically adapt themselves to widely divergent political contexts, apart from creating an opportunity to enlarge the respective movement's appeal, to some extent transcending class and replacing it with community.

The narrow definition of fundamentalism has to be distinguished, however, from attempts to cover a wider range of political movements using the concept of fundamentalism. One of the most important distinctions in this regard concerns the role of religion: Fundamentalism in the narrow definition is stringently tied to religious doctrine. Religious debate and the interpretation of religious scriptures (or other authoritative sources) takes an important place in the political and ideological discourse of narrowly defined fundamentalist movements, despite the lay character of many fundamentalist movements and its ambivalent relationship to religious orthodoxy (Riesebrodt 2000).

Many movements which are labelled as fundamentalist do not show any strong preference for religious debate even in their internal discourse. Instead, they are strongly concerned with identity, which tends to be denoted in religious terms but is, in fact, closer to the concepts of ethnicity and nationality.[7] These movements may still originate from the narrowly defined fundamentalist spectrum or may have been influenced by it, but have certainly developed core features that set them apart from the latter.

The aim of social (and moral) reform in accordance with a utopian ideal state of society is superseded for these movements by the goal to challenge the politically dominant concepts of identity and group membership. The opposition to secularism is not anymore based on its perceived threat to the moral and ethical foundations of modern life, but instead on the secular concept of national identity by citizenship which places a political system (the state) above cultural criteria.[8]

Religion becomes a more or less notional criterion for inclusion within and exclusion from the community for political movements that are classified as fundamentalist according to the broad definition of the term. Moreover, these movements often display a tendency to weaken the role of religion further by including non-religious cultural attributes, including language and origin, and by excluding certain religious attributes like sect or loyalty to religious schools of thought.[9]

The debate on Huntington's 'clash of civilisations' (Huntington 1993) hypothesis and criticisms of the concept by a variety of authors (including Sen 2006; Said 2001; Berman 2003) as well as efforts to counter the term's increased political utilisation by establishing new definitions, though obviously needed, have instead reinforced the conceptual opacity of fundamentalism.

A relatively recent trend has been the equation of fundamentalism with fanaticism.[10] The equation is partially due to the linkage of fundamentalism with terrorism in much of the public discourse, even more so with regard to terrorist acts associated with the style of Al Qaeda.[11] In turn, the trend of equating fundamentalism with fanaticism has been fuelled further by scholars critical of the mainstream discourse on the topic, leading to the emergence of terms such as 'market fundamentalism' (Soros 1998; French-Davis 2000).

Other authors have focussed on explaining the rise of movements propagating culturally defined concepts of identity without strongly referring to the fundamentalism paradigm. As an example, Lapidus (1997) argues that a variety of movements have recently emerged that can be understood as both a reaction against modernisation in their respective societies and an expression of modernity and modernisation. These comprise religious revival movements, especially among Muslims but also among Hindus, Christians, and Jews, as well as non-religious populist, nationalist, or nativist movements. With reference to Islamic revival movements, Lapidus argues that these follow a traditional model for alternative political movements that have drawn upon cultural and religious identities for the purpose of political mobilisation in times of rapid socio-economic change.

A distinction has to be drawn here between classifications based on the differences in religious and cultural heritage and attempts to establish new conceptual terms in cross-cultural comparison of movements focussing on traits that are not specific to one particular area or culture. The former often emerge from area study-oriented disciplines and the general pre-occupation of the discourse on fundamentalism with Islamist movements.[12] These concentrate on providing information with regard to the specific movement's ideological heritage in view of the larger debate on fundamentalism. Attempts to establish new classifications for distinct clusters of movements in cross-cultural terms are significantly fewer in number.

Notable examples for the latter category of works include Keddie's concept of New Religious Politics (Keddie 1998) and Nasr's concept of Muslim Democracy (Nasr 2005). Nasr's work is of special relevance here as it consciously implies structural similarities between strands of Islamism and Christian Democracy, an argument which is also inherent in the theoretical approach used here.[13]

For Nasr, the degree of adaptation to liberalism and secularism shown nowadays by Christian Democratic parties characterises their success in the transformation to the modern world, but does not constitute a pre-requisite for classifying Islamic parties as Muslim Democratic parties:

> The depth of commitment to liberal and secular values that democratic consolidation requires is a condition for Muslim Democracy's final success, not for its first emergence. As was the case with Christian Democracy in Europe, it is the imperative of competition inherent in democracy that will transform the unsecular tendencies of Muslim Democracy into long-term commitment to democratic values.
>
> (Nasr 2005: 15)

A common aspect in these two theoretical approaches to recently emergent movements that have often been characterised as fundamentalist is that both authors perceive the movements they are working on as a distinct type of movements, set apart from the concept of fundamentalism which, by and large, is rejected by them for explanation. The almost simultaneous emergence of these movements as major political forces in vastly different political contexts is uniformly noted. Thus, Keddie notes that 'it is striking how many of them developed rapidly beginning in the late 1970s' (Keddie 1998: 718). These newly emergent movements apparently share a number of characteristics and should be subsumed under a single category distinct from the concept of fundamentalism.

The discussion above has indicated several problems with associating non-secular, typically right-wing political movements in developing countries as fundamentalist. The opacity of the concept of fundamentalism as used in the discourse on the topic results in ambiguities as to what actually forms the main characteristics of a fundamentalist movement. Fundamentalism in the narrow definition of the term is clearly not applicable on a political party like the BJP and similar political parties or movements outside India. In the broad definition of the term fundamentalism, cultural identity supersedes religion as both the origin and the aim of non-secular ideologies. The emphasis on religion which is implicit in the use of the term fundamentalism accordingly cannot be justified.

The classification of political movements in developing countries as fundamentalist mostly signifies these movements' opposition to established secular nationalist political actors which have been dominant in large parts of the developing world after de-colonisation. The political recourse to culture and – to a significantly lesser degree – to religion by movements often associated with fundamentalism has to be viewed in the context of this opposition.

New cultural identitarian political movements

The emergence and evolution of NCIPM

Movements that follow the model of development shortly outlined above are characterised here as New Cultural Identitarian Political Movements (NCIPM). Key features of an NCIPM include a discourse oriented towards a projection of culturally defined identity in opposition to secular nationalism, and economic pragmatism with a generally vague preference for free market policies. NCIPM are dominated by either the middle or the lower classes but nevertheless comprise select segments from among the respective other social strata and are, accordingly, partially class transcending. Another crucial feature of NCIPM is constituted by the willingness to participate within the established political systems, both nationally and internationally, notwithstanding possible deviations from certain norms and conventions of accepted political behaviour, especially in the case of political violence.

The emergence of NCIPM as viable political alternatives in some areas of the world is linked to the decline of dominant secular nationalist political forces

---

Box 2.1 Rents and the state class

The following analysis is to a significant extent based on an interpretation of theoretical constructs which so far have not been widely used in the discourse on Indian politics: rents and the state class. A short characterisation of the two concepts in the way they are used here is necessary before proceeding:

Rents: Rent is distinguished from profit as a form of surplus generated under conditions of imperfect markets. Several sub-types of rents are distinguished. In this work, rent equivalents – forms of surplus which cannot technically been defined as rents but have similar effects – are subsumed under the term rent. The concept is used here mostly with reference to its political dimension. A common feature of distinct types of rents is that rents due to their generation under conditions of market imperfection are susceptible to political contest, since political means are instrumental in sustaining the market imperfections that allow their generation and acquisition. By being susceptible to political contest, rents form an important element in political processes, especially since they enable political actors who can influence the rent allocation process to gain support from social sections in return for the allocation of benefits. In turn, social sections can attempt to maintain or increase their socio-economic status by emphasising political organisation over individual economic competition (rent seeking). States where rents constitute a substantial, though not the only important, ingredient of the political process are characterised here as semi-rentier states.

State class: A state class is defined as the social strata exercising significant control over the generation and allocation of rents. This primarily includes the political and bureaucratic elite from the local to the national level. The state class is distinct from other elite sections of society in that its socio-economic status is dependent mostly on its political predominance. It tends to act as a class in itself in ensuring the continuance of this political predominance.

---

established as anti-colonial liberation movements due to the latter's rent distribution-dominated political strategies and the failure of import substitution development strategies to provide sufficient rents to co-opt newly assertive social strata. Depending on the structure of their respective social support bases, the scarcity of rents may result in the NCIPM turning towards free market policies as a way to safeguard economic interests of their core supporters: Scarcity of rents prevents to a significant degree the co-optation of numerically large rising lower middle class sections into the political structure of rent distribution which remains dominated by the established state classes, while access to this structure is furthermore contested from politically organised lower class interests. The turn towards free market policies removes economic segments from political contest, and in this way benefits groups that have attained comparative advantages with regard to information and formal education, once their political predominance cannot anymore be sustained.[14]

In this way, the (pragmatic) articulation of economic interests increases in importance for political strategy, thus resulting in a gradual turn of NCIPM towards a moderate political agenda: The cultural identitarian elements of the movement's ideological heritage are more and more transformed into a discursive framework providing legitimacy for economic policies benefiting certain sections of society.

Since lower class groups in semi-rentier states will not, as a rule, benefit directly from liberalisation policies – due to the lack of the very comparative advantages which makes liberalisation beneficial to middle classes – NCIPM dominated by lower class groups will tend to focus on increasing benefits accruing from rent allocation to their respective supporters. This places lower class dominated NCIPM in direct opposition to the established elite, unless available rents remain sufficient to ensure the co-optation of the NCIPM. Correspondingly, the evolution of NCIPM as political actors to a large extent depends on two factors: (1) the structure of their social support base, and (2) rent scarcity or sufficiency. The interaction of these two factors permits a distinction of four different patterns in the evolution of NCIPM.

Matrix 1 provides a rough illustration of the various possibilities in the evolution of NCIPM which serves to highlight some general trends. Other factors influencing the evolution of NCIPM may lead to different outcomes. This is especially likely regarding the first mentioned outcomes for each pattern – inclusion, exclusion, and co-optation – as these depend not only on the behaviour of the NCIPM but even more so on the behaviour of the established elite.

NCIPM can still emerge under conditions of rent sufficiency, but in this case are not likely to evolve into viable contenders of political power. Instead, the established elite possess the means to co-opt sections of the NCIPM, thereby increasing its legitimacy. Which section of an NCIPM is co-opted by the established elite depends to a large extent on the context, especially the respective strength of the various wings of the NCIPM. Both lower class and middle class dominated sections can be co-opted. The co-opted section of the NCIPM will tend to turn towards de facto moderation, while opposing sections are likely to turn towards radicalism. Essentially, this process institutionalises a split in the NCIPM political spectrum.

In this case, NCIPM are placed in a dilemma: The economic interests of their supporters demand participation in governance as this forms the basis for

	Rent scarcity	Rent sufficiency
Middle class dominance	Inclusion Moderation	Co-optation Moderation
Lower class dominance	Exclusion Radicalisation	Co-optation Moderation

Matrix 1 Patterns in the evolution of NCIPM.

participation in the system of rent allocation. This system is, however, still dominated by the established elite which will tend to use co-optation as an instrument to ensure their continued socio-economic dominance, in effect weakening the incentive for NCIPM supporters to continue their support. Once popular support to the NCIPM is weakened sufficiently, the incentive for the NCIPM's continued co-optation decreases as well, so that the co-opted section of the NCIPM over time ceases to form a significant political player. The section which was not co-opted can continue to mobilise support under a radical agenda, but is likely to remain at the fringes of the political mainstream unless rents become scarce.

This case is best illustrated by the NCIPM in Algeria. There, rent generation based mainly on natural resources is by and large sufficient to enable the established elite to co-opt newly assertive social sections, but remains dependent on an external factor: the oil price. In the mid-1980s, a significant and rapid decline in oil prices resulted in temporary rent scarcity. Social segments which could no longer be co-opted turned towards the *Front Islamique du Salut* which was prevented from coming to power by a military coup d'etat. With oil prices increasing after the early 1990s, the conditions of rent scarcity were gradually overcome, and the established elite were able to re-assert their primacy. The elite then turned to co-optation of parts of the Islamist spectrum, especially the MSP and *El Islah*, the former being dominated by middle class sections and the latter including a substantial lower class segment.

Both these parties kept their respective ideological discourse but, in essence, turned towards political moderation regarding policy. The Islamist political spectrum in Algeria split into the two main moderate parties and a variety of radical organisations. Co-optation weakened the popular support of the moderate NCIPM which were summarily excluded from the ruling alliance by the still dominant secular nationalist parties. Accordingly, a re-assertion of NCIPM in Algeria would depend on renewed rent scarcity. Since rent scarcity in Algeria depends on conjunctural factors and thus cannot be expected to be durable, self-sustained political assertion by NCIPM in Algeria remains unlikely. Institutionalisation of NCIPM as major contenders for political power to a large extent depends on sustained rent scarcity, which also creates the conditions for a stable path-dependent turn towards political moderation.[15]

The BJP forms an NCIPM which operates under the conditions of rent scarcity and predominantly middle class support. This scenario forms the basic grid for the subsequent analysis of the BJP and, accordingly, is stressed in the subsequent discussion of the evolution of NCIPM.

Though rent sufficiency or scarcity and middle or lower class dominance within the NCIPM form the most important factors, other variables affect the evolution of NCIPM. These include the preference of established elites vis-à-vis accommodation, co-optation or exclusion in their political strategy, the degree of openness and stability of the political system, the role of external actors, internal cohesion of and discipline within the NCIPM, and the potential for integration into the mainstream which is inherent in the respective NCIPM's ideological heritage. The influence of these other variables can be seen in the development of the various NCIPM which emerged in Northern Africa, the Middle East, and South and Southeast Asia especially since the early 1990s, which will be discussed below.

In summary, NCIPM form political movements in developing societies whose polities were strongly dominated by co-optation of segments of the population through rent distribution by politically dominant secular nationalist movements. These political movements propagate a culturally defined nationalism (or other community identity). They utilise this promulgation to advance the economic interests of social sections that could not be included in the established system of distributing benefits arising from political participation due to rent scarcity arising out of the relative failure of import-substitution oriented economic development policies to generate sufficient rents to satisfy the aspirations of rising lower and lower middle strata of society.

Under conditions of rent scarcity, they turn towards free market policies, though in a pragmatic way which provides opportunities to include moral economy elements in order to include select lower class segments. At present, NCIPM have become influential political actors in parts of South Asia, the Middle East and Northern Africa, and Southeast Asia where they are expected to assert significant influence on the future development of the countries they are operating in.

Historically, NCIPM emerged as alternatives, if not an antithesis to secular nationalism. Their basic ideological foundations were formulated – as is the case with secular nationalism in post-colonial societies – from approximately the late nineteenth century to the early twentieth century. In opposition to the mainstream secular nationalist movements, these NCIPM sought to project an alternative concept of identity, including national identity, which laid emphasis on select cultural traits of the respective society and its indigenous historical experiences. In this, these movements differed sharply from the relatively unquestioning adaptation to Western political thought displayed by many modernising, secular nationalist movements.

Core features of these cultural nationalisms comprise (1) the transfer of broad cultural criteria derived from community identities apart from ethnic, racial or linguistic attributes to the respective new alternative conception of national identity propagated by the NCIPM, and (2) a preference for a combination of descent, birth, and self-profession of membership in the national community over citizenship as the relevant criteria for an individual's nationality, with variations regarding the specific combination of these features among NCIPM.

Politically, while NCIPM emerged during approximately the same period as their secular nationalist rivals, they remained rather insignificant political actors for several decades. They emerged as viable contenders for political power from the mid-1970s onwards due to the crisis of the secular nationalist project in certain post-colonial societies.[16]

Variables affecting the evolution of NCIPM

As indicated above, several features impact the emergence and subsequent evolution of NCIPM. Table 2.1 lists seven variables influencing the evolution of NCIPM in different cultural contexts: (1) rent scarcity or sufficiency, (2) the dominant social support base, (3) preferred behaviour of established elites, (4) openness of the political system, (5) stability of the political system, (6) the influence of external actors, and (7) the ideological potential for integration into the national political context. While all eight variables influence the evolution of NCIPM, variables 1 and 2 – rent scarcity or sufficiency, and the dominant social support base – are interpreted here as constituting the primary factors explaining the evolution of NCIPM.

Table 2.1 of necessity constitutes only an approximation of the current situation regarding the emergence and evolution of NCIPM which serves to highlight certain trends and patterns in this evolution. These trends and patterns form a grid for evaluating the relative importance of factors affecting NCIPM.

In Table 2.1, columns 2–8 describe variables affecting the evolution of NCIPM in various political contexts, while columns 9–11 describe the current scenarios faced by NCIPM in these contexts. Options have been restricted to two or three cases each to enable successful comparison. This necessitates simplifications in some cases. Columns 2 (Rents) and 3 (Social Support) – rent scarcity/sufficiency and the dominant social support base – have already been discussed. Options include Scarcity, Periodic Sufficiency, and Sufficiency for column 2, and Middle Class and Lower Class Dominance for column 3.

Column 4 (Elite Reaction) indicates the overall strategic preference of the established elite in dealing with rivals and, accordingly, implies a general pattern which still allows significant exceptions. Options include Inclusion, Co-optation, and Exclusion. Column 5 (External Actors) indicates the importance of external actors in influencing the behaviour of established elites vis-à-vis an NCIPM and the political positioning of the NCIPM itself by various means including but not restricted to violent coercion. External actors also include radical (and often more militant) competitors in violent or instable polities such as Pakistan. Options include Not Significant, Partially Significant, and Significant. Column 6 (Political System) describes the degree of openness of the political system in terms of democratic political participation. Options comprise Open, Partially Open, and Restricted.

Column 7 (Stability) indicates the stability of the political system. Options include Stable, Partially Stable, and Instable. Column 8 (Integration) indicates the inherent potential in the ideology of a respective NCIPM for integration into the specific political framework of the country it is operating in. Accordingly, *Hamas* is depicted as operating in the Palestinian territories, not as operating in Israel, i.e. outside the occupied territories. Options include High, Average, and Low. Options for columns 9–11 include Exclusion, Inclusion, and Co-optation for column 9, Moderation, Partial Moderation, and Radicalism for column 10, and Durable Assertion, Dependency, and Marginality for column 11.

Table 2.1 Factors influencing the evolution of NCIPM

(1) Country NCIPM	(2) Rents	(3) Social support	(4) Elite reaction	(5) External Actors	(6) Political system	(7) Stability	(8) Integration	(9) Outcome A	(10) Outcome B	(11) Outcome C
India BJP	Scarcity	Middle Class	Inclusion	Not Significant	Open	Stable	High	Inclusion	Moderation	Durable Assertion
India Shiv Sena	Scarcity	Lower Class	Inclusion	Not Significant	Open	Stable	High	Partial Inclusion	Partial Moderation	Durable Assertion
Algeria MSP	Periodic Sufficiency	Middle Class	Co-optation	Not Significant	Partially Open	Partially Stable	High	Co-optation	Moderation	Dependency
Algeria El Islah	Periodic Sufficiency	Lower Class	Co-optation	Significant	Partially Open	Partially Stable	Average	Co-optation	Moderation	Dependency
Turkey AKP	Scarcity	Middle Class	Co-optation	Significant	Partially Open	Stable	High	Inclusion	Moderation	Durable Assertion
Turkey SaP	Scarcity	Lower Class	Co-optation	Significant	Partially Open	Stable	Average	Co-optation	Radicalism	Marginality
Morocco PJD	Scarcity	Middle Class	Exclusion	Partially Significant	Restricted	Stable	Average	Exclusion	Moderation	Durable Assertion
Egypt MB	Scarcity	Lower Class	Exclusion	Partially Significant	Restricted	Stable	Average	Exclusion	Partial Moderation	Durable Assertion
Egypt Al Wasat	Scarcity	Middle Class	Exclusion	Partially Significant	Restricted	Stable	Average	Co-optation	Moderation	Dependency
Jordan IAF	Scarcity	Middle Class	Inclusion	Partially Significant	Partially Open	Stable	High	Inclusion	Moderation	Durable Assertion
Palestine Hamas	Scarcity	Lower Class	Inclusion	Significant	Partially Open	Instable	High	Exclusion	Radicalism	Durable Assertion
Lebanon Hizbullah	Scarcity	Lower Class	Inclusion	Significant	Partially Open	Partially Stable	High	Inclusion	Radicalism	Durable Assertion
Pakistan JI	Scarcity	Middle Class	Co-optation	Significant	Partially Open	Partially Stable	High	Co-optation	Partial Moderation	Dependency

Table 2.1 shows several general trends with reference to the variables affecting the evolution of NCIPM in different contexts. Most importantly, it establishes that the variables indicated in columns 2 and 3 constitute the primary factors explaining NCIPM evolution and, accordingly, the accuracy of Matrix 1 as the basic grid for the analysis of NCIPM. The other variables form modifying factors on the basis of the conditions set by the scarcity or sufficiency of rents and the dominance of middle or lower classes. The patterns arising from the interplay of the primary variables in isolation are discussed below. Here, it is important to note that no combination of variables depicted in Table 2.1 excluding the primary factors permits a more accurate explanation of the depicted outcomes in the various cases than the combination of the primary factors.

The modifying factors impact the evolution of NCIPM to various degrees. Again, it is possible to discern some general trends in this from Table 2.1. Some factors show a relatively low modifying effect. Starting from the end, the potential for integration of an NCIPM into the respective national political system inherent in an NCIPM's ideological heritage influences the outcomes to a significantly lesser degree than a number of other factors. Both *Hamas* in the Palestinian territories and *Hizbullah* in Lebanon have a high potential for integration, but have respectively been excluded and included.[17] In these cases, the outcome is strongly modified by the high significance of external actors. In Egypt, both the Muslim Brotherhood and the *Al-Wasat* have an average potential for integration, but have been excluded and co-opted respectively.

The modifying factors depicted in columns 7 and 8 similarly have a low impact on the evolution of NCIPM which illustrates the high capacity of NCIPM for adaptation to different political contexts. While a high degree of openness of the political system an NCIPM is operating in is certainly conducive to its growth, it does not significantly affect the NCIPM's turn to moderation or radicalism, the most likely outcome affected by the variable. Similarly, the stability of a political system does not significantly affect the outcomes.

This leaves the strategic preference of elites for dealing with rival organisations and the significance of external actors – depicted in columns 4 and 5 respectively – as the major factors modifying rent scarcity or sufficiency and the dominant support bases of NCIPM. Examples for the, at times, strong modifying effect on the evolution of NCIPM of the influence of external actors are constituted by the Palestinian territories, Turkey, and Pakistan which also provide an indication of the various ways in which external actors are capable of influencing NCIPM evolution. In the Palestinian territories, the influence of Israel and the western countries has led to the exclusion of *Hamas*, and continues to form an obstacle in a possible turn away from radicalism by the latter. In contrast, the role of the European Union in Turkey has tended to reinforce the inclusion and political moderation of the AKP. In Pakistan, the large militant Islamist spectrum deriving sustenance from the ongoing conflict in Afghanistan and other factors continue to pose an obstacle to a possible turn towards moderation by the JI,[18] despite sustained rent scarcity and substantial middle class support to the NCIPM.

Similarly, the strategic preference of elites for behaving towards rivals may significantly modify the effect of the primary factors. This is illustrated by the examples of Morocco and Lebanon: In Morocco, the PJD continues to be excluded from the political system, despite the fact that the primary variables would indicate the potential for inclusion with other modifying factors reinforcing this potential. In Lebanon, the strategic preference for inclusion has led to the inclusion of *Hizbullah*, despite the latter's radicalism and significant contrary influence of some important external actors. The strategic preference of elites does not, however, need to be followed by the elites in every case, as the example of *Al-Wasat* in Egypt shows.

The moderation and assertion of middle class dominated NCIPM in contexts characterised by rent scarcity

In general terms, NCIPM became politically influential forces in a part of the 'developing world' stretching from Northern Africa to Southeast Asia, especially those which relied heavily on middle class support under conditions of (at least temporary) rent scarcity. In this area, mainstream secular nationalism began to face a dual crisis of legitimacy due to its failure to co-opt both newly emerging middle classes as well as newly assertive segments from the lower classes into its political project. This is not to preclude the possibility of NCIPM emerging as influential actors outside the specified area or under different circumstances, but to define the broad contextual parameters of NCIPM assertion in historical terms and from a global perspective.

In the area outlined above, the dominant secular nationalist political organisations emerged as advocates of a modernising project that – broadly speaking – combined socio-politically liberal orientations with a preference for import-substitution and state interventionism as a strategy for economic growth and restructuring. The project's legitimacy, apart from the historical legacy of its main proponents' leading roles in the respective struggles against colonial rule, was based to a large extent on the ability to protect the social and economic status of its supporters while at the same time being capable of co-opting newly assertive groups. In order to achieve this, secular nationalist organisations in the area outlined above mainly took recourse to a strategy of rent allocation, aided by moderate economic growth and the central role occupied by the state in economic development. The dominant political organisations developed into ideologically flexible umbrella (or catch-all) parties that centred on the maintenance of patron–client relations and networks of patronage distribution.

Political economy from Northern Africa to Southeast Asia increasingly became orientated towards political-bureaucratic control over the acquisition and distribution of rents. This control was established either by direct central administrative control over rent providing resources (especially oil and gas) or, in the absence of these resources, by indirect and often decentralised state control over economic activity, exemplified by India's 'license-permit-raj' regime,[19] and a public sector which – as it was described in India – occupied the 'commanding heights' of the economy.

The distinction between dependency on natural resources and regimes of indirect control over the economy for the generation of rents is crucial in two respects: (1) Countries which possess large-scale natural resources which supply rents are more likely to be able to sustain rent sufficiency, at least in conjuncture phases in which prices for these commodities are relatively high. They are also more likely to have centralised control over rent generation. This means that opposition forces cannot rely on establishing themselves at the local and regional level first. (2) While rent generation in states relying for it on natural resources is often able to sustain rent sufficiency, rapid decreases in the prices of these commodities which are often associated with external factors can lead to temporary rent scarcity which reduces the state class's capacity for co-optation and contributes to the exit of groups from the social coalition supporting the state class which may re-establish itself after prices for the respective commodities have risen again. For the evolution of NCIPM, these two aspects have significant implications:

- In contexts with sustained rent sufficiency – whether dependent on rents generated by the exploitation of natural resources or by indirect control of economic activity – NCIPM can be expected to turn towards political moderation only when striving to be co-opted by the ruling state class and to turn towards radicalism when attempting to overcome the state class in order to establish themselves as their successors.
- In contexts with sustained rent scarcity – which is more likely if rent generation is not dependent on the exploitation of globally traded natural resources but instead on indirect control over the economy – NCIPM can be expected to strive for inclusion (as distinguished from co-optation) into the political system as viable contenders for political power. Political moderation or radicalisation then largely depends on the interests of the NCIPM's support base, with middle class-dominated NCIPM more likely to turn towards moderation.
- In contexts with alternating phases of rent scarcity and rent sufficiency – which is more likely when rent generation depends on the exploitation of globally traded natural resources – NCIPM can be expected to turn towards radicalism if attempting to replace the established state class, i.e. especially in times of rent scarcity when the state class's capacity for co-optation is low. In turn, NCIPM can under these conditions be expected to turn towards political moderation when aiming at being co-opted by the established state class which is more capable of doing so in times of rent sufficiency.

In essence, both rent scarcity and rent sufficiency can lead to either the political moderation or increased radicalism of an NCIPM. Rent scarcity can lead to political moderation if it is sustained and the NCIPM is therefore capable of competing with the established ruling parties. In a context of temporary rent scarcity, it can instead be expected to lead to a turn towards radicalism on the part of the NCIPM since the latter can attempt to replace the weakened established elite by radical political activities including violence. Under conditions of rent sufficiency, an NCIPM can turn towards moderation due to the ruling elite's attempts at co-opting it. If the political moderation of an NCIPM is dependent on co-optation by the ruling elite it is likely to be sustained only under conditions of sustained rent sufficiency. In contrast, the political moderation of an NCIPM under conditions of sustained rent scarcity can lead to a stable and path-dependent turn towards moderation. Accordingly, for the case of rent scarcity, Matrix 1 has to be modified as follows:

The matrix' outcomes correspond to the examples cited above for India and Algeria. In India, under conditions of sustained rent scarcity, the middle class-dominated BJP has been included in the political system and has turned towards political moderation. The lower class-dominated *Shiv Sena* has been partially included and has to a lesser extent turned towards political moderation. In Algeria, under conditions of temporary rent scarcity, both the middle class- and lower class-dominated wings of the FIS were excluded and turned towards radicalisation. Once temporary rent scarcity had been overcome (by the late 1990s), the two most important successors of the FIS – the middle class-dominated MSP and the lower class-dominated *El Islah* – reverted to the pattern of evolution anticipated under conditions of rent sufficiency in Matrix 1.

As in the case of Matrix 1, the possible modifying effects of other variables depicted in Table 2.1 have to be kept in mind. Still, Matrix 2 also serves to illustrate the primary factors influencing NCIPM evolution under conditions of rent scarcity and, accordingly, the basic pattern of NCIPM evolution which is then affected by the modifying variables.

In countries which did not possess natural resources for generating sufficient rents, exemplified by India, the failure of import-substitution strategies to achieve self-sustained levels of economic growth capable of providing sufficient surpluses to extend rent allocation to newly assertive social segments resulted in rent scarcity from approximately the 1970s onwards. These countries became subject to increasingly competitive political mobilisation over access to rent allocation. Established state classes and politically dominant sections increased their

	Temporary rent scarcity	Sustained rent scarcity
Middle class dominance	Exclusion Radicalisation	Inclusion Moderation
Lower class dominance	Exclusion Radicalisation	Partial inclusion Partial moderation

Matrix 2 Patterns in the evolution of NCIPM under conditions of rent scarcity.

efforts at competitive vertical mobilisation of previously excluded social groups, while the latter began to form increasingly effective political organisations of their own to participate in the systems of rent distribution in their own right, at least partially eliminating their clientelistic dependence and accordingly leading to an increase in horizontal mobilisation.[20]

The modernising project of secular nationalism thus became perceived to be illegitimate by a variety of social groups. Newly assertive sections from among the lower classes were mobilised increasingly over the state's failure to ensure sufficient access to public resources. The newly emerging middle classes began to question the validity of the state's role in the economy including the overall development strategy of import-substitution, favouring a model of political economy were state control over resources was much reduced and politicians were thus less capable of transferring resources to the numerically larger assertive segments from among the lower and lower middle classes.

In this context, NCIPM became perceived by large and diverse sections of society as viable alternatives to the established secular nationalist organisations. Accordingly, under these circumstances NCIPM were increasingly able to attract middle class support and, in turn, were increasingly able to turn towards political moderation. Apart from their previous exclusion from the 'Establishment' there are two key factors explaining this shift in public preferences towards NCIPM: (1) By championing broad alternative concepts of national identity that were moreover based on indigenous and thus more familiar cultural heritages, NCIPM were able to rise (at least rhetorically) above particularistic demands for rent allocation as well as socio-economic cleavages. The construction of (imagined) internal and/or external enemies also assisted the formation of new, heterogeneous and cleavage-transcending political support bases. (2) The emphasis on cultural-identitarian issues displayed by these movements corresponded to a distinct vagueness with regard to concepts of political economy, which allowed an enormous flexibility in pragmatically adapting to diverse interests and changing circumstances.

Having emerged as viable contenders for political power, NCIPM are now placed in a strategic dilemma. As with the previously dominant secular nationalist political parties, their support bases include vastly different economic interests, and with rent allocations remaining insufficient to ensure political legitimacy, the articulation of economic interests is becoming central to gaining political power.

The dominant sections of society prefer 'moderate' economic policies (and usually a corresponding moderation of political idioms), and increased inclusion into the political establishment, while the NCIPM's initial success was based on the radicalism of their alternative conceptions of identity, opposition to the established order, and their general refusal to formulate positions on economic policy which might strengthen divisions within their support bases. In short, in order to remain contenders for political power, NCIPM are compelled to become increasingly moderate but – at the same time – will have to carry along most of the constituents of their respective support bases as well as safeguard their ideological distinctiveness vis-à-vis the previously dominant secular nationalist political organisations.

In case of success in this respect, NCIPM can be expected to emerge as the regional equivalents to Christian Democratic parties in continental Europe. Inability to carry out the balancing act described above will in all probability lead to divisions within the respective movement and the emergence of various splinter groups. NCIPM form a major political force in contemporary post-colonial societies and will continue to exert significant influence on the further development of the political (as well as socio-economic) systems of Northern Africa, and West and South Asia.

Christian democracy, Iberian corporatism and NCIPM

There are strong similarities between NCIPM and Christian Democratic parties with strong corporatist roots in continental Europe, especially on the Iberian peninsular, despite the obvious differences between the African, Asian and European cultural heritages these movements draw upon. The example of Christian Democracy, however, is used in the following mainly as an analogy for the expected future evolution of NCIPM towards political moderation and integration into the global system, keeping in mind the difficulties arising out of the use of analogies for analysis.

Similarities between early Christian Democracy and NCIPM are striking: Both operated in a context of rapid socio-economic and political transition which challenged the pre-eminence of previously established social segments. Both were essentially conservative in character, but not to a degree which prevented an adaptation to changing contexts and an extension to newly assertive social groups. Both provided models of the good and ordered society which included a strong role for government and were based on community, not the individual. In this, they employed ideas of organic linkages between communities which tended to leave established hierarchies intact. Lastly, both comprised ideologies whose main features were drawn from a re-interpretation of the traditional heritage of their respective societies without, however, being restricted to a narrow interpretation of this heritage. Both Christian Democracy and NCIPM included representatives who were close to fascism, but have successfully participated in democratic polities as well.

The similarities between Christian Democracy and NCIPM are especially strong when considering the case of Iberian corporatism which formed one of the main features of both Christian Democracy and fascism in Spain and Portugal where the influence of community and group membership on national politics has traditionally been accentuated (Wiarda and Mott 2001: 3). Corporatism was perceived by its proponents as a 'third way' between liberal and Marxist conceptions of society which was based (in Spain and Portugal) on Catholic socio-political ideas, but also drew on non-religious ideas and traditions (Wiarda and Mott 2001: 42). The interpretation of Iberian corporatism by Wiarda and Mott, devoid of its cultural context, illustrates the proximity between Iberian

Christian Democracy and Islamist and Hindu nationalist thought as propagated by NCIPM:

> Corporatism in this sense means a political world view derived from Aristotle and St. Thomas Aquinas: that government is good and natural; that it need not, therefore, be checked and balanced; that all groups and individuals are secure and fixed in their station in life. Corporatism thus pictures society as an organic whole with all its parts interrelated. A corporatist political system is made up of corporately organized groups recognized in law as having juridical personality and having duly recognized rights and responsibilities.
>
> (Wiarda and Mott 2001: 42–3)

Corporatism as an ideology was strongly associated with the Franco and Salazar regimes. Still, it continues to have a significant impact on Christian Democracy in the Iberian peninsular today, especially in the form of neo-corporatism (Wiarda and Mott 2001: 196). Corporatism, while forming an element of Iberian fascism, is distinct from fascism as the example of German fascism shows. In essence, while the two concepts have been related at times, both fascism *sans* corporatism and corporatism *sans* fascism are easily conceivable.

The analogy between the concept of NCIPM and Christian Democracy, especially the corporatist strand of Christian Democracy, is interesting precisely because it implicitly shows that both concepts comprised radical and moderate strands. The radical strands of corporatist Christian Democracy were highly compatible with fascism as experienced in southern Europe. The moderate strands of corporatist Christian Democracy were and are highly compatible with democratic politics in continental Europe.

Structural characteristics of NCIPM

The main structural similarity between the various NCIPM discussed above is the initial refusal to commit themselves to a distinct economic agenda. The failure (or unwillingness) to do so reflects both a strong emphasis on issues of cultural identity and a tendency to perceive politics in communal (and cultural) as opposed to class (and economic) terms. It also reflects the composition of the NCIPM's core constituencies: NCIPM, while usually being dominated by certain classes, tend to prefer to mobilise support across class divisions. This is both due to their ideological outlook and to electoral (or similar solely political) considerations, since middle classes in many post-colonial societies remain an insufficient base for gaining political power.

This does not prevent the emergence of dominant groups within NCIPM based on class or occupational background. Various case studies on organisations classified here as NCIPM have described their support bases as being dominated respectively by the urban middle classes, especially new middle classes, or by (again mostly urban) 'losers' coalitions.' The respective dominant groups' economic interests naturally define the NCIPM's actual economic policies to a large extent. Still, the compulsion to ally with groups outside the respective dominant classes as well as the ideological preference for issues of cultural identity places restrictions on the formulation of comprehensive economic programmes.

To balance divergent economic interests within its support base, an NCIPM's economic agenda will have to remain flexible and only moderately preferential to specific groups. It is to be expected that an NCIPM dominated by new middle classes will tend to prefer a larger private sector role in the economy but will, at the same time, favour state intervention in specific areas as well as move only incrementally on the state's disengagement from the economy as a whole. It will tend to prefer the liberalisation of those economic sectors which provide (well paid) employment to the middle classes and where the middle classes possess sufficient comparative advantages over lower class competitors for gaining employment so that the removal of these sectors from political contest is not detrimental to middle class interests.

While a middle-class dominated NCIPM would prefer a free market economy, it will certainly not be averse to be engaged in rent distribution in order to gain political support. As a consequence, NCIPM favour a mixed economy, which includes moral economy policies, economic policies based primarily on national security perceptions, the maintenance of certain patronage structures within the political economy and free market economic policies.

NCIPM thus tend to formulate a conglomerate of economic policies, pragmatically justifying these by taking recourse to select (and sometimes seemingly arbitrarily selected) cultural and religious traditions, norms and values from among the respective society's cultural heritage as well as nationalistic considerations. The economic policies actually chosen from among this conglomerate at any particular moment in time depend less on the movement's ideology, but rather on the political context as well as internal leadership conflicts.

The most readily identifiable feature of NCIPM consists of their projection of cultural-identitarian issues. NCIPM take recourse to the promotion of select cultural and religious traditions, norms and values from among the respective society's cultural and religious heritage. These may be (and usually are) coupled with elements of Western political practice and thought – which anyway often form part of these societies' historical experiences. While the promotion of indigenous cultural traits certainly is regarded valuable in itself by its proponents, their principal function is to balance diverging interests within the NCIPM and society. The projection of a glorified (and sanitised) indigenous heritage enables the NCIPM to unify large parts of society in a context of substantial political division.

The preference for indigenous, non-western tradition is not to be interpreted as a failure to adapt to modernity. On the contrary, it is part of a rational political strategy, reminiscent of early Christian Democracy in continental Europe, and thus structurally very much in accordance with modern political practice. By promoting indigenous traditions, NCIPM provide their supporters a cultural identity, creating community sentiment around a set of often rather vaguely articulated core beliefs.

The provision of cultural identity serves both to include supporters within the community and to exclude predetermined enemies, a fixed 'Other' which can easily be identified. Most importantly, though, the provision of cultural identity prevents the exclusion of social segments on class lines, since all classes can be represented both within the community of supporters and among their enemies.

The notion of non- or even anti-modernity regarding NCIPM – unless based on the use of political violence or, rather arbitrarily, on the latter's projection of select practices that appear anachronistic or even repulsive to western or westernised audiences – seems to rest principally on this importance attributed to community rather than the individual. The emphasis on community instead of individuality certainly places these movements outside the liberal spectrum. The way community is created (or intended to be created) by NCIPM, however, reinforces their position as modern conservative movements.

The cultural identity NCIPM provide to their supporters usually includes elements related to nationalism, ethnicity and religion. With nationalism being a modern concept, the notion of non-modernity with regard to the cultural-identitarian character of NCIPM has to be discussed in the context of their use of the latter concepts of ethnicity and religion. Here, it is apparent that NCIPM strive to create broad communities that are, in fact, transcending traditional ethnic and religious boundaries as long as these are unrelated to the projected enemy communities.

The relationship between NCIPM and the established order is ambivalent. On the one hand, NCIPM pose a challenge both to the hegemony of previously dominant political actors and to the ideological basis of the states they are operating in. NCIPM were excluded from the respective 'Establishments' for most of the time of their existence, and they tend to attack these, especially for their alleged corruption, decadence, and complacency.

At the same time, NCIPM can hardly be considered revolutionary or even (in most respects) social reform movements. NCIPM may resort to radicalism and militancy, especially if lower class segments form a major part of their support base, but usually in support of dominant or status quo-oriented social groups which perceive themselves to be threatened by changing circumstances or assertive rival groups. The support base of NCIPM primarily tends to comprise social segments that benefited to some extent from rent allocations in the past (though not sufficiently to ensure continued loyalty to secular nationalism), but feel threatened due to the increasingly contested process of rent distribution.

Moreover, the cultural identitarian issues espoused by NCIPM had often been part of the overall political discourse for several decades, and usually had made inroads into the establishment by the time NCIPM became politically influential, mostly in the early 1990s. The many similarities between the support bases of secular nationalist and cultural-identitarian organisations as well as the umbrella character of the former facilitated the emergence of cultural-identitarian fringe groups within the main secular nationalist organisations. These acted as links to the established political actors, and later facilitated NCIPM integration into the mainstream.

The spread of cultural-identitarian values among the middle classes and the establishment in general has often been linked to increased perceptions of insecurity that emanated from rapidly changing contexts both at the national and the global level. Militancy (mostly in the form of sporadic, but locally organised political violence) among largely conservative sections of society forms both a response to feelings of insecurity in the face of these rapid changes as well as an attempt to reaffirm the established social order which is perceived to be threatened. The relationship between NCIPM and the established order reinforces the proposed analogy between these movements and early Christian Democracy in continental Europe. If NCIPM are included into the political system, NCIPM militancy tends to threaten their respective designated enemies, not the established order itself.

The concept of NCIPM used here cuts across cultural contexts and distinct geographic regions. It associates movements that operate under vastly different political circumstances. And, finally, it links Hindu nationalist organisations to Islamist ones, highlighting their commonality with early Christian Democratic movements. It should, however, be noted that the specific cultural contents, the particular norms, values and traditions promoted by these movements do not form an important part of the conceptualisation of NCIPM, despite the undoubtedly high relevance for many of their proponents within these movements (as well as the latter's critics.)

What is important for classification, here, is the structure, not the contents. The very selectivity of the respective traditions, norms and values championed by particular NCIPM within their specific cultural contexts and their combination with western ideas and practices reinforces the argument that these projections are driven by political utility. In essence, they form instruments for class-transcending mobilisation. An NCIPM is not so much characterised by the content of the cultural and religious values, norms and traditions it espouses, but rather by the process of doing so.

The vagueness in articulation of the values propagated by NCIPM, the selectivity of the recourse to cultural heritage and morality, and the opacity of the process of selecting the specific values and traditions NCIPM are utilising for political mobilisation at any given time are in part due to the absence of a strong religious character of these movements. Since debate on specific religious or other cultural norms does not form an important part in the internal discourse of NCIPM, the morality and moral reform advocated by these movements remains devoid of strong philosophical reasoning and foundations. It cannot but stay vague. Instead, it becomes a broad moral conception of socially acceptable behaviour, and in this regard does not differ strongly from the moral discourses of other NCIPM, or of some of their rivals.

Since the religious and philosophical foundations of their cultural identitarian and moral discourse remain vague, the actual values propagated by NCIPM show strong similarities, despite their different religious and cultural origins and contexts. The differences lie for the most part in the terminology used for articulation.

Conclusion: NCIPM and the BJP

The discussion above indicates the complexity of NCIPM as a single category and has already illustrated a number of sub-categories. In the following chapters, the analysis will focus on a single NCIPM, the *Bharatiya Janata Party* in India. The BJP stands out within the spectrum of NCIPM as it forms the most important non-Islamic organisation characterised here as NCIPM in terms of sustained political influence both at the national and at the global level. In many other respects, however, the BJP constitutes a highly exemplary NCIPM of the sub-category characterised by sustained rent scarcity and strong middle class support.

One of the reasons for this exemplary pattern of NCIPM evolution discernible in the BJP is the development of the Indian polity and Indian political economy after independence, which is discussed in the following chapter. Indian political and economic development since independence illustrates many of the stages and turning points that formed the preconditions for the emergence of NCIPM as viable contenders for political power in the area outlined above. The moderate, but not overwhelming success of Indian development after independence forms the context in which the evolution of NCIPM can be analysed up to a comparatively advanced stage. India, as an example, so far constitutes one of the very few countries where an NCIPM has been able to reach out in a significant way to highly educated elite sections of society and gain support from these sections.

The BJP and the larger Hindu nationalist movement – as any NCIPM – form a highly complex political force with various, at times even conflicting strands. The interplay of diverse interests within and outside the party to a significant degree determines its future development. It is not argued here that the factors which led to the emergence, assertion and increasing political moderation of the BJP and similar NCIPM predetermine their future political course and relevance. Instead, it is argued that these factors contribute to the establishment of path-dependency which reduces the likelihood of patterns in the evolution of the BJP and similar NCIPM strongly divergent from the model outlined above and analysed in greater detail for the Indian case in the following.

3   Context

Politics in India

The genesis of modern India

The emergence of politically and socio-economically modern structures in India primarily took place during British colonial rule and the subsequent decolonisation process. Early colonial rule by the East India Company was by and large characterised by the super-imposition of British practices in select areas – mainly in trade and production as well as the related corpus of law – on the previously established order which otherwise was left in place as long as it was not perceived to contribute to resistance against colonial rule.[1] The cohabitation between the colonial and the previously established regimes was given up by the British after the uprising of 1857, which led to the removal of the remains of India's higher nobility from positions of influence outside the Princely States, and the transferral of sovereignty from the East India Company to the British crown. British control was extended and British practices, especially in law and education, were implemented to a much larger degree.[2]

The removal of the established Indian elite after 1857 left the colonial rulers without an indigenous social segment capable of acting as an intermediary between the British and the population of British India. This vacuum was gradually filled by an emerging middle class, principally made up of a social segment which collaborated with the British, was educated in the new British-inspired institutions (or in the UK itself), and held intermediate positions in the judiciary and the colonial administration (Joshi 2001: 23–58). Due to the necessities of colonial ruling practices and a British perception that Indian society was largely organised communally and divided on ethnic, social and religious lines, the British also began an enumeration process (the Census of India) which significantly contributed to the consolidation of ethnic, caste and sect identities in India (Dirks 2001).

Within Indian society, the defeat of the established order and the emergence of a western-style educated middle class led to efforts to establish modern political organisations. In the nineteenth (and early twentieth) century, these attempts largely took the form of social, religious and educational reform movements, exemplified among others by the Brahmo Samaj, Arya Samaj, and the Deobandi school.[3] While these movements originated from among the largely urban middle class, they soon began to extend their reach to include parts of the rural hinterland.

Middle class collaboration with the British was, at first, largely a local phenomenon. It became institutionalised at the all-India level with the founding of the Indian National Congress (INC) in 1885, which was set up to provide the colonial regime with an indigenous counterpart, while at the same time forming the basis of an indigenous Indian political system under British tutelage and control. The INC originally formed a moderately nationalist assemblage of notables mostly comprising representatives from the urban middle class and (mostly upper caste) community leaders from the rural and semi-urban areas. The INC became divided in the early twentieth century between a moderate wing and a radical section led by Bal Gangadhar Tilak, which called for Indian independence and started a violent campaign in this regard including acts of sabotage and terrorist attacks.

The radical phase of INC politics peaked during the first world war, especially with regard to sabotage against industrial units which were set up partially to contribute to the British arms production. The latter formed the basis for the emergence of large-scale Indian industry and contributed to the appearance of an initially small segment of urban industrial workers and the resulting migration of rural workers to the urban centres of India. The economic opportunities especially for the lower castes and classes provided by industrialisation also began to affect rural power structures already in the early decades of the twentieth century.[4]

The division of the INC into a radical and a moderate wing was overcome to a large extent in the 1920s due to the emergence of Gandhi as the most important Congress leader. Gandhi managed to combine the radicals' aim of Indian independence with a preference for non-violent means and an engagement with the British rulers as opposed to militant resistance. Most importantly, however, Gandhi initiated the transformation of the INC from a party of notables and the indigenous political elite to a mass-based movement, and successfully built up a corresponding party organisation that extended across most of India.

The main rival of the Congress in the pre-independence era was the Indian Muslim League (ML).[5] The Muslim League became antagonistic to the Congress on the issue of separate Muslim and Hindu electorates for the election of regional parliaments in the 1930s which were to be set up as a concession by the British to the nationalist movement. With the commencement of the political reforms of the 1930s, Indian political organisations began to transform themselves from political movements to established political parties including parliamentary wings.

In the late 1930s and during the Second World War, the Indian political system became increasingly polarised. The prospect of a division of British India into India and Pakistan further heightened communal tensions in India, which were exploited by Hindu nationalist organisations, leading to outbreaks of large-scale violence and, hence, reinforcing the Muslim demand for the creation of an independent Muslim state.

Political Hinduism formed an alternative to the secular nationalism espoused by most of the Congress leadership. The first expressly Hindu political organisation at the all-India level, the *All India Hindu Mahasabha* (HMS), was founded shortly before the First World War. The most important HMS leader, Vinayak Damodar Savarkar, formulated the *hindutva* ideology in the early 1920s, and in doing this, shifted the emphasis of political Hinduism from communal to national identity. The HMS, however, failed to have a significant impact politically already in the 1930s. Instead, Hindu nationalism became centred on the *Rashtriya Swayamsevak Sangh* (RSS), which was founded in the early 1920s and rejected involvement in electoral politics in order to avoid the latter's perceived corrupting influence.

The foundations of politics in independent India

At the time of independence, real power in the INC had shifted from Gandhi to Jawaharlal Nehru and Vallabhbhai Patel already in the years preceding independence. After Gandhi's assassination, the two leaders jointly dominated the INC until Patel's death in 1950. The evolving Indian polity, especially the economic structure of the Indian state, to a large extent resembles a compromise formula between the ideas of both, although the actual formulation of the Indian constitution was to a significant degree influenced by Bhimrao Ramji Ambedkar.

India opted for the establishment of a federal polity, albeit with a strong role of the central government which was enabled to exert significant influence on the various state governments both via financial and legal means, the latter including the option of dismissing state governments for a variety of reasons on the advice of centrally appointed state governors.[6] The Indian president took over the ceremonial role of the former British viceroy, but real power rested with the prime minister. Elections to the *Lok Sabha* (the lower house of parliament) as well as the various state legislatures (*Vidhan Sabha*) were to be held according to the British model under a single member simple plurality (SMSP) electoral system.

The strategy for economic development that was formulated under the leadership of Nehru was characterised by a preference for import substituting industrialisation, while agricultural policy was relatively neglected apart from efforts at land reforms. Economically, India opted for a mixed system, combining a strong interventionist role of the state including a large public sector of the Indian economy and central economic planning with a private sector. The latter, however, was regulated by the state to some degree by an evolving regime of licences and permits, the so-called license-permit-raj. In contrast to central planning by the Planning Commission, the latter regime functioned as a decentralised system of control, which enabled local and regional politicians and bureaucrats to exert significant influence on economic activity. This system had considerable implications for the evolution of Indian politics: Quintessentially, economic success and therefore social upward mobility became to a significant degree based on the successful political mobilisation of interests. In turn, political success was by and large founded on access to government and its mechanisms of economic control, which provided the requisite financial resources for electoral mobilisation.

The dominant position of the INC ensured its control of the state apparatus, and thus provided it with the means to maintain its predominance vis-à-vis the opposition parties. The Congress opted early on for a strategy of co-opting local notables, often community leaders, who could 'deliver' the votes of social segments depending on them to the INC (Brass 1965; Kothari 1964: 1163). The capacity to create and maintain networks of highly personalised relationships with these local leaders became one of the most important criteria for political success within the party as well. Elections evolved into a process of bargaining between politicians and local leaders over the distribution of state-controlled resources and privileges. The two most notable forms of political organisation that developed from this process are clientelism and factionalism.[7] With minor exceptions, this model of organising political activity was copied by the major opposition parties.

The spectrum of political parties in India comprises six major categories of political parties: the INC, and socialist, ethno-linguistic, communist, Dalit, and Hindu nationalist parties.[8] The various socialist parties originated from within the Congress, and were organised as a separate wing in the Congress Socialist Party (CSP) until 1946, when the CSP split from the Congress to form the Socialist Party. The socialist spectrum has since split apart and reunified on a number of occasions, and has incorporated several non-socialist movements or parties, mostly of Gandhian origin or caste and farmers' movements, and various splinter groups of the INC. In the process, the socialist political spectrum has shed most of its original ideology, and has evolved into a political competitor to the INC in distributing state resources and privileges without having a distinct ideology. Ethno-linguistic parties evolved in much the same way in some Indian regions, utilising sub-national identities for political mobilisation as opposed to the Congress' propagation of national identity.[9] In fact, parties from both spectrums have often created alliances at the central level. Ethno-linguistic movements and parties successfully compelled the central government to implement a restructuring of the Indian federal polity, leading to the creation of several states based on linguistic criteria since the 1960s.

Dalit parties evolved out of the political legacy of Ambedkar. After independence, Ambedkar founded the Republican Party of India (RPI), which later split into several factions and, barring some areas of Maharashtra, has been largely marginalised since. At present, the most important Dalit party is the Bahujan Samaj Party (BSP), whose political agenda and strategy deviates to a great extent from Ambedkarian tradition in that it is almost exclusively focussed on gaining and maintaining access to the system of distribution of state-controlled resources.[10]

With the failure of the HMS to gain political influence, the Hindu nationalist spectrum became centred on the RSS. The RSS soon after independence evolved a strategy of creating ideologically affiliated but organisationally separate entities, which together form the so-called *Sangh Parivar*, among them the *Vishwa Hindu Parishad* (VHP). In order to create an electoral alternative, but maintain its own isolation from the corruption allegedly associated with parliamentary politics, the *Bharatiya Jan Sangh* (BJS) was formed, which in the early 1980s evolved into the *Bharatiya Janata Party* (BJP). The previously ethno-linguistic *Shiv Sena* also adopted Hindu nationalism, without however becoming part of the *Sangh Parivar*.

In the 1950s, partially successful land reforms considerably contributed to a shift in the structure of power relations in the Indian countryside. The state abolished the system of absentee landlords, introduced land ceilings, and attempted to redistribute surplus land among small and marginal farmers. In general, it can be noted that areas where land reforms were implemented by and large successfully tend to show a much better progress of development than areas where the implementation of land reforms failed, mostly in eastern India. As a result, landlords lost most of their political power, which shifted to the owners of mid-sized farms, often from the intermediate castes.[11] The latter were, however, not incorporated proportionately into the INC-dominated system of clientelist distribution of state resources, especially in North India, largely on the grounds of upper caste domination of the Congress party in this region. The partial neglect of land-owning social segments provided an opportunity for the opposition parties to challenge Congress dominance (Hasan 1998: 70–120; Frankel and Rao 1989; 1990).

The decline of the established political order

The hegemonic position of the INC in the early decades after independence is characterised in political science as a system of one-party dominance. In the Indian political discourse it is usually described simply as the 'Congress System.' The main characteristic of this system is the ability of the dominant party to occupy the centrist position in the political spectrum, pragmatically shifting its political agenda to partially incorporate moderate left- or right-wing positions. By doing this, the dominant party can gain enough votes to ensure the electoral defeat of the ideologically divided opposition, and emerges as the only viable party for government formation despite multiparty competition (Kothari 1964).

To counter this system, the leading socialist politician Ram Manohar Lohia in the 1960s propagated the unity of opposition forces from both the left and the right against Congress dominance. In the Indian political discourse, this was termed 'anti-Congressism.' Mostly in northern and western India, the main socialist parties entered into electoral arrangements with right-wing political parties, especially the BJS, and managed to form generally short-lived minority governments with support from the latter, the *Samyukta Vidhayak Dal* (SVD) governments. Lohia also affected a shift in socialist political strategy: From the 1960s onwards, socialist parties began to emerge as the main representative of political interests of the intermediate castes, especially those that had benefited from the land reforms outlined above, e.g. Yadavs and Jats in much of northern India (Hasan 1998). In parts of the Hindi heartland, this corresponded with the emergence of the socialist influenced, but essentially caste-based *Bharatiya Lok Dal* (BLD). With Congress dominance challenged in the South by ethno-linguistic parties, by the communists in Kerala and West Bengal, and the socialist-led SVD governments in the Hindi heartland, opposition parties began to emerge as viable contenders for political power, in effect largely destroying the system of one-party dominance.

Nehru's death in 1964 and the death of his successor as Prime Minister, Lal Bahadur Shastri, at the end of the peace negotiations with Pakistan in Tashkent left the Congress without a central leadership capable of uniting the various factions and regional party leaders. Effective power within the party shifted to a group of regional leaders, the so-called Syndicate, who opted for Indira Gandhi as consensus prime ministerial candidate. Apart from her family background, Indira Gandhi was selected by the Syndicate precisely because of her lack of a support base in the organisational wing of the party, in order to ensure her continuing dependence on the regional leaders.

Indira Gandhi ensured her own primacy within the Congress by engineering a split within the INC in 1969, quintessentially dividing the party into its organisational apparatus – which evolved into a separate party under the Syndicate's leadership and later merged with the socialist spectrum – and its parliamentary wing which was controlled by her. Instead of relying on the elaborate system of clientelist networks the Congress had created, Indira Gandhi opted for left-wing populism, including the centralisation of decision-making within the party and the government. The latter ensured that her primacy in the party could not be challenged from within, since the remnants of the party apparatus were prevented from producing a second line of leadership, and political success depended on proximity to her and her advisors. In doing so, however, Indira Gandhi severely weakened her own party, and in the long run enabled the opposition parties to establish themselves as the main representatives of organised political interests, especially regarding the structure of clientelist networks.[12]

Utilising the Indian success in the 1971 war with Pakistan and her leftist rhetoric, Indira Gandhi managed to win a clear majority in the ensuing general elections, but afterwards failed to contain increasing efforts at mobilisation by the opposition parties, led by Jayaprakash Narayan, one of the main socialist leaders of the independence movement. In 1975, after having been convicted in a case of misuse of government resources in her election campaign, she declared emergency rule, and proceeded to arrest most opposition leaders and a vast number of opposition party cadres.

Economically, Indira Gandhi opted for increased industrialisation with a preference for direct state intervention, in some instances including the nationalisation of certain sectors, notably banking which, in turn, provided the resources for her industrialisation policies. The most important economic policy shift under her rule was the implementation of the so-called Green Revolution, in essence the capitalisation of agricultural production,[13] including increased use of fertilisers and machinery. The Green Revolution in a very short time turned India from a net importer of agricultural produce to a major exporter of the latter. Food sufficiency significantly contributed to Indian industrialisation, especially regarding the generation of resources from agriculture and the increased availability of labour. Concerning the power structure in rural India, especially in the areas which adapted early to the new policies, the Green Revolution consolidated the effects of the earlier land reforms, the rise of the numerically large, land-owning and politically organised intermediate castes.[14]

After her large-scale repression of the opposition, Indira Gandhi called for general elections in 1977 which she lost to a unified opposition, the Janata Party (JP), which included most former socialist parties, the old organisational wing of the INC, and the erstwhile *Jan Sangh*. The JP split in 1979, leading to the re-emergence of the *Lok Dal* and the founding of the BJP as the successor to the BJS.[15]

The emergence of the current political system

After the split of the JP, Indira Gandhi returned to power in 1980 due to a once again divided opposition, and in the wake of militant secessionist movements in the Punjab and Kashmir shifted the political stance of the Congress party from left- to right-wing populism, including a political rhetoric borrowing from Hindu nationalist ideology. The latter is classified as 'soft *hindutva*' in the Indian political discourse. The second Indira Gandhi government militarily suppressed the Punjabi secessionist movement. After the military attack on the *Hari Mandir* in Amritsar, Indira Gandhi was assassinated by her own Sikh bodyguards.[16]

The Congress chose her remaining son, Rajiv Gandhi, as her successor, and called for general elections in the wake of a Congress-organised pogrom against Sikhs in Delhi.[17] The elections produced a massive majority for the Congress in parliament. The right-wing populism and 'soft *hindutva*' stances appealed to much of the Indian middle class, which by then apart from dominating most political institutions had emerged as a significant electoral constituency as well. Rajiv Gandhi went further to consolidate the party's hold on the middle class by projecting a political rhetoric based on technocratic terminology and appealing to middle class interests. Though the reform measures under Rajiv Gandhi were soon discontinued, the discourse on economic policy shifted away from its previous socialist roots and state intervention, preparing the ground for the shift towards liberalisation which, however, became the dominant theme of economic policy in India only from the early 1990s onwards.[18]

The opposition reacted by utilising emerging agricultural movements led by those segments of rural Indian society which had benefited the most from the Green Revolution, but also encompassing weaker social sections from the countryside. The emergence of substantial *kisan* (farmer) movements[19] went along with a political mobilisation of intermediate and lower castes, the so-called

Other Backward Classes (OBC), which propagated an extension of existing positive discrimination regimes covering Dalits (Scheduled Castes) and Tribals (Scheduled Tribes).[20] Constitutional provisions for this extension existed, but had not been enacted due to a lack of consensus on the precise classification of OBC groups and a lack of political expediency. The socialist opposition parties now began to articulate a demand of implementing the recommendations of the so-called Mandal Commission, which had favoured reservation for OBC groups on a caste basis, including most of the relatively prosperous land-owning castes.[21]

Rajiv Gandhi by and large continued the 'soft *hindutva*' rhetoric used by his mother, but at the same time attempted to counter the ensuing discontent among Muslims, a major electoral base of the INC, by selectively serving organised Muslim political interests, especially regarding the continued validity of Muslim Personal Law.[22] The Congress party also had to contend with substantial corruption scandals, including the notorious Bofors scandal.[23] On this issue, the former Congress leader V. P. Singh left the Congress and emerged as the leading political figure of the opposition. In the late 1980s, he formed the *Janata Dal*, re-unifying various socialist splinter groups including the *Lok Dal*. In alliance with several regional parties and with electoral arrangements with both the BJP and the communists he won the ensuing general elections in 1989, and formed the so-called National Front government, which included outside support from the BJP and the Left Front. To consolidate his electoral base, and also to marginalise intra-party rivals, V. P. Singh implemented the Mandal Commission report. This led to substantial social unrest among the upper castes, especially upper caste students, since OBC quotas were to be introduced in educational institutions.

The Mandal controversy placed the Congress and the BJP in a significant dilemma: Both parties relied in several important state units on solid upper caste support, while on OBC support in others. While the Congress largely failed to react, leading to large-scale disenchantment with the party among its upper caste and middle class supporters, the BJP under the leadership of L. K. Advani reacted with developing a complex counter-strategy: While the party officially welcomed the implementation of reservation for OBC communities, its leaders (especially at the local level) began to participate in the anti-Mandal campaign.[24] The party also used a strategy of social engineering, derived from Hindu nationalist ideology which perceives all castes as harmoniously linked in an organic fashion despite hierarchical differences and, hence, incapable of being in conflict with each other, projecting party leaders from the OBC communities as proof of its commitment to the OBC cause.[25]

Apart from this, the BJP embarked on a major diversion, using a decades-old local controversy over a mosque in the North Indian town Ayodhya to organise one of the biggest mass movements in independent India along with its sister organisations from the *Sangh Parivar*. The Ayodhya campaign was accompanied by large-scale communal violence encompassing most Indian regions, while the central government's reaction to it provided the BJP with the opportunity to withdraw support, leading to the collapse of the V. P. Singh government. While the Congress managed to form a minority government under the leadership of P. V. Narasimha Rao after the 1991 elections, the BJP emerged as the largest opposition party and was able to form state governments in parts of northern and western India.

The twin controversies, Mandal and *mandir* in the Indian discourse, formed the most significant political planks until the mid-1990s, despite the fact that one of the most important policy shifts was the turn towards economic liberalisation, which was implemented by the Congress government but supported strongly by the BJP.[26] Liberalisation formed a way to consolidate middle class dominance despite the state's positive discrimination policies and the numerical superiority of the lower classes, in that it removed certain economic sectors from political interference. This, in turn, increases middle class employment opportunities in these sectors, since this social segment possesses advantages especially regarding education and information over lower class competitors.

With the destruction of the Babri Masjid in Ayodhya in late 1992, the BJP began to moderate its political positions, most importantly shifting towards the articulation of middle class economic interests.[27] However, the party remained largely isolated, which became apparent after the 1996 general elections in which it had emerged as the single largest party but found itself unable to gain support from smaller parties to form the government. Instead, the Congress agreed to support a Janata Dal-led government including most socialist and regional parties, the United Front, from the outside. After the Congress withdrew its support in 1998, the BJP managed to overcome its isolation, and formed the National Democratic Alliance (NDA) which included several socialist and regional parties to form the central government with A.B. Vajpayee as its prime minister.

With the BJP in power between 1998 and 2004, the Congress shed its aversion to forming alliances with smaller parties and set up the United Progressive Alliance with several socialist and regional parties including some former allies of the BJP. The UPA managed to form a minority government with outside support from the Left Front in 2004 with Manmohan Singh as prime minister and (in a different composition of the alliance) also won the 2009 general elections. While the Indian party system has appeared bipolar in the last decade, in fact, the strength of the smaller parties, mostly socialist, ethno-linguistic, and Dalit parties has by and large continued to increase.

Indian politics and the contest over participation in rent allocation

The historical narrative of Indian politics outlined above can be conceptualised by the application of the concepts of the state class, rent allocation, and rent scarcity following Elsenhans.[28] Quintessentially, India after independence formed a semi-rentier state in which the relative lack of sources for the generation of rents was partially compensated by the establishment of a large public sector and the regime of state interference in the private sector – the so-called license-permit-

raj. Political power rested to a large extent with a state class – the political and administrative elite segments from the local level upwards – which was able to use its political power to indirectly generate resources from interfering in economic activity in both the public and the private sector. These resources were then partially reinvested in order to sustain political dominance and the resulting access to the process of rent allocation, in effect generating legitimacy.[29]

In contrast to rent allocation regimes in many other countries,[30] the Indian system of rent allocation of necessity had to be decentralised: State interference in economic activity largely took place at the local level and the rents being generated by this interference were partially passed upwards by local politicians and bureaucrats in order to ensure continued patronage from politicians at the higher levels. The regime of rent allocation played an important role in state formation in India: It enabled the former independence movement, the Indian National Congress (INC), to transform its moral authority into real political power in that it provided the means to integrate diverse and often divergent interests within the framework of its party organisation and, hence, into the structure of the Indian state. It provided a major incentive for participation within the legal and constitutional framework of the Indian polity and helped to marginalise groups which resisted this integration.[31] The system of rent generation and distribution was maintained (and enlarged) later, since it also formed the most important instrument to achieve and maintain the pre-dominance of the INC as the ruling party and the social segment which principally and most directly benefited from it, the state class. In essence, the decentralisation of control over rent allocation served to integrate diverse political interests in the process of nation-building but, eventually, also facilitated the rise of opposition forces against the dominant INC. Lacking large-scale natural resources for the generation of sufficient rents, increasing demands for participation in the rent allocation process led to rent scarcity as the demand for rents outstripped supply.

Historically, rent scarcity became increasingly acute from the late 1960s onwards, since political participation before – at least meaningful participation in the Indian state's decision-making apparatus – remained restricted to elite sections of society and the higher and intermediate levels of the Indian administration. Political competition among the elite led to the gradual extension of this participation to the politically more organised social groups, at first by co-optation, which later emerged as contenders for political power in their own right, without a need for intermediaries from the established elite. This continuing process is often expressed in terms of an emancipatory movement against traditional patterns of discrimination against certain social sections – the 'social justice' discourse – which is why the Indian political discourse appears largely pre-occupied with identity at first glance.

The state class tends to reinvest rents in order to maintain its dominant position in the rent allocation system by using rents to consolidate the respective political support bases. Rents are thus redistributed among the population in accordance with political relevance.[32] Since maintenance of the status of political actors in the rent allocation process is essential, political loyalty becomes important vis-à-vis the redistribution of rents. To ensure continued loyalty, the redistribution of rents tends to take place through clientelist networks.

Clientelist networks are formed in two distinct ways: in personalised networks (factions) and group loyalties to specific political leaders and parties, the latter most often in the form of caste and religious communities. Factions are formed as loose personal networks between politicians (including local notables who act as power brokers) usually within a party, but in some cases also transcending party membership. Factions include hierarchical relationships between factional leaders and their followers, based on personal loyalty, but also act as platforms for the articulation of common political interests for their respective members. Since factions rarely become institutionalised to a significant degree, their composition and relevance often fluctuates. However, factional loyalty is often more important to political success than party discipline, so that intra-party factional conflicts often lead even to formal party splits.

In India's democratic polity, voting plays a significant role in rent distribution.[33] While in the early decades after independence the co-optation of local notables remained one of the most important reasons for political success, competition between factions and political leaders led to the extension of political participation by incorporating previously less organised segments of society, whose emerging leaders where incorporated into the various parties and factions. Politically organised segments tended to be organised and mobilised in terms of communal or caste identity. Within the rent distribution process religious community and, most importantly, caste was used to facilitate the redistribution of rents to the respective support bases of political leaders since, at least at the local level, community membership is readily identifiable for political parties. While every community can, in principle, be organised politically, most are organised only at the local level.[34] A number of politically important castes have, however, linked themselves to certain factions and political parties, usually at the regional level. These castes provide the core electoral support for a variety of parties, including the Congress and the BJP. Smaller regional parties, most often from the socialist or ethno-linguistic spectrum are more openly basing their support on specific castes, and have often been labelled as 'casteist' parties by their rivals in return.

Caste has evolved to form an instrument for the rent distribution process, since clientelist networks based on caste are much less complex to maintain than the mere co-optation of local leaders into factional networks. Long-term linkages between castes and political parties also offer politicians a core support base, which tends to stay loyal regardless of shifts in a leader's or party's popularity arising out of everyday politics. For these castes, initially only the dominant or entrenched castes at the local level,[35] the linkage with party politics, in turn, provides the means to maintain their status, at least as long as the respective party is perceived to have a viable chance of staying in or coming to power. In part, the democratic process in India has provided rising social strata opportunities to challenge this initial predominance. For certain lower caste groups, caste has accordingly become an 'instrument for equalisation' (Varshney 2003: 4).

The Indian middle class was originally largely based on administrative professions. The same is obviously the case with the state class, which incorporated a large part of the original middle class. The social and economic status of the original middle class was accordingly based to a large extent on the system of rent allocation. With India constituting a semi-rentier state the total amount of rents available was limited at the outset. The moderate success of Indian import-substituting industrialisation enabled the Indian state for a time to extend the rent allocation system to co-opt newly assertive social segments, especially the emerging new lower middle classes. Rents became increasingly scarce, however, from the mid-1960s onwards, since demand by newly mobilised social segments began to outstrip the supply of rents, and Indian economic policy was not capable of producing sufficient increases in rents.

The two most important factors for this rise in demand for rents were the rise of lower middle classes in the urban and rural sectors, due to industrialisation and the main agricultural policy initiatives after independence, land reforms and the Green Revolution. Both led to the creation of politically organised, relatively prosperous social segments which were, however, prevented from fully participating in rent allocation, since their full incorporation would have significantly reduced the socio-economic position of the old and politically dominant middle classes. At the same time, political assertion of select lower class groups, especially with regard to the state's efforts at positive discrimination to overcome traditional social and economic backwardness, placed further pressure on the overall rent base of the Indian state.

The democratic polity of India enables newly assertive groups to challenge established, previously dominant social segments via participation within the political system if they are numerous, politically organised and in possession of sufficient material means to overcome resistance by the established order.[36] The political history of India between the mid-1960s and the early 1990s can by and large be interpreted, accordingly, as a struggle between previously established dominant groups from the old middle class and newly rising lower middle classes which benefited from agricultural reforms and industrialisation but were, at the same time, threatened by lower class political organisation. In the public discourse, the challenge of newly assertive against established social sections was usually couched in a political idiom centring on 'social justice.' In turn, the established sections attempted to resist this challenge of their political predominance discursively by propagating the concept of 'merit.'

The old middle classes largely managed to prevent political parties representing the newly assertive sections from coming to power until the late 1980s, especially in North India where the caste-wise composition of society was more even, with a substantial segment of society belonging to the upper castes (Hasan 1998: 9). With the failure of this strategy to prevent the access of newly assertive groups to state-controlled resources becoming apparent in the late 1980s, and lower class political organisation reaching a level where lower class mobilisation presented a viable challenge to the middle classes, the latter began to turn towards a new strategy of maintaining their socio-economic positions, embracing globalisation and attempting to partially dismantle the structure of state intervention in the Indian economy. In the public discourse, the two main paradigms of 'social justice' and 'merit' – which initially had been antagonistic in character – increasingly co-existed harmoniously, enabling political parties to combine elements from both these discourses in reaching out to their respective supporters.[37]

The middle classes with a relatively high standard of formal education and networks of information possess significant competitive advantages over lower class groups in their access to jobs in the most important economic sectors affected by liberalisation.[38] State intervention in these sectors would negate these advantages to some extent, as employment would partially become politically contested. The attempt to remove certain economic sectors from political contest strongly benefits the Indian middle class, apart from having contributed to higher overall growth rates which once again have benefitted mostly the middle classes.

Liberalisation includes two different measures: divestment of the public sector and deregulation of the economy. The former is a straightforward process of privatisation. This is beneficial for large parts of the middle classes because private sector companies do not have to adhere to the regime of positive discrimination for 'backward' sections of society, providing enhanced employment opportunities. It also benefits the economic elite who can invest into acquiring substantial industrial units at comparatively low prices. Deregulation dismantles the structure of rent allocation, and is accordingly resisted strongly by those benefiting from rent allocation, including much of the political elite. Both measures continue to be resisted by a variety of political forces. Especially deregulation, however, divides the middle classes and the elite itself: The administrative segments among the middle classes and the elite still benefit the most from rent allocation and, hence, do not have a stake in its dismantling. Free market-oriented middle class and elite segments, at the same time, tend to prefer deregulation. Apart from removing select economic sectors from political contest, this provides an opportunity to increase their social and economic status at the cost of the administrative segment which had been dominant previously.[39]

Liberalisation was initiated by the Congress, rhetorically in the 1980s with the shift to a technocratic terminology under Rajiv Gandhi, and implemented as economic policy in the early 1990s under Narasimha Rao. It is unsurprising that the two main champions of liberalisation in the Indian political spectrum are precisely the parties which depend most on middle class votes: the Congress and the BJP.[40] Within both parties, however, liberalisation remains partially contested by groups and leaders who draw their main support from either the lower classes or the administrative segment of the middle classes and elite. The process of liberalisation, hence, tends to go forward in spurts and has often been restricted to mere divestment. Still, the paradigm shift to liberalisation has continued, with no political group being willing or capable to go against middle class interests too far.

Political parties in India with minor exceptions do not openly appeal to class interests, despite the presence of lower class-based parties and movements and the strong influence on Indian politics by the middle class.[41] In fact, the latter constitutes one of the main reasons for this lack of class cleavages in the political rhetoric. The middle class dominates both political institutions and the political discourse, but despite its significant growth since independence is not capable of determining electoral results. Since the early 1990s, there is a trend of decreasing middle class participation in elections in contrast to increases in lower class participation. However, this does not lead to significant shifts in economic policy in India.

Middle class domination is partially due to the comparatively high standards of formal education and competitive advantages in gaining information. However, with rent allocation being based so strongly on caste divisions, most benefits of this system are acquired by the respective middle class segments among these castes and caste groups since highly paid employment in the public sector and the administration is restricted by a system of classifying positions according to the formal educational qualifications required. In the political discourse in India, identity often replaces economic policy as the main instrument for political mobilisation. The recourse to identity is generally safe for the middle classes, because the numerous divisions within Indian society allow the formation of politicised communities which are transcending class divisions. Middle class domination within these communities is less open than it would be in class-based mobilisation, and rhetorically overcome by the bonding effect of communal identity.[42]

Political parties in India, as a rule, appeal to four different forms of community identity: (1) secular nationalism, (2) cultural nationalism (exemplified by Hindu nationalism but, in fact, also present among the religious minorities), (3) ethnic or linguistic sub-nationalism, and (4) caste identity.[43] In all four cases, community membership is vast and encompasses various segments, most importantly the middle classes who emerge as leaders of the respective communities. Community membership, however, is multiple and often over-lapping, creating a relatively complex web of political allegiances in many cases. Identity obviously also serves as an instrument for emotional appeals. Its function to maintain class hierarchies, at the same time, is of enormous importance to understand the, at first glance puzzling, lack of openly articulated class interests in India.

The structural factors shaping Indian politics discussed above result in a political process which is mostly devoid of ideological divisions in actual day-to-day politics, despite the enormous importance attributed to some ideological cleavages, most importantly the cleavage of secular in contrast to Hindu nationalism and caste cleavages, in political rhetoric. The factional composition of party organisations coupled with the fluctuations caused by usually caste-based distinct voting blocks in society devoid of clear ideological leanings and primarily interested in gaining and maintaining access to state-controlled resources result in frequent party splits (and mergers). These lead to the emergence of a highly fractionalised party system whose components with some exceptions can come together to form short-lived alliances, thus enabling government formation.

The turn towards liberalisation is slowly undermining the rentier state base of the Indian polity. But with the dominant middle classes shying away from open articulation of class-based interests, and lower class mobilisation mostly aiming at participation in the rent allocation process, the emergence of a polity based on distinct class interests is unlikely in the near future. Instead, political mobilisation overtly will remain focussed on issues of identity which provide a cover for diverging economic policy interests. In this, Hindu nationalism forms one of the most potent concepts in contemporary India.

4 Ideology and political practice of Hindu nationalism

The evolution of Hindu nationalism and secularism in India

Hindu nationalism comprises a relatively broad spectrum of political, social and moral ideas which are mainly linked by shared views on Indian and Hindu identity. These form an alternative to the secular nationalist concept of national identity prevalent in the Indian polity. This leads to the establishment of a secularism-Hindu nationalism cleavage in the Indian party system. While this cleavage remains relevant for the positioning of Indian political parties, strict analytical separation between a secular and a Hindu nationalist segment in Indian politics tends to obscure certain developments with regard to the main ideologies represented in the Indian polity that affect the significance of this cleavage. Furthermore, it tends to disregard the evolution of both Hindu nationalism and secularism in the political practice of their respective proponents. To understand the concept of Hindu nationalism, it is therefore necessary to trace its ideational evolution (and that of secularism in India) as well as the development of the concept in Indian party politics.

The formation of conceptions of Indian national identity

The origin of both Hindu nationalism and secular nationalism in India can be traced to the emergence of a variety of reform movements and educational projects in the second half of the nineteenth and the early twentieth century that operated in the context of socio-economic transformation under colonial rule, especially the emergence of a modern middle class. Prominent among these are the Arya Samaj and Brahmo Samaj among Hindus and the Deobandi school among Muslims, as well as educational reformers like Madan Mohan Malaviya and Syed Ahmed Khan.[1] While these reform movements represent a wide variety of social, religious or political ideas, they can be interpreted as various strands of a larger modernising project in Indian society that arose from the perception of defeat of the previously established socio-political order by the British in the wake of the colonisation of India, especially in the rebellion against the East India Company of 1857. A number of authors, most importantly Dirks (2001), have also noted the importance of British colonial policy during the same period of time, especially enumeration practices, for the creation of communal political identities in India.

Social and political conceptions of identity that originated from this modernisation process can largely be subsumed into the classifications of secular and cultural nationalisms, although these were (and continue to be) supplemented by various forms of sub-national, including ethno-linguistic, regional and communal identities. The main differences between the two conceptions of nationality, in both ideological and practical terms, relate to the mode of inclusion of religiously defined minority communities into the conceptual framework of Indian nationality.

Secularism as a concept was introduced into the Indian political discourse by the British colonial rulers, and was taken up and strongly advocated by the dominant section of the Indian nationalist movement and most of its important leaders. However, the concept of secularism underwent significant changes with its adaptation to the Indian political context, even in the British political practice. As mentioned above, the British enumeration policies in India, especially with regard to the decadal census (starting from the late nineteenth century), influenced the formation of social and political identities by attempting to define and categorise communities. This recognition of disparate communities formed part of a realisation by the British colonial rulers that British dominance in India could best be preserved by co-opting community leaders, especially at the local level. In this way, the British at least partially gave recognition to the idea that Indian society was constituted on the basis of a multitude of distinct communities, defined primarily by religion, caste and – in some cases – tribe.[2] In this interplay of community-based social and political forces, the British assumed the role of an arbiter, ideally an impartial arbiter. Secularism as a political concept became increasingly deprived of its original laic content, and instead became increasingly based on the idea of equal and fair treatment of all communities by the state.[3]

Aiming at the composition of a unified nationalist movement comprising all sections of Indian society and a vast variety of divergent interests, the Indian National Congress incorporated this interpretation of secularism into its political strategies and ideological outlook. Instead of attempting to mobilise Indian society as a single entity for the nationalist cause, the INC effectively mobilised Indian society segmented by communities, and thus accepted the association of secularism with impartiality vis-à-vis community, including religiously defined communities. The INC began to include religious elements in its political strategy early on. The adoption of religious (generally Hindu) religious symbolism into the party's political rhetoric at an early stage was apparent in the politics of Bal Gangadhar Tilak.

The concept of political secularism evolved under the twin challenges of expressly Hindu politics (even within the INC) and the Two Nation Theory of the Muslim League. Among the most influential political leaders, Gandhi, with his emphasis on often religiously derived morality in politics and the central place accorded to an idealised version of Indian village society in his political approach epitomised the transformation of secularism as a concept by its adaptation to Indian politics. Gandhian secularism did not in the least exclude religion from politics but rather attempted to establish its raison d'être from religious doctrine itself, using an ecumenically inspired interpretation of the latter to overcome the inherent sectarian divisiveness of religious practice. Stressing the basic doctrinal unity of all religions on the principles of moral behaviour, Gandhi endeavoured to include relevant religious doctrines and practices from all major religions in India into the political discourse while treating them and their respective believers as equals. This stance was often contested by representatives from both the religious minorities and the religious majority as being biased to the detriment of the respective group.

In comparison to Gandhian thought, the Nehruvian conception of secularism was closer to its European laic origins. Nehru favoured the exclusion of religion at least from the legal framework of the polity and generally attempted to reduce the political utilisation of religion by the Indian National Congress. Nehru generally desisted from projecting religious symbolism, while cultivating his image as a modern, moderately left-wing nationalist leader. After independence, his position of predominance within the INC was challenged on account of this orientation by leaders of the party's conservative spectrum, especially from the Hindi heartland, though in the end unsuccessfully.[4]

In the run-up to independence the mainstream secular orientation of Indian politics was challenged by the Muslim League which mobilised support with the help of the Two Nation Theory as well as by advocates of more openly religious and communal politics from among the Hindu majority community, and to a lesser extent from among the Muslim and Sikh communities. The concept of secularism as it is usually interpreted in contemporary India, by emphasising equal treatment to all communities (Madan 1997: 189), reinforces an often conciliatory and accommodative approach to issues of identity which has served the Indian state well on several occasions, most notably the ethno-linguistic demands for a reform of the federal polity in the early decades after independence (Dasgupta 2001; Mitra 1996). However, proponents of the 'strong' state, whether secular or Hindu nationalist, have tended to perceive the, at times, accommodative character of state responses as a sign of weakness in the face of perceived threats to Indian national and territorial integrity.[5]

'Strong' responses by the state to the politicisation of sub-national identity may take the form of police or military repression. Ideologically, however, these responses are complemented by a desire for the creation of a strong, unified national identity. Within the secular political spectrum, this desire stresses Indian nationality as an overarching common identity under the slogan of 'unity in diversity.' Hindu nationalism, while giving recognition to the existence of multiple communities and community identities in India, is appealing to proponents of the 'strong' state by its aim of creating a unified national identity drawing upon select elements of the Hindu majority community's traditional heritage.

Hindu nationalism developed as an alternative conception of national identity to secular nationalism in a period of rapid social and economical transformation

as a counter ideology to the increasing assertion of Muslim and lower caste political interests and the perceived weakness (or unwillingness) of the nationalist
movement to counter this assertion. Socio-economically, it originated from the
small town petty bourgeois milieu in the Indian hinterland, from among communities whose social and economic position was comparatively precarious and,
hence, more threatened by increasingly assertive lower social strata. The constituency of Hindu nationalism was made up to a large extent from among the upper
castes, especially Brahmins and Banias. These possessed high religious status in
the traditional order, while their political status was threatened by the imminent
transition to mass-based political mobilisation. The recourse to religiously
defined and sanctioned community identity and the corresponding ideal social
order which characterises Hindu nationalism is, under these circumstances,
hardly surprising.

Gooptu (1997: 887) notes that the precarious situation of the lower classes
created tensions between Hindu and Muslim workers. While Hindu nationalism
benefited Hindu lower classes to some extent, its unifying aims helped the petty
bourgeoisie to overcome (at least partially) the threat of lower class assertion,
since it resulted in the incorporation of Hindu lower classes in a political project
dominated by the urban lower middle classes. The ideological rejection of
secular nationalism by the Hindu right in the first half of the twentieth century
thus formed part of a political strategy to maintain its main constituency's socio-
economic status in a rapidly changing context. In this regard, early Hindu nationalism can be interpreted as an attempt to overcome the challenge posed by lower
caste and class assertion by creating and strengthening a unified Hindu majority
community, partially incorporating traditional hierarchies, against an imagined
enemy community, Indian Muslims.[6] While Hindu nationalists certainly took
part in the anti-colonial movement, if mostly at the fringes, Hindu nationalism as
an ideology remained largely pre-occupied with an internal enemy, not the
British colonial legacy (Hansen 1999: 79–80). Western cultural and ideational
influence was strongly opposed only to the extent that it formed the ideological
basis of the secular nationalist movement, the main rival of Hindu nationalism.

Hindu nationalism and secularism: the secular cleavage

The cleavage between Hindu nationalism and secularism appears insurmounta-
ble at first glance, but has been much less so in political practice. This is partially
due to the constraints the Indian polity poses to Hindu nationalists in order to
operate freely.[7] These constraints necessitate the adaptation of Hindu nationalism to the concept of secularism as it is spelt out in the Indian constitution as
well as legal and constitutional provisions regarding civil liberties including
those of minority communities. Apart from adherence to constitutional norms,
political practice places constrictions to Hindu nationalists regarding the acceptance of the overall ethnic and cultural diversity of India, including the existence
of multiple layers of identity which inhibit the formation of a single, unified
majority community. In sum, political viability in India limits the feasibility of

exclusionary political strategies to some degree and forces non-secular political actors to respect a minimal interpretation of secularism.

The partial ideological adaptation of Hindu nationalism to secularism is facilitated by the specifically Indian interpretation of the latter concept, outlined above, which implicitly recognises the political role of community. It is further enhanced by the principally identitarian character of Hindu nationalism which allows its proponents a highly flexible approach to religious doctrine. Hindu nationalist ideology attempts to express and justify its partial adaptation to secularism, mainly by proposing that Hinduism inherently incorporates secularity in that it accepts the diversity of religious doctrines and customs prevalent in the Hindu religious spectrum (Bhatt 2004: 138). In this argumentation, secularism reinterpreted as doctrinal religious diversity becomes a specifically Hindu concept which, in turn, allegedly distinguishes Hinduism from other religions, especially Islam.

In addition, by approximating the conceptions of Indian national and Hindu communal identity, Indian-ness and Hindu-ness, Hindu nationalism includes an ambiguity which allows the incorporation of non-Hindu groups into its fold as long as the (dominant) contribution of Hinduism to Indian culture is acknowledged and no extra-territorial loyalties are suspected. The conditions to the inclusion of non-Hindus into the Hindu nationalist spectrum are highly compatible with the profession of love of the motherland, as stipulated by Savarkar as one of the main criteria for Indian- and Hindu-ness (Madan 1997: 220).

The suspected disloyalty to the Indian motherland of some communities, especially Muslims and certain Christian sects, by Hindu nationalists finds its expression in a distinction between 'Indian' and 'foreign' religions. In short, 'Indian' religions like Buddhism, Jainism and Sikhism are considered part of the overall Indian religious tradition, which is dominated by Hinduism. These religions are thus perceived to be related to Hinduism and Indian tradition in general. 'Foreign' religions are perceived to have originated from other cultural contexts. In Hindu nationalist parlance, since these religions' centres lie outside the Indian cultural entity, their adherents' loyalty to India over their loyalties to other countries cannot be taken for granted. Individual adherents of 'foreign' religions are not considered to be anti-national per se, but their loyalty to the Indian motherland has to be proven (Jaffrelot 1996: 26–32).

Accommodative practices vis-à-vis the minorities and measures of positive discrimination towards traditionally disadvantaged Hindu communities are ideologically suspect from the point of view of a Hindu nationalist. The former are often labelled as 'minority appeasement.' In fact, Hindu nationalists have generally attempted to counter these practices by taking recourse to the secular argument of equal treatment of all citizens, regardless of their religion, by the state. This line of argumentation is exemplified in the Hindu nationalist discourse on Muslim Personal Law.

The Indian constitution accepts the co-existence of community-specific personal laws with the Indian Civil Code, though only as a temporary provision. After independence, the Indian state abolished Hindu Personal Law. With the implementation and (by and large) successful enforcement of the Hindu Code Bill, the continued legal validity of Muslim Personal Law became one of the main political planks of Hindu nationalist organisations who argued in favour of Muslim Personal Law's abolition. In this specific instance, a strong commonality in argumentation exists between progressive secularists and Hindu nationalists. Since to date successive Indian governments, mostly dominated by secular nationalist political parties, have not been able or willing to follow the constitutional stipulation of reforming the personal laws, Hindu nationalists have been able to question the commitment of secular nationalist parties to the principle of secularism. In the Hindu nationalist discourse, the refusal to reform Muslim Personal Law indicates that secular nationalists use secularism only selectively. Accordingly, they are depicted as 'pseudo-secularists,' with an implication that Hindu nationalism should be considered as the only truly secular political ideology.

The Hindu nationalist argumentation vis-à-vis the perceived lack of commitment to secularism by the secular nationalist parties was reinforced in the 1980s by the controversy over the so-called Shah Bano case. Here, the Congress government under the leadership of Rajiv Gandhi intervened politically to circumvent the assertion of the common civil code's supremacy over Muslim Personal Law by the Indian Supreme Court, ostentatiously in order to placate conservative Muslim political interest groups (M. Hasan 1998: 224–5). The Shah Bano case emerged as a major political plank of Hindu nationalist organisations who equated secularism as practised by the Congress party with 'minority appeasement.' The BJP managed to position itself as a progressive political force, claiming to care for Muslims suffering under the allegedly illiberal and anachronistic social order codified by Muslim Personal Law (Jaffrelot 1996: 344). The BJP publicly began to focus on the socio-economic development of the Muslim community, instead of its rights of cultural self-determination.

The clear distinction between secularism and Hindu nationalism implied in the supposition of a corresponding cleavage is compromised in political practice not only by the partial adaptation of Hindu nationalism to the secular nationalist dominated Indian polity. Some secular politicians have tended to articulate policies in a way that closely resembles the Hindu nationalist idiom, while examples of alliances between secular and Hindu nationalist organisations are far more common than implied by the postulated cleavage.

Political discourses by secular nationalist organisations and politicians which include references to Hindu nationalist topics or sentiments are usually classified as 'soft *hindutva*' and are, at times, strategic in character: Secular nationalist parties attempt to limit the political space available for Hindu nationalism, or find it inopportune to take clear stances against Hindu nationalist sentiments among the majority community on particular issues. A related aspect is the inclusion of politicians close to Hindu nationalism into secular nationalist political parties. The INC as an umbrella organisation encompassing politicians with various divergent ideological positions included a number of relatively high profile leaders with soft *hindutva* leanings from the outset and is continuing to induct politicians from the Hindu nationalist spectrum even nowadays.[8]

Indira Gandhi initiated a repositioning of the INC in the early 1980s which resulted in a shift away from the party's left-leaning populism of the early 1970s towards a right-leaning populism, including a preference for strong state responses to internal disorder and soft *hindutva* rhetoric. This shift was partially continued by Rajiv Gandhi, although he attempted to gain support among the minorities by simultaneously articulating organised Muslim interests. The 1980s thus form a period in which soft *hindutva* stances became established even at the top level of the Congress leadership (Banerjee 2007: 3194). Soft *hindutva* is usually associated with the Congress party, although a number of other parties have tended to utilise soft *hindutva* idioms. A notable example in contemporary India is the Dravidian *All India Anna Dravida Munnetra Kazhagam* (AIADMK), one of the two main contenders for political power in Tamil Nadu.[9]

While soft *hindutva* positions are most often related to political strategies by the INC to extend its support among the majority community, leaving aside local exceptions the question of allying with the BJP does not arise for the Congress, largely due to the national and state level competition between the two parties. The Congress has, at times, gained tacit support by the RSS and other Hindu nationalist organisations, most notably in the 1984 general elections (Jaffrelot 1996: 329–30; Malik and Singh 1994: 188). The phenomenon of alliances between secular and Hindu nationalist political parties has been restricted to the Congress' rivals. The concept of coalitions between the left- and right-wing rivals of the Congress party was championed in the 1960s by the socialist leader Ram Manohar Lohia as a strategy to overcome one-party dominance in India. Until the early 1990s, the process of formation and collapse of left–right coalitions to keep the Congress out of power formed one of the main patterns of the Indian political process. The rise of the BJP in the wake of the Ayodhya movement led to the temporary formation of a reverse alliance system, where the Congress supported a JD-led coalition, the United Front, the first alliance arrangement in Indian politics ostentatiously founded on the principle of secularism.

As shown above, a stringent division between secular and Hindu nationalism, as implied by the application of cleavage theory, has not been in place during much of India's recent political history, with regard to both political discourse and political strategy. The cleavage concept is, however, helpful to some degree in discussing electoral politics in India, especially voting preferences and electoral alignments between political parties.

Hindu nationalism as a political ideology

While the origin of Hindu nationalism can be traced back to the nineteenth century, its formulation as a distinct political ideology took place between the 1920s and the early 1940s. The first significant Hindu nationalist organisation, the *Akhil Bharatiya Hindu Mahasabha* (HMS), was founded in the early twentieth century, but at this time still lacked a coherent political ideology (Madan 1997: 218). It was conceived primarily as an organisation which aimed at countering the perceived threat posed by increasing Muslim political organisation, and as such can be interpreted rather as a communal organisation than a Hindu nationalist one.

The first major attempt to create a comprehensive ideological foundation of political Hinduism was carried out by Vinayak Damodar Savarkar, the most notable HMS leader. While in prison, he composed the pamphlet '*Hindutva*: Who is a Hindu?' Published in 1923, it remains one of the most significant contributions to the ideational development of Hindu nationalism.[10]

Savarkar created an ideological outline for political Hinduism and, most importantly, supplied one of its core features: the emphasis on by and large culturally defined Indian national identity. In this way, Savarkar shifted the focus of early political Hinduism on the articulation of diffuse community interests, mostly in reaction to various perceived injustices, towards the formation of a unified national community defined by select elements of its Hindu cultural heritage. To achieve this, Savarkar in his writings attempted to equate Indian-ness with Hindu-ness, while at the same time extending the scope of his concept by incorporating into it a non-cultural feature derived from western nationalism, the profession of national instead of communal identity. In doing so, Savarkar formed the basis for the inclusion of non-Hindu communities into the project of Hindu nationalism, while at the same time creating an ideological argument which aimed at overcoming the multiple fractures within the Hindu community, most importantly divisions by caste and sect.

The *Hindu Mahasabha* lost its leadership role in the spectrum of Hindu nationalism after it unsuccessfully attempted to challenge the predominance of the INC and the Muslim League in parliamentary elections in the 1930s. This leadership role was instead taken up by the RSS. Its first *sarsanghchalak*,[11] Keshawar Baliram Hedgewar, stressed the importance of non-parliamentary political organisation for the creation of a unified Hindu community. The RSS under his leadership advocated instilling national pride, defined culturally by using select elements of Hindu tradition, into its members and the overall Hindu community. In RSS parlance, the emphasis was laid on 'character-building' (Hansen 1999: 92). The seclusion of the RSS from parliamentary politics and its perceived corrupting influences was further reinforced by Hedgewar's successor, Madhav Sadashiv Golwalkar, despite his contribution to the founding of the *Bharatiya Jan Sangh* (BJS). The latter, in fact, was consciously designed to provide the RSS with a parliamentary arm, while still keeping the organisation itself away from the corruption associated with parliamentary politics.

Under the leadership of Shyama Prasad Mookerjee, the early BJS remained pre-occupied with the immediate fallout of the partition of British India, both in terms of its relationship with Pakistan, especially concerning the conflict in Jammu and Kashmir, and the status of Muslims remaining in India. The ideational development of Hindu nationalism was further advanced by Deendayal Upadhyaya, another founding leader of the BJS. Upadhyaya's concept of integral humanism to date provides one of the most comprehensive interpretations of Hindu nationalist ideas. Most importantly, while maintaining the emphasis on culturally defined national identity, Upadhyaya incorporated socio-economic ideas into the ideology of Hindu nationalism, thus creating a full-fledged ideological alternative to the Nehruvian vision of an Indian developmental project prevalent at the time.

Socio-economically, Upadhyaya included Gandhian ideas of the good society based on religiously derived morality and based on the model of an idealised Indian village community (Hansen 1999: 85–6). In contrast to Nehruvian thought, modern technology, while being welcomed in general, was valued by him only insofar as it could be adapted to the Indian context, i.e. without threatening the proposed organic fabric of Indian society. Upadhyaya's concept of integral humanism emphasised the organic character of social relations in a way that closely resembles corporatist ideas, in fact attributing a key role to organic linkage between various social strata in its socio-economic agenda.

The incorporation of a socio-economic element in Hindu nationalist ideology in the concept of integral humanism is clearly spelt out by Upadhyaya while introducing the concept in a series of lectures in Bombay in 1965. Drawing on select components of Hindu cultural tradition and contrasting these to the prevalent discourse on development at the time, Upadhyaya here presents an alternative approach to capitalist and socialist thought, which attempts to link individual, communal and national prosperity and happiness by taking recourse to the allegedly organic character of society inherent in Hindu tradition. The organic linkage of social relationships is depicted as follows:

> [T]he first characteristic of Bharatiya culture is that it looks upon life as an integrated whole. It has an integrated view point. To think of parts may be proper for a specialist but it is not useful from the practical standpoint. The confusion in the West arises primarily from its tendency to think of life in sections and then to attempt to put them together by patch work. We do admit that there is diversity and plurality in life but we have always attempted to discover the unity behind them.
>
> (Deendayal Upadhyaya)[12]

The proposed organic linkage of social relations is perceived to lead to the establishment of a harmonious society, made up from distinct communities which perform roles necessary to the overall advancement of society as a whole and free from conflict:

> Classes do exist in a society. Here too, there were castes, but we had never accepted conflict between one caste and another as fundamental concept behind it. In our concept of four castes, they are thought of as analogous to the different limbs of Virat-purusha. [...] There cannot be any conflict in the different parts of the same body. [...] These limbs are not only complementary to one another, but even further, there is individual unity. There is a complete identity of interest, identity of belonging. The origin of the caste system was on the above basis. If this idea is not kept alive, the castes,

instead of being complementary, can produce conflict. But then this is [a] distortion. It is not a systematic arrangement, rather it is absence of any plan, any arrangement. This is indeed the present condition of our society.

(Deendayal Upadhyaya)[13]

Politically, this society is considered by Upadhyaya to be governed by a variety of institutions – usually based on community – at various levels which function largely autonomously from each other, again without strife, since each institution is attuned to performing distinct roles and in itself legitimate in performing these tasks due to their accordance with Hindu culture.[14]

Economically, Upadhyaya proposes a model of development close to Gandhian thought, which emphasises decentralisation and self-reliance. The prevalent Nehruvian model of development is perceived to be contrary to the Indian ethos and, hence, not suitable to India and in the end counter-productive:

> Upadhyaya's concept of integral humanism provides the most comprehensive system of Hindu nationalist thought, formulating a utopian vision of social and economic goals to be achieved under Hindu nationalist guidance. Integral humanism was incorporated as a key ideological principle in the BJP constitution in 1980, while the resemblance to Gandhian socioeconomic thought formed the basis of the BJP's early emphasis on select Gandhian ideas, especially moral economy elements and the economic nationalism associated with the *swadeshi* concept.
>
> (Hansen 1999: 158)

With the increased emphasis on communal identity politics in the wake of the party's radicalisation in the late 1980s and early 1990s and the subsequent shift to economic liberalisation, the socio-economic principles of integral humanism have lost to some extent their immediate utility for the party's politics. However, they still form the moral and ideological basis for Hindu nationalist economic policy as a set of principles used in articulating the legitimacy of BJP policies.

The organisation of political Hinduism

While some ideas of political Hinduism were formulated and used by leaders of the Indian National Congress, the foundation of the All India Hindu Mahasabha marks the advent of organised political Hinduism as a distinct alternative to secular nationalist organisations. The HMS can be interpreted, especially in its early form, as an attempt to organise, unite and extend Hindu communal networks and organisations previously restricted to acting at the local or, at most, the regional level. In contrast to the RSS, its design as a political party and the antagonism of its support base towards the INC obstructed the possibility of securing its role as the leading Hindu nationalist organisation.

In the 1951 general elections, the HMS contested 31 seats and won four with an overall vote percentage of 0.95 per cent.[15] With the inability of the HMS to compete in elections with the INC already apparent in the 1930s, the leadership of the Hindu nationalist movement began to pass to the *Rashtriya Swayamsevak Sangh*, whose refusal to participate in elections, generally less antagonistic relationship with the INC and broader support base made it more suitable for this leading role.

The Rashtriya Swayamsevak Sangh *and the* Sangh Parivar

The RSS was founded in 1925 in the central Indian town of Nagpur which to date remains the location of its headquarters. At the time of its foundation, the RSS formed an alternative concept of Hindu nationalist political organisation vis-à-vis the *Hindu Mahasabha*: It eschewed direct participation in everyday politics, and instead opted to present itself as a mostly educational organisation and aimed at the creation of a large cadre base which would contribute to the spread of nationalism, defined culturally in opposition to secular nationalism, and the unification of the Hindu community under Hindu nationalist leadership. As an organisation, the RSS included strongly centralised, if not authoritarian features.

Apart from the national level organisation, the RSS is mainly constituted around an elaborate network of local cells. These local cells centre on *shakas*, meeting places for RSS members in the localities, which serve as forums for discussion as well as ideological and physical training (Andersen and Damle 2005: 35–7). The physical exercise regime at *shakas* is highly regulated and comprises amongst others training with *lathis*, the batons used also by the Indian police. This is often compared to similar exercise practices employed by fascist organisations in Europe, although its origins can be traced to the practices of physical training at Indian schools which were introduced under British colonial rule, and are still practised there. There are also similarities to the training regime at wrestling gymnasiums, the *akharas* (Alter 1994; Jaffrelot 1996: 37–8). While physical training forms an important part of daily routines at *shakas*, it is perceived mostly as an educational supplement to the ideological and moral instruction of RSS cadres.

The RSS was banned after the assassination of Gandhi in 1948 by the Indian government, which alleged a link between the murderer, Nathuram Godse, and the organisation. The ban was revoked soon afterwards, but the RSS was compelled to adopt a formal constitution in line with Indian constitutional stipulations. The adoption of a formal constitution by the RSS, however, did not significantly change the real power structure within the organisation, and internal decision-making processes remain highly opaque to outside observers (Jaffrelot 1996: 88–90).

After the revocation of the ban on the RSS, the organisation started to grow rapidly. It currently forms one of the most important civil society organisations in India in terms of membership. At the outset, its social base was dominated by upper caste, middle class social segments, especially from non-metropolitan urban centres in northern and central India. The RSS represented a significant segment of the petty bourgeoisie. Its initially urban character insulated the RSS from the effects of the restructuring of agrarian social hierarchies in the wake of the land reforms of the 1950s, which formed one the main reasons for the decline of the *Hindu Mahasabha*. Another notable feature was the strong RSS base among private sector employed urban (lower) middle classes, middle class sections which by and large were integrated to a lesser extent in the social base of the Congress party, compared to administrative and public sector oriented middle class segments. Apart from the latter's dominance in the Congress party, which contributed to blocking integration of private sector oriented middle classes, the combination of free market and moral economy elements within Hindu nationalist ideology, in contrast to the INC's preference for state intervention appealed to this segment of society. At the same time, restrictions against formal RSS membership when applying for administrative posts, and the imperative to be close to the ruling party, limited the appeal of the RSS to administrative and public sector oriented middle classes.

The RSS managed to expand significantly from its initially limited social base, especially to the metropolitan areas, less so to rural India. However, its key support base remains the private sector oriented petty bourgeoisie. Caste-wise, upper castes (especially Brahmins and Banias) continue to be strongly represented in the organisation, but the organisation has made conscious efforts to expand its base among OBC, Dalit and Adivasi communities as well as Sikhs and Jainas. The gradually changing composition of RSS cadres is to some extent masked in public perception by the composition of its leadership. Here, a very slow fluctuation in leadership positions contributes to the perception that the RSS cadre base is still made up mostly of Brahmins who continue to dominate the national level leadership. Similarly, the slow fluctuation in its leadership significantly obstructs the political assertion of more moderate RSS leaders vis-à-vis the 'old guard,' a fact which is magnified in public perception which focuses on the public faces of the RSS, especially the *sarsanghchalak*.[16]

Apart from the *shakas*, the RSS is strongly involved in the Indian educational sector, setting up schools and colleges.[17] In part, these educational institutions are controlled directly by the RSS while others are controlled by (generally local) organisations and trusts which are linked to the RSS, or close to its ideology. RSS-influenced educational institutions cover a broad range of subjects, including technical and science education, and are not limited to providing moral or ideological teaching. They provide an opportunity for formal education especially in smaller towns and to social sections which cannot afford to pay for other private-sector educational institutions, but do not have access to equally good public schools or colleges. The elaborate network of educational institutions is providing the RSS both with a significant influence on education policies and with a large reservoir for the recruitment of cadres.

After the revocation of the RSS ban, the organisation decided to assist in the founding of ideologically linked organisations working in specific areas to advance the Hindu nationalist movement's position in civil society and politics without directly involving the RSS. The latter was perceived, on the one hand, to protect the RSS from possible corrupting influences and to ensure that it continued to concentrate on its original agenda. On the other hand, it formed a strategic decision to limit the risks of renewed state action or legislation against the RSS or the Hindu nationalist movement (Jaffrelot 1996: 116–19). The decision to set up a network of ideologically linked organisations which profess their proximity to the RSS led to the creation of the so-called *Sangh Parivar*. While the newly created organisations are formally independent of the RSS, with the latter providing assistance and guidance, de facto the RSS possesses a number of ways of influencing decision-making within these organisations. This has, at times, been interpreted as an exertion of significant direct control over the whole *Sangh Parivar*.[18] In fact, the question of RSS control is much more complex: The RSS can, in some circumstances, exert control even against contrary preferences by the organisations concerned. It is, however, much more likely to influence the guiding principles of social and political actions in a relatively circumspect way. This provides the organisations in the *Sangh Parivar* with a certain amount of autonomy, as long as they do not deviate too far from the RSS agenda and, at times, they can even assert their autonomy against RSS pressure (Bhatt 2001: 151).

The *Sangh Parivar* comprises a large number of organisations ranging from local and one-point agenda organisations to large and highly influential organisations operating in various areas of national society, politics, and economics. The former in many cases include organisations linked to specific local level campaigns and are often short-lived. These small and relatively obscure organisations can, at times, also be used in order to provide larger Hindu nationalist organisations with a cover, enabling Hindu nationalists to engage in forms of agitation, including political violence, which the larger *Sangh Parivar* organisations cannot in certain contexts employ directly (Berglund 2006). Other small organisations within the *Sangh Parivar* are set up to represent local issues or deal with local civil society. This does not necessarily involve the higher level leadership of the larger organisations. Since no formal relations exist between the various organisations within the Hindu nationalist network, the number of *Sangh Parivar* constituents and their exact relationship to each other can only be estimated, and is likely to show significant fluctuation over time.

The larger organisations within the *Sangh Parivar* include the BJP and its predecessor, the *Bharatiya Jana Sangh* (BJS), as well as several other major Indian organisations. The most prominent among these, apart from the BJP and its predecessor, include the *Vishwa Hindu Parishad* (VHP),[19] its youth wing, the *Bajrang Dal* (BD),[20] the *Bharatiya Mazdoor Sangh* (BMS),[21] and the *Swadeshi Jagran Manch* (SJM).[22]

Especially in areas with a strong presence of Hindu nationalist organisations, professional, community or neighbourhood associations can be strongly influenced by Hindu nationalism. Varshney has noted the importance of cross-communal membership in civil society to prevent communal violence (Varshney 2002). Apart from facilitating communal violence at times, these groups facilitate recruitment of cadres and mobilisation of electoral support as well as influence the public perception of Hindu nationalism and help to spread of Hindu nationalist thought among society, if often in relatively vague forms. The elaborate networks of Hindu nationalist influenced civil society associations which permeate Indian society constitute a potent factor in Hindu nationalism's success as an ideology and political movement. Among other aspects, it contributes to the temptation of secular nationalist parties in India to take recourse to soft *hindutva* positions.

Apart from formal civil society associations, the Hindu nationalist movement at the local level functions in a milieu of informal individual and group relationships. It can rely on informal systems of mutual assistance which facilitates the work of the *Sangh Parivar* constituents in many ways. Brass has shown the importance of these systems in the management of communal violence with his concept of institutionalised riot systems, in essence an informal system of labour division with certain tasks in the instigation, conduct and interpretation of communal riots (Brass 1997; 2003).

The Bharatiya Jan Sangh

In political terms, the *Bharatiya Jan Sangh* (BJS) and especially its successor, the BJP, emerged as the most important organisations within the *Sangh Parivar*. As mentioned above, the *Jan Sangh* was founded with assistance by the RSS to provide a platform for the Hindu nationalist movement's participation in political institutions and to act as a safeguard against attempts by the state to re-invoke the ban or employ similar legal measures against the RSS.[23]

The early BJS was closely associated with a number of emotive political campaigns, among them partition related campaigns, the campaign against cow slaughter and, most importantly, the campaign for the removal of Article 370 which grants a special status to the state of Jammu and Kashmir within the Indian Union from the Indian constitution. The latter still forms one of the three alleged 'core issues' of the BJP. The campaign for the removal of Article 370 from the Indian constitution was linked to both the Pakistan issue and the first Indo-Pakistani conflict over Kashmir. Shyama Prasad Mookerjee, the *Jan Sangh*'s first president, became strongly associated with this campaign (and the related question of the treatment of Hindu fugitives from the Kashmir valley.) Mookerjee was imprisoned while campaigning in Jammu and Kashmir, and died in prison shortly afterwards. Some Hindu nationalists continue to perceive Mookerjee's death in prison as a political murder or, at best, as due to malevolent neglect by the government authorities. His death and the subsequent allegations by Hindu nationalists certainly served to increase the emotive appeal of the issue, especially to the *Jan Sangh*'s core supporters.

Economically, the BJS opposed the state interventionist direction of Nehruvian economic policy. While the party due to the importance attributed by it to national security agreed on the need to maintain state control over strategically relevant economic sectors, the strong role accorded to central planning was opposed. In general, the BJS expressed a preference for market economy wherever this did not compromise the party's nationalistic stances or the moral economy foundations of Hindu nationalist thought (Jaffrelot 1996: 169–72). The latter, as mentioned above, where articulated comprehensively in the 1960s by one of the most important BJS leaders, Deendayal Upadhyaya, in his concept of integral humanism. Opposition to state interventionism in the economy was highly compatible with the economic interests of one of its main constituencies, small traders and industrialists in the non-metropolitan urban areas. In contrast to the HMS, the BJS did not strongly oppose the implementation of land reforms in the 1950s. Its predominantly urban character insulated the party from the changes in agrarian hierarchies which resulted from the land reforms and which severely weakened the *Hindu Mahasabha* (Jaffrelot 1996: 172).

Vis-à-vis foreign policy, the BJS tended to prefer a closer relationship with the USA over non-alignment. After India's defeat in the 1962 Sino-Indian border conflict, the strident propagation of a perceived Chinese threat to India – next to the threat by Pakistan – became one of the major foreign policy themes of the party, although it has to be stated that in both these respects, the BJS did not differ significantly from other mainstream political parties in India.

The BJS vociferously propagated the pre-eminence of national over regional identities, especially in its stances towards the restructuring of the Indian federal polity and the status of regional languages, Urdu and English vis-à-vis Hindi as the national language. BJS policies, apart from the party's economic policy, are probably best summarised by one of the party's most well-known slogans: 'Hindi – Hindu – *Hindustan*.'

Electorally, the BJS had a significant presence especially in northern, central and western India. At the national level, the party was usually unable to gain the support of 10 per cent of the electorate, except in 1962. This support remained insufficient to emerge as a viable contender for political power, in part due to India's SMSP electoral system. While Congress dominance remained relatively unchallenged until the late 1960s, the role of the main opposition was mostly played by the various socialist parties. The gradually growing electoral support of the party as the main opposition part to the right of the INC was temporarily challenged by the *Swatantra Party*, a conservative party close to political Hinduism but not associated with Hindu nationalism, especially of the *Sangh Parivar* variety, which received significant support in the 1960s especially in eastern India.[24]

In the late 1960s, the *Jan Sangh* became the main right-wing partner in the socialist endeavour to form anti-Congress electoral alliances in order to overcome Congress dominance. The BJS participated in several attempts to form

Table 4.1 Vote percentages of the Bharatiya Jan Sangh in *Lok Sabha* elections

1951	1957	1962	1967	1971
3.06	5.97	16.73	9.31	7.35

Source: Election Commission of India.

left–right non-Congress state governments, labelled as *samyukta vidhayak dal* (united legislative party) governments. Attempts to form lasting left–right anti-Congress coalitions failed but, at the same time, served to reduce the isolation of the BJS within the Indian party system which arose from its association with the RSS. The socialists, regional parties and Congress splinter groups at the time by and large did not receive strong Muslim support so that alliances with the BJS were not detrimental to their electoral success. Moreover, these parties often represented interests of agrarian rising social strata which had not been incorporated fully by the Congress into the Indian system of rent allocation. Since the BJS received significant support from similarly not fully incorporated urban social strata, the interests of the respective parties' supporters were relatively congruent. The failure to form lasting *samyukta vidhayak dal* governments is related to the inability of the BJS and the socialists to maintain coalition arrangements on the grounds of the vast differences in their respective ideological outlook. While this appears obvious at first glance, given the differences between socialism and Hindu nationalism, certain congruencies did exist and the recent example of the second National Democratic Alliance government – which functioned moderately well for most of a full legislative term – suggests that other reasons for the collapse of SVD governments have to be taken into account. Partially, the collapse of SVD governments can be explained by attempts from both sides to emerge as the dominant element within the non-Congress party spectrum and Congress attempts to split the alliances by selective co-optation of factions from among the socialist spectrum and Congress splinter groups.

The creation of the *Janata Party* can be interpreted as the culmination of efforts to create anti-Congress coalitions. The BJS, at first, did not participate prominently in the movement against Indira Gandhi's rule which was dominated by the socialist parties and the Congress (O) and strongly influenced by the leadership of Jayaprakash Narayan. But the decision to include the BJS – and by extension to be able to draw support from RSS cadres and networks as well – significantly increased the strength of the JP movement. Hindu nationalists often claim that a large part of people imprisoned due to their participation in the JP movement were from the BJS or the RSS. Hindu nationalists were thus able to present themselves as a force for democracy (Bhatt 2004: 135). The collapse of the subsequent Morarji Desai government on the question of dual membership, i.e. a ban on simultaneous membership in the JP and the RSS, is commonly attributed by Hindu nationalists to a conscious attempt at excluding the former *Jan Sangh* members from the *Janata Party* after receiving their assistance in overcoming the Indira Gandhi regime.[25] Once again, it is likely that ideological divergence and political strategy (from both sides) went hand in hand to lead to the split in the *Janata Party*.

After the split in the *Janata Party*, the former BJS members of the JP opted to set up a new party – the BJP – instead of reviving the *Jan Sangh*. The decision to found a new party was supposed to demonstrate that the BJP had been part of the JP movement as well and would carry on the legacy of the struggle against the emergency regime. The BJP strongly expressed its intention to carry forward the JP movement's legacy by giving a central role to Gandhian socialism in its political programme and constitution, although this concept was based more on Upadhyaya than on Jayaprakash Narayan's political thought.[26] The newly founded party comprised some former socialists and former members of the Congress (O) but mostly former BJS cadres and leaders. One of the most important changes between the BJP and its predecessor was the conscious attempt to enlarge the social base of the party by overcoming its traditional reliance on the small town petty bourgeois milieu, especially by incorporating rural social strata and rising OBC groups strategically using both 'sanskritisation' and 'social engineering' (Jaffrelot 1998a).

The ideology of Hindu nationalism in its political practice

The political practice of Hindu nationalist ideology in India is often perceived by observers to be limited to a small number of issues. These comprise communal violence (against Muslims and Christians), the propagation of a unified Indian national identity based on Hindu culture, campaigns against conversion and aiming at re-conversion to Hinduism, campaigns centring on Hindu religious or cultural symbols exemplified by agitation against cow slaughter, the equation of Muslim identity with terrorism, campaigns against privileges for religious minorities, and resistance against separatist movements. The various issues of Hindu nationalist political practice are often subsumed under three so-called core issues of Hindu nationalism which serve as illustrations for Hindu nationalist political practice, apart from their high symbolic importance for the constitution of the secular cleavage: (1) the abrogation of Article 370 of the Indian constitution which grants a special status to Jammu and Kashmir, (2) the creation of a unified civil code which would result in the abrogation of Muslim Personal Law, and (3) the construction of a grand Ram temple at Ayodhya in place of the *Babri Masjid*. These issues certainly form a large part of the public perception of Hindu nationalism, and possess a high emotive appeal to Hindu nationalists while, at the same time, they are strongly resented by representatives of Indian secular nationalism. The larger appeal of Hindu nationalism to a substantial part of the Indian electorate cannot, however, be explained by this limited agenda.

National identity, national security and national cohesion

Early political Hinduism focussed for the most part on the articulation of community interests. In doing this, it remained largely limited to the local level, and divided by the various factors which dissect the Hindu community, especially caste, sect, and region. The focus on traditional values went together with an emphasis on the protection of traditional hierarchies since political Hinduism drew an important part of its support from upper castes and the small town petty bourgeoisie whose socio-economic status was threatened by increasing lower caste and class assertion. This is notwithstanding the origin of political Hinduism from among Hindu reform movements: The aim to strengthen the Hindu community by reforming select aspects of Hindu tradition was perceived by the main protagonists of political Hinduism as wholly compatible with maintaining social hierarchies due to the alleged organic linkages inherent in this social order.

The turn away from localised community interests towards national identity associated with the work of Savarkar proceeded simultaneously with the increased political organisation of Muslim interests in India, and the demand for the creation of Pakistan. National identity and national cohesion emerged as a major element of the Hindu nationalist agenda. The focus on traditional values became increasingly submerged in the struggle over the definition and identity of India. Some elements of the earlier focus on traditional values remain relevant even today but, as a rule, underwent a significant transformation as a result of the shift towards national identity, and their incorporation into the new, nation-wide agenda of Hindu nationalism. The selectivity of the Hindu nationalist recourse to Hindu tradition is partially due to strategic considerations – and therefore generally pragmatic – but equally to the inability of Hindu nationalism to encompass the myriad local manifestations of communal values that form the basis of Hindu religion and culture. Some of these can be resurrected on occasion, when this appears politically opportune, but only a few of these issues possess the capacity to serve for nation-wide political mobilisation, across the divisions by caste, sect, and region.

The rapid modernisation of India before and after independence contributed to the – all in all – limited electoral appeal of Hindu nationalism since it significantly reduced the authority carried by the early Hindu nationalist constituency in rural India, thus temporarily limiting the Hindu nationalist movement to the small town petty bourgeois milieu out of which it had originated. The ideology of the Hindu nationalist movement survived this period of intermittent relative decline by adaptation to the changing structure of Indian politics (Jaffrelot 1996: 158–9). As mentioned above, the RSS strategy to focus on the constitution of a committed cadre base, instead of attempting to pose an electoral challenge to the INC significantly contributed to this survival.

This strategy not only served to conceal the temporary weakness of the movement in terms of electoral appeal but increased acceptance of Hindu nationalism in Indian society by the growth and institutionalisation of social networks influenced by the movement. Crucially, the RSS strategy provided the basis for Hindu nationalism's accommodation within the newly emergent structure of Indian politics dominated by the INC. Bhagavan (2008) has noted the extent to which Hindu nationalist thought was incorporated – and spread to larger audiences – by INC politicians even while the RSS itself remained banned after the assassination of M. K. Gandhi in his work on K. M. Munshi. While the spread of Hindu nationalist ideology – even if sometimes in diluted form – was carried forward by the RSS and select Congress (and even socialist) politicians, the BJS as the movement's representative in electoral politics was provided with the time to adapt to the socio-economic transformation of Indian society, and to reach out to social sections which were neglected by the INC.

The socio-economic transformation of India after independence was characterised to a significant extent by the emergence of rising lower caste, lower middle class strata intent on full participation in the system of rent allocation which necessitated political organisation within the political system of India. The attempt to gain support from these strata led to a further dilution of the Hindu nationalist's movement capacity to lay emphasis on the traditional values associated with early Hindu nationalism, since these strata often took recourse to traditions and values which were at variance with the upper caste (and urban) interpretations of Hindu culture which had been predominant in Hindu nationalism earlier.

The Hindu nationalist movement reacted to this by increasing efforts at sanskritisation. Sanskritisation constitutes a process by which lower caste (and tribal) communities attempt to gain higher status by replicating upper caste behavioural codes. Since sanskritisation does not openly challenge traditional hierarchies – in that it accepts the ideational basis for their legitimacy even if it attempts to overcome the economic restrictions which result from these hierarchies – it is generally preferred by Hindu nationalists to other modes of lower caste emancipation. By and large, sanskritisation remained insufficient to incorporate newly rising strata comprehensively, and had to be complemented by non-preferred modes of incorporation into the Hindu nationalist project which diluted the predominance of upper caste interpretations of Hindu cultural heritage (Jaffrelot 1998a: 22–3; 36).

The extension of the Hindu nationalist movement to newly rising social strata also reinforced the necessity and willingness to operate within the restrictions of the Indian political system, including the democratic political process and the articulation of particularistic economic interests. Given the Hindu nationalist movement's role in communal violence in India and the opaque power structure within the RSS, its characterisation as a democratic actor appears to be hollow at first glance. In many other respects democratic processes have, however, been embedded to a significant extent within the movement. The discursive frame for the articulation of particularistic economic interests within the bounds of Hindu nationalist ideology was formulated soon after independence, as mentioned above especially by Upadhyaya.

The modernisation of India's system of law after independence further limited the capacity of the Hindu nationalist movement to restrict itself to community issues. The Hindu Code Bill abrogated Hindu personal laws which otherwise could have served for communal political mobilisation and provided a firm anchorage for (Hindu) community issues within the framework of secular law.

The developments outlined above give an indication of the factors contributing to the gradual assertion of Hindu nationalism with its emphasis on national identity as defined by Savarkar vis-à-vis political Hinduism and Hindu communalism. The national identity conception formulated by Savarkar, however, evolved in opposition to Muslim political assertion and the demand for the creation of Pakistan, and became strongly focussed on national cohesion and accordingly the struggle against perceived internal and external enemies. Political

Hinduism and Hindu communalism might conceivably have developed in a way in which Muslims would have served as an imagined 'Other' perceived to be necessary for community unification by exclusion without necessarily creating a durable obstacle to inter-communal harmony – and accordingly a relatively benign form of exclusionary political ideology.

The emphasis to national cohesion in opposition to Muslim political assertion, however, entrenched the perception of Muslims as an enemy community, and served to obscure the boundaries between internal and external 'enemies.' Efforts to overcome this attitude (at least partially) within the Hindu nationalist attitude to Muslims have only begun recently, and were only possible after generational indifference to the partition of British India and the resulting violence became politically significant, and the proportional under-development of Muslim communities in India partially removed the threat perception by the now firmly dominant Hindu communities.

The prominence accorded to Muslims as both internal and external enemies led to ambivalence regarding other possible targets which could have been more forcefully designed as enemies: In comparison to many Islamist groups, 'the West' and liberal, westernised Indians are much less targeted by the Hindu nationalist movement. Attacks on Indian Christians and Christian institutions in India have increased especially since the 1990s, but are due more to the agitation against conversion than a generally negative perception of western culture, much less an effort to design 'the West' as an enemy on the part of the Hindu nationalist leadership. The increasingly westernised lifestyles of urban, especially metropolitan young Indians (or among the Indian diaspora communities in Europe and Northern America) has led to a certain amount of resentment within the movement among hard line cadres and leaders but, at the same time, has never been allowed to emerge as a major plank for political agitation.

In contrast, the Hindu nationalist movement's designation of the People's Republic of China (PRC) as an enemy state after the 1962 border conflict has remained a durable feature of Hindu nationalist political discourse. Many Hindu nationalists (but also secular politicians like George Fernandes, at the time defence minister) strongly linked the need for nuclear tests in 1998 and nuclear armament afterwards to the danger posed by China to India despite a general *denouement* in Sino-Indian hostility since the early 1990s.[27] The increasing normalisation of relations between the two countries which was given a strong impetus by the second NDA government was accepted as being due to economic and geo-strategic reasons by many cadres and leaders, but has so far not resulted in assuaging vague and often latent fears vis-à-vis the PRC among Hindu nationalists. It has to be stressed, however, that the threat perception concerning China is not particular to the Hindu nationalist movement, but shared among many politicians and a large part of the Indian middle class. Jaffrelot (1996: 178–80) notes that the BJS positioning on the PRC in the early 1960s led to notable defections from the Congress party.

The question of national cohesion and territorial integrity of India – defined by Hindu nationalists as *akhand bharat* (indivisible India) and in some interpretations merging with ideas of a Greater India which encompassed not only Pakistan but stretched into Central Asia (Brosius 2005) – remained relevant not only because of the creation of Pakistan but due to other actual or potential conflicts or separatist movements which arose at intervals in the decades after independence. These included the Kashmir conflict, the Indian invasion of Hyderabad and Junagadh, the 1962 border conflict with China, the ethno-linguistic demands for a reform of the federal polity especially in South and West India, the *Khalistan* movement among Punjabi Sikhs, and the various separatist movements in North-Eastern India.

The issues of national identity (and cohesion) and the integration of the Muslim minority remaining in India are illustrated by the Hindu nationalist movement's shifting stance on linguistic diversity. The *Jan Sangh* gave prominence to the slogan Hindi-Hindu-*Hindustan*, combining all three factors mentioned above to mark its interpretation of national identity. In essence, the movement mobilised support for the declaration of Hindi as the national language.

The position accorded to Hindi as the national language vis-à-vis the regional languages of India underlines the strong support the movement received from northern India, especially the Hindi heartland. The opposition against the prominence accorded to Hindi by the Indian state from the non-Hindi speaking regions was strongly associated with linguistically defined sub-national identity and, hence, was at least partially perceived as a threat to national cohesion by Hindu nationalists. The state's by and large accommodative policy on the regional languages, however, proved helpful in averting what could have evolved into a major crisis of the newly independent Indian state (Dasgupta 2001: 49–50). The strong emphasis on Hindi as the national language by Hindu nationalists is often seen in the context of the movement's strong base in the Hindi heartland and its smaller presence in the southern and eastern regions. It has to be stressed, though, that the emphasis on Hindi was connected equally to the economic interests of Hindu nationalism's small town petty bourgeoisie constituency which was not able to compete for employment in the Indian administration against the established middle classes as long as English language skills remained of high importance in the selection of candidates.

The two most unambiguous examples of Hindu nationalism's cultural identitarian agenda – the quest to establish a unified national identity defined by cultural attributes derived selectively from Hindu tradition – are found in education policy and the movement's policy towards the electronic media. During the terms of the two NDA governments, the most important central ministries in these regards were held by the BJP.

The education policy formulated by M. M. Joshi, at the time Human Resources Development minister, strictly followed the Hindu nationalist movement's agenda on education policy. Accordingly, it was strongly contested by secular nationalists, and became intensely debated by academics from both sides of the political spectrum.[28] This debate by and large showed a lack of common ground between the two poles, even where the new education policy's changes were less drastic, with both sides sticking to maximum positions. In essence, the BJP government prepared the ground for reforming India's education policy by according key positions within several academic and educational bodies decisive for the formulation of national curricula with academics close to the *Sangh Parivar*. These appointments were justified by the party as an attempt to remove an alleged earlier bias caused by the predominance of secular nationalist and Marxist scholars in Indian academics. Critics strongly condemned this move, apart from their concern over an anticipated re-orientation of education and research on the grounds that the appointments in some cases were alleged not to be based on academic merit but political loyalty. This, in turn, was rejected by academics close to the Hindu nationalist spectrum. Apart from the political dimension, the controversy showed the segregation of Indian academics between an increasingly globally oriented, metropolitan based section dominated by secular nationalists and Marxists and a section based mostly in the lesser known (but much more numerous) academic institutions outside the major cities which is increasingly being influenced by Hindu nationalist ideology.

The controversy predictably turned towards changes in text books prepared for the national curricula. The changes affected in school and college text books by the NDA government did not, in fact, add up to a comprehensive overhaul of older text books. Observers sympathetic to the government have pointed out that most passages were left unchanged, and even outstanding representatives of secular nationalist and Marxist influenced academics had been incorporated. Many alterations in text books were, however, placed strategically to cover issues with a high symbolic value to Hindu nationalists. Critics of the new education policy in their turn pointed out that these changes added up to a significant reinterpretation of India's cultural heritage and in related areas. The NDA governments' education policy can be interpreted as an inevitable attempt to correct the official interpretation of India's historical and cultural heritage – given the increased presence and influence of the Hindu nationalist movement in Indian society and, as importantly, the gradual shift in the ideational foundations of Indian nationalism, especially within the middle classes, towards the incorporation of cultural attributes. Since it poses a direct and highly symbolical challenge to the self-perception of the largely metropolitan and upper middle class social strata whose dominance in the Indian discourse had not been contested to such an extent before, the intensity of the reactions to the NDA education policy and the overall debate on it is hardly surprising.

Alterations in I&B policy were, by comparison, less high profile. Still, the I&B ministry, at times, attempted to strengthen 'ethical' broadcasting in media outlets and to effect a gradual shift towards the increased broadcasting of films which portrayed values and an interpretation of cultural and historical heritage close to Hindu nationalism.[29]

The emphasis on national cohesion coupled with the various crises and conflicts which occurred at intervals after independence went together with strident rhetoric on national security and the maintenance of law and order on the part of the Hindu nationalist movement. Again, this was shared among large parts of the secular nationalist spectrum, and is anyway not surprising in any right-wing movement. With the conflict over Jammu and Kashmir and the general deterioration of Indo-Pakistani relations, the Hindu nationalist stance on national security was often accompanied by communalist overtones, however, which set Hindu nationalism apart from secular nationalism to some extent (Navlakha 1998: 64–7). As with the larger nationalist discourse in India, hard line national security rhetoric is combined with the glorification of the Indian military, especially the common soldier – the '*jawan.*' This did not, however, lead to the development of positive images of a politicised military which, again, is hardly surprising given the predominance of Hindu nationalism's secular nationalist rivals for most of the history of independent India. By now, the civilian character of governance in India has been established to such an extent that the idea of a larger military role in politics does not even appear to arise within the Hindu nationalist movement.[30]

Law and order

Law and order in Hindu nationalist parlance is strongly associated with national security and national cohesion. It covers anti-terrorist measures and, with terrorism being associated with Islamic movements from within and outside India by Hindu nationalists (and many secular nationalists), easily fits into Hindu nationalist rhetoric. It also covers action of police and paramilitary forces against militant left-wing movements such as the Naxalites, and separatist movements in Jammu and Kashmir and the north-eastern states. Law and order is further invoked in Hindu nationalist campaigns against allegedly illegal immigration into the north-eastern states from Bangla Desh where a linkage with anti-Muslim stances can be constructed (Malik and Singh 1994: 121–2). Since the biggest north-eastern state, Assam, is also the state with the largest proportion of Muslims after Jammu and Kashmir, Bangladeshi (and hence Muslim) immigration is perceived by many Hindu nationalists as a conspiracy to transform the demographic situation there, and eventually pose a new threat to national cohesion.

Domestic law and order has been accorded much less prominence by the Hindu nationalist movement, for most of the time. A notable exception were state elections in the large Hindi heartland states where the BJP made law and order a major campaign plank, concentrating on the alleged 'jungle *raj*' of its then ruling secular nationalist rivals, the *Samajwadi Party* in Uttar Pradesh and the *Rashtriya Janata Dal* (RJD) in Bihar.

Another feature of the Hindu nationalist movement's law and order agenda has been the alleged criminalisation of Indian politics, the growing linkages between (usually local or state-level) politicians and the underworld and the entry of alleged criminals into Indian politics. This, in turn, is linked to corruption. The criminalisation of Indian politics can be interpreted as a sign of increasing rent scarcity which led to an extension of contest over rent allocation from elections and control over the bureaucracy to the inclusion of criminal practices and the resulting formation of linkages between politics and organised crime. Indian political parties have by and large been caught in a vicious cycle where linkages with alleged criminals are perceived necessary for electoral success but, at the same time, are highly unpopular especially among the middle classes who dominate the political discourse. While the BJP places a strong emphasis on its clean image – the 'party with a difference' – and has, at times, attempted to project its willingness to get rid of alleged criminals, it has by no means succeeded in doing so to a significantly higher extent than many other political parties.

The criminalisation of Indian politics is closely linked to corruption, although the former is a more recent phenomenon. While corruption is a recurrent feature in societies with a strong rentier character (Ades and Di Tella 2005), in India under-regulation of party funding has resulted in corruption emerging as a major factor in political success (Ghosh 1999: 64–5): While rent allocation processes can be conducted legally – and comparatively straightforward – in many respects, the transfer of rents to politicians in order to finance their activities is, at times, conducted by corrupt means. The Hindu nationalist movement throughout its existence has strongly propagated anti-corruption measures, especially in the 1980s and early 1990s when several corruption scandals were uncovered. However, similarly to the socialist parties, the BJP had been an opposition party at the time, while one-party dominance had institutionalised the INC as the party in control of rent allocation and the main political beneficiary of corruption.

The BJP-led governments at the centre and at the state level have often not been able to resist the temptations of their new positions of power. Several corruption scandals were uncovered during the two NDA governments at the centre, although some were centred on politicians from among its socialist and regional allies. It should be noted that within the Hindu nationalist movement, participation in corruption still has a more negative image than in some other political parties. Apart from violating the moral code of conduct expected especially from RSS *swayamsevaks*, a large part of the movement's support base is made up from private sector oriented lower middle classes who are more often at the receiving end of corrupt practices than beneficiaries themselves, and view corruption accordingly.[31]

While increased access to power has coincided with the evolution of a certain pragmatism regarding corruption, moral pressure from the RSS and the economic interests of the BJP's most important social constituency can still be expected to contain corruption within the party to a larger extent than in many other parties. Anti-corruption campaigns by the BJP have been instrumental in rallying middle class support and contribute to positive media coverage.

Given the importance attributed by it to law and order, the movement is obviously placed in a dilemma regarding communal violence. As a rule, official documents by the BJP stress social harmony and the maintenance of the rule of law. In order to defend incidents of communal violence and even large-scale pogroms against Muslims, the movement tends to express – often obliquely – an incapacity to react in the face of spontaneous outbreaks of violence to which people are induced by prior provocation on the part of the victims. The violence is then often linked to the right of self-defence and, while it may be portrayed as excessive, is accordingly to be perceived as an at least partially justified reaction. This interpretation of communal violence constitutes a recurrent feature in Indian history (Brass 2003: 306–7). In the relatively recent case of attacks on Christian institutions in India, the obviously pre-planned character of these acts of violence and the limited number of perpetrators accentuate the problems of subsequent justification. Here – and in some cases regarding the often larger scale violence against Muslims – conspiracies by external agents are often invoked, partially as a means to justify the violence and partially as an attempt to shift the debate to other topics: In the case of attacks on Christians the larger debate on conversion and the role of missionaries can be utilised, while implications of the alleged role of Pakistan and especially the Pakistani military intelligence service ISI serve the same purpose with regard to violence against Muslims.

The BJP has strongly criticised communal violence on occasion, if the Hindu nationalist movement was not responsible for it as in the case of the anti-Sikh pogrom in Delhi. As a rule, communal violence can be beneficial in winning elections in certain circumstances, and can help in maintaining and enlarging the cadre base of the Hindu nationalist movement even if it is not beneficial electorally.[32]

Economic policy

Regarding economic policy, the Hindu nationalist movement until the late 1980s has often been depicted as the representative of what is termed the Brahmin-Bania network, or of traders. In class terms it represented the small town petty bourgeoisie (Hansen 1999: 115). In terms of the Indian political economy, what these depictions have in common is that the constituency represents social strata which have achieved a certain social status but had not been fully incorporated into the system of rent allocation in India, and were accordingly in opposition to the INC. Their strategies for social upward mobility included claims for access to rents proportional to what other middle class sections had acquired. But given the general market economy orientation especially of traders and small-scale industrialists and manufacturers, under conditions of increasing rent scarcity and lower class political organisation the Hindu nationalist movement and its parliamentary arm – the BJS and the BJP – placed more emphasis on market economy and economic liberalisation than the INC and the centre-left political spectrum.[33]

As mentioned above, early Hindu nationalism did not accord much prominence to economic policy. The comprehensive articulation of Hindu nationalist thought vis-à-vis economic policy was carried forward by Upadhyaya only in the 1960s, and even nowadays the hard line cultural identitarian wing and a large part of the cadres of the BJP are only partially concerned about economic policy (Chhibber 1997: 635).

The rejection of state interventionist strategies in economic policy by the *Jan Sangh* was articulated early on. It was also clearly stated by Upadhyaya. This rejection was modified only with regard to the strategic sector of the Indian economy which shows the over-riding concern about nationalism and national security, but also fits easily with the economic interests of the Hindu nationalist core constituency, since this constituency had no stake in large-scale industry and, accordingly, was not concerned about employment in the strategic sector being open to political contest. The opposition to state interventionism from the Hindu nationalist movement was from the outset pragmatic and not ideological in character.

Hindu nationalist economic thought as articulated by Upadhyaya heavily incorporated moral considerations based on its conception of the good and ordered society and the organic linkages of communities within it. Moral economy elements in Hindu nationalist economic thought remain vague, though, and provide a useful instrument to articulate the economic interests of particular social strata or organised interest groups and to adapt flexibly to newly articulated demands. An analysis of BJP election manifestos does not provide a strict guideline as to the extent and the circumstances in which the party's proposed economic policies are presented in a moral economy idiom. In fact, the proposed BJP economic policy always constitutes an amalgamation of moral economy, economic nationalism, the more or less open propagation of particularistic economic interests and a free market, development oriented jargon. An analysis of the work of the BJP legislative parties in the *Lok Sabha* and *Rajya Sabha* regarding economic policy, especially of questions posed during Question Hour, shows a strong emphasis on day-to-day single issues, associated with a distinct lack of ideologically driven economic policy. The party's normalcy in this regard in comparison to secular nationalist parties is remarkable.

The BJP has particularly used elements of moral economy and economic nationalism in its argumentation when attempting to protect the interests of its key constituencies, small- and medium-scale industrialists and traders and mid-level employees especially in services in the private sector. Recent examples for this discourse include the campaign against the introduction of VAT or the opposition against foreign direct investment (FDI) in certain economic sectors dominated by these social strata like retail.

After experimenting with a pronounced emphasis on moral economy until the late 1980s when the party was strongly propagating Gandhian socialism, the BJP began to shift towards economic liberalisation. The party's co-operation with the INC-led government on the introduction of the economic reform package including de-regulation and divestment in 1991 serves as a landmark in this shift. The co-operation during the introduction of liberalisation measures marks an open embrace of economic reform which was reinforced by the economic policies adopted by the NDA governments between 1998 and 2004.

De-regulation and divestment form an important part of middle class strategy to safeguard its socio-economic status. Liberalising economic sectors with a high growth potential, especially IT and telecommunication related services had the added value of creating high growth sectors. The re-interpretation of the party's economic policy was accordingly easily possible within the parlance of economic nationalism, involving a shift from the emphasis on self-sufficiency inherent in Gandhian socialism towards achieving rapid all-out development (and the resulting great power status) by integration into the global economy.

The shift towards liberalisation was not only beneficial in electoral terms, but followed a nationalist impulse which facilitated the acceptance among party supporters, especially from among the cultural identitarian wing of the party. It is important to note that the likelihood of BJP members justifying the party's economic policies in terms of economic nationalism increases with closer association with the cultural identitarian wing both among cadres and the leadership.

While the transition from Gandhian socialism to economic liberalisation was both relatively rapid and marked, both strands actually co-exist within the party's heritage of economic thought (Desai 1994). Already the BJS had propagated free market oriented reforms and policies and opposed the 'over-regulation' of India's economy.

In the mid-1980s, middle class economic interests in India began to shift from protecting their disproportionate benefits derived from rent allocation which was increasingly contested from organised lower class groups towards liberalisation. In essence, liberalisation as a political strategy removes certain economic sectors, usually those providing highly paid employment, from political control and, accordingly, from a political contest in which the middle classes were not anymore able to compete successfully. Instead, employment opportunities in these economic sectors become restricted by 'merit,' the term used in Indian middle class parlance which denotes a combination of qualifications in communication, information and formal education where the middle classes possess significant competitive advantages (Upadhya 2007).

Newly rising lower middle classes especially outside the metropolitan areas – the core constituency of Hindu nationalism – had not yet achieved participation in the rentier economy proportionate to that of established middle class groups, the pivotal demand of these social strata prior to the advent of economic reforms. Still, these social sections were compelled to shift alongside the established middle classes by the severity of rent scarcity in India in the late 1980s which arose from the moderate, yet insufficient success of economic development policies in India: The formation of numerous rising social strata which could not anymore be co-opted into the rentier economy but, at the same time, could not anymore be excluded from participation in India's comparatively open political system. The BJP simultaneously began to shift its economic agenda in accordance with middle class interests: from a focus on moral economy and economic nationalism which were utilised to express demands for greater incorporation of its core supporters in the system of rent allocation towards liberalisation which was now needed to protect and advance the socio-economic status of Indian middle classes.

The shift in middle class economic interests from maintaining control over rent allocation to selective dismemberment of the rentier economy necessitated a corresponding reinterpretation of the Hindu nationalist economic agenda by the BJP. This led to increasing strains between the various *Sangh Parivar* outfits – between those organisations which remained strongly attached to moral economy and economic nationalism and those increasingly propagating economic liberalisation and integration with the global economy – and even within the BJP which still comprises a moral economy oriented wing.

These strains did not become openly apparent at first, especially due to the efforts to interpret the shift in the BJP agenda within the bounds of Hindu nationalist ideology and the general disinterest in economic affairs by many representatives of the cultural identitarian wing. Tensions, though, became evident after the formation of the first BJP-led government at the centre. The first NDA government was continuously criticised by several *Sangh Parivar* outfits including the RSS, at the surface mostly on its unwillingness to place greater emphasis on the cultural identitarian agenda but also on its economic policies. The difficulties within the *Sangh Parivar* in reconciling the shift in BJP policies towards middle class interests can be seen in the following excerpt from the Organizer:

> Generally two conflicting views prevail in the society about the role and character of the middle class. One is that the middle class is the backbone of humanity everywhere in the world and is the harbinger, catalyst and agent of change and custodian of morality. The other one is just the opposite. The middle class is only vocal, corrupt and corrupting, exploitative, self-seeking, do-nothing, ever-grievancing and change resistant. While much can be said on both sides [...] the former appears less convincing and more aggrandising and the latter more realistic and truthful, especially in the present context.
>
> (Surya Narain Saxena. 'A Role for the Middle Class,' Organizer, 24 April 2005)

The Kargil conflict and the consequent rallying of the whole Hindu nationalist movement against a perceived massive threat to national security served the BJP well to avoid an open escalation of tensions over its economic agenda at this time. Tensions, however, continued to surface until well into 2003 when the NDA government finally managed to enforce *Sangh Parivar* acquiescence to its policies by fabricating a massive media hype with strong nationalistic overtones on the success – alleged or otherwise – of its economic policies: the 'India Shining' campaign. The subsequent electoral defeat of the NDA by a Congress-led alliance in 2004 only served to reinforce dissent with the economic agenda from within the *Sangh Parivar*. Criticism now became openly based on demands to place greater emphasis on moral economy aspects which would help to reintegrate lower class sections of society into the Hindu nationalist movement which were perceived to have deserted the party.

Strains between the two wings regarding economic policy can be expected to persist. Still, the lobby to continue (and accentuate) economic liberalisation is, at present, very strong within the BJP, and middle class interests have remained strongly linked with liberalisation.[34] Periodic and selective recourses to elements from the movement's cultural identitarian agenda, including communal violence, can also serve to placate the internal critics of the BJP economic agenda, since this section within the party and the movement is often placing greater importance on the advancement of the cultural identitarian agenda than the direction of economic policy.

5   The rise of the BJP

The foundation of the BJP

The *Bharatiya Janata Party*'s emergence as a viable contender for political power at the level of national politics in India and one of the two major poles in the Indian party system in the late 1980s and early 1990s was largely unexpected by observers of Indian politics at the time. Indian politics since the late 1960s had been comprehensively dominated by the struggle between the Congress and the various counter-alliances led by the centre-left political spectrum, with government formation oscillating between the two sides, between the centrist and the centre-left. The right-wing opposition to the Congress and the Indian political establishment had, at times, supplemented centre-left alliances, but had not been perceived as an equally significant force in its own right despite occasional worries over the spread of the RSS on the part of secular nationalists. The rapid growth of the BJP in terms of *Lok Sabha* seats and the ferocity of the BJP-led Ayodhya campaign – possibly not the largest popular movement in Indian history as claimed by its leaders but certainly one of the larger ones – coupled with a number of recent crises which had been portrayed by Atul Kohli as a general crisis of governability (Kohli 1990) created an impression of a political wave which threatened to overturn the very foundations of Indian politics.

This sense of an inexorable rise of right-wing politics, if not downright religious fanaticism which is strongly inherent even in academic literature published in the early and mid-1990s appears odd when contrasted with the image of the BJP in the years after 2004: a dejected and disoriented political party unable to come to terms with its own electoral defeat, a quarrelling leadership and a disenchanted cadre base.

In between lies the emergence of India as a major global player in the eyes of the western world – and in the eyes of India's own middle class whose rapidly growing economic capacity forms the basis of this perception. The evolution of the BJP between its founding in 1980 and today cannot be explained without taking into account the socio-economic development of India in this period and the consequent transformation of India's political economy.

The *Janata Party* interlude between 1977 and 1979, on the part of the Hindu nationalist movement, was not only forced upon it by the specific circumstances which necessitated the unification of opposition parties. It also formed a strategic decision only partially to prevent the establishment of comprehensive dominance by Indira Gandhi (and compel her return to democratic processes), but further-more to enlarge the movement's acceptability in the secular nationalist domi-nated political mainstream (Hansen 1999: 130). This reinforces the argument that the Hindu nationalist movement's politics during the second half of the 1970s was strongly aiming at overcoming political isolation and that the even-tual decision to join the JP – even accepting the dissolution of the *Jan Sangh* in the process – was based on this strategy.

In the event, this strategy proved only partially successful. The conflict within the JP over dual membership of RSS members posed a direct challenge to Hindu nationalist cohesion within the *Janata Party*: As long as membership in the RSS was permitted for JP members the dissolution of *Jan Sangh* structures of polit-ical organisation hardly mattered as the RSS provided a common platform for Hindu nationalists in the JP. This challenge negated the advantage of relative cohesion the Hindu nationalists enjoyed over the former *Lok Dal* and Congress (O)-dominated wings which possessed larger electoral appeal at the time and comprised the majority of JP members. The decision to split away from the JP and form a new party constituted a second best option. The newly founded BJP not only included some former socialists and Congress (O) leaders and cadres, but due to its participation in the struggle against the emergency regime could claim a part of the legacy of the JP movement which significantly boosted the moral perception of Hindu nationalist politics by the general public that had suf-fered after the assassination of M. K. Gandhi (Bhatt 2004: 135).

The JP interlude also provided Hindu nationalist leaders their first experi-ences in governance – leaving aside Mookerjee's short-lived inclusion in the first government of independent India. With Atal Bihari Vajpayee as the foreign minister and Lal Kishan Advani as Minister for Information and Broadcasting, two important former *Jan Sangh* leaders were included in the central govern-ment. As a result, both leaders were accorded higher public attention than previ-ous *Jan Sangh* leaders.

For the former *Jan Sangh* members, the JP interlude constituted a significant step in the evolution of their respective careers, and was perceived as a major contribution towards the spread of Hindu nationalism in Indian society. In inter-views with leading actors at the time, the perception of bitterness regarding their treatment within the JP is palpable, but the importance attributed to the experi-ment for the emergence of Hindu nationalism as a major part of the Indian polit-ical spectrum by Hindu nationalist leaders is equally clear. This is exemplified by J. P. Mathur, a founding leader of the BJP and erstwhile *Jan Sangh* leader:

'[D]uring Emergency, wrongly or rightly, we merged together, the Janata Party was formed and it broke apart. We had to do it [split away from the JP], because during the Emergency it was agreed that RSS issues would not be raised. That means that those who had an RSS background, they would not be barred from holding any office, this was agreed. But the Socialist

Party people and some Congress (O) people, they went back on their word. And we said: "No, we have had contact with you only for a few days, but with the RSS we are a sort of aligned organisation." So we came out, and BJP was formed. But still there was a change, without – as I said – in any manner losing our roots, our hindutva.'

(Interview with J. P. Mathur, 7 March 2007, Delhi)

When the BJP was founded in 1980, the party leadership attempted to construct a new party identity by supplementing the *Jan Sangh* agenda with the newly inherited legacy of the struggle against the emergency regime. This included a greater emphasis on social and economic elements derived from the JP movement – the basis for this line of thought had already been created by Upadhyaya, but its implementation into the party constitution was significantly advanced only with the founding of the BJP. The attempt to overcome political isolation had been temporarily blocked by the centre-left political spectrum on the issue of dual membership and did not figure prominently in the party's strategy for a number of years, despite the pre-eminence of A. B. Vajpayee – often called the 'moderate face' of the party – as party president until 1986. The importance attributed to overcoming the party's political isolation within its leadership can be seen in the resumption of these attempts in the late 1980s which led to seat-sharing agreements with the *Janata Dal* – this time led by the 'radical' L. K. Advani, before the BJP consciously suspended these efforts between 1990 and 1993.

The party's development from 1980 to 2008

The historical development of the BJP after 1980, summarised below, shows several recurring features which give an indication of the internal and external compulsions the party is and has been facing and depicts patterns within the party's development which allow certain predictions with regard to its future course. Amrita Basu (Basu 2001; further Jaffrelot 2005a: 292) perceived the BJP as a party which passed cyclically through recurring phases of political moderation and radicalisation. In her view, the advancement of the Hindu nationalist agenda and the corresponding increase in support from hard line Hindu nationalists is pulling the party towards radical politics while, at the same time, involving significant political costs in terms of acceptability among the larger Indian public, institutional reactions and political isolation which necessitate course corrections at periodic intervals. Written by Basu when the BJP had once again turned towards political moderation after its radical phase between 1990 and 1993 which, in turn, had followed a period of political moderation, the argument of cyclical development appears plausible at first glance. After the electoral defeat in 2004 and especially after the Jinnah controversy had compelled L. K. Advani to resign as party president, the idea that the BJP was once again entering a radical phase was widely shared among observers of Indian politics. The argument, however, neglects aspects of path-dependency in the interpretation of the party's evolution which will be discussed in Chapter 7. Still, the interplay between moderation, radicalisation and normalisation forms a recurring element in the historical narrative of the party's evolution after 1980.

The first phase of moderation: the BJP between 1980 and 1985

As outlined above, the BJP followed a course of accentuated political moderation in its early years which can be seen in both the party constitution and its 1984 general election manifesto. The spread of Hindu nationalist ideology in society was deemed to be facilitated by moderation and integration into the mainstream political spectrum. In many respects, Indira Gandhi's turn to right-wing populism during her second turn in government from 1980 to 1984 managed to outflank the BJP on issues of hard line national security and cohesion (Jaffrelot 1996: 330). Her conscious efforts to utilise a soft *hindutva* idiom highlight both the success of Hindu nationalist strategy regarding the spread of its ideology and the risks involved concerning the BJP.

In contrast to Indira Gandhi's right-wing shift, the newly founded BJP opted to highlight its hopes for arrival in mainstream Indian politics by electing A. B. Vajpayee as its first president. Vajpayee had been president of the *Jan Sangh* between 1969 and 1973, succeeding Deendayal Upadhyaya, but had, in turn, been succeeded by L. K. Advani who led the party until its dissolution into the *Janata Party*. In contrast to Advani, Vajpayee was strongly associated with a moderate course of the party. His higher acceptability among potential allies indicates the importance attributed to integration with mainstream politics. It has to be noted, however, that the choice of Vajpayee as party president also followed his larger stature in public perception as former foreign minister in the Morarji Desai government.

The conscious efforts at positioning the BJP as a relatively moderate political party is exemplified by the party's projection of Gandhian socialism in economic policy and its reaction to the secessionist *Khalistan* movement among Punjabi Sikhs. The former formed a recourse to a political idiom which especially since the return of Jayaprakash Narayan to national-level Indian politics had been strongly associated with the socialist political spectrum and included, at a time when the INC was gradually turning towards a political idiom of liberalisation and economic reform, a strong emphasis on economic nationalism in its *swadeshi* concept – in essence a proposition of autonomy from the global economy while the Congress was beginning to highlight increased integration with the latter.[1]

The *Khalistan* movement formed the first major threat to Indian national cohesion which could not easily be interpreted by Hindu nationalists as an illustration of Muslim disloyalty to the Indian motherland. Despite a strong emphasis on the role of 'the foreign hand' – in the form of the Pakistani state – Sikh secessionism challenged the Hindu nationalist idea that 'Indian' religions were different from 'foreign' religions in this respect. Sikh secessionism certainly endangered national cohesion, and the terrorist campaign of parts of the *Akali*

Dal – directed amongst others against Punjabi Hindus – threatened law and order, but the BJP by and large managed to pursue a relatively balanced and accommodative approach to the crisis.

While the INC tried to legitimise the pogrom against Sikhs in Delhi in 1984 much in the same way the BJP later tried to justify the 2002 pogrom in Gujarat – as a understandable if maybe excessive spontaneous reaction by the aggrieved populace against prior provocation – the BJP propagated a combination of accommodation and strict enforcement of law and order while, at the same time, maintaining social harmony:

> The BJP shares the agony of Punjab with the Punjabis. It congratulates the people of Punjab on maintaining the peace in the Punjab in the face of grave provocation. The BJP holds the Congress (I) squarely responsible for encouraging separatist and terrorist elements in the Punjab. As a result, for four long agonising years, the State has been subject to an orgy of murder and mayhem. The tragic murder of Prime Minister Mrs Gandhi, and the bestial carnage which followed in its wake, also, are poison-fruits of Government's Punjab policy. The BJP wishes to declare unequivocally that the nation shall not allow another assault on the country's integrity, and that there can be no compromise with those who talk of Khalistan. At the same time, the BJP will not suffer any harm being done to innocent people, Hindu or Sikh. The Punjab problem is basically political and we will solve it politically; [s]eparatism and terrorism will be sternly dealt with; [w]e will adequately compensate the sufferers of violence during the last three years; [t]he BJP will refer territorial claims and counterclaims, river waters and other outstanding issues, to the Chief Justice of India, for arbitration within one year.
>
> (BJP election manifesto, general elections 1984)

The BJP performed poorly in the subsequent general elections, both in terms of vote percentage and seats. It managed to gain support of less than 8 per cent of voters and won only two constituencies.[2] The right-wing turn of the INC, large-scale sympathy among the public after the assassination of Indira Gandhi, the fresh and clean image of Rajiv Gandhi as prime ministerial candidate and a low level of opposition unity translated into a wave of support for the INC which won almost 50 per cent of votes. The election results effectively undermined the position of Vajpayee within the party, paving the way for his eventual replacement by Advani in 1986.

The interaction of radicalisation and moderation between 1985 and 1990

Advani's party presidency is often perceived to mark the beginning of the party's radicalisation although the BJP under his leadership continued its efforts towards integration into the political mainstream until the commencement of the party's

Ayodhya campaign.[3] The culmination of these efforts was the inclusion of the BJP into the pre-electoral system of seat adjustments with the *Janata Dal*-led National Front and the subsequent provision of outside support to the V. P. Singh government. The sense of gradual radicalisation of the BJP during the second half of the 1980s is to a large extent due to a relatively small number of issues which, however, were accorded great prominence by the party leadership, involving the question of the treatment of the Muslim minority and national cohesion.

The treatment of the Muslim minority in India took centre-stage in Indian politics once again with the debate on the Shah Bano case in the mid-1980s. In essence, the Rajiv Gandhi government had continued to some extent the right-wing turn of the last Indira Gandhi government in the first half of the 1980s including its tendency to take recourse to a soft *hindutva* idiom and the enactment of a number of highly symbolical measures which aimed at accommodation with organised right-wing Hindu interests. This included among others the opening of the *Babri Masjid* in Ayodhya to Hindu worship. This policy was supplemented by measures designed to placate organised Muslim interests, especially conservative Muslim interests. In the Shah Bano case – a case on alimentation after the divorce of a marriage between Muslims – the Indian Supreme Court had reinforced the supremacy of secular Indian law over Muslim Personal Law in cases of disagreement between the two. Conservative Muslim interest groups protested against this decision, ostentatiously on the grounds that this violated minority rights. The Rajiv Gandhi government intervened on the side of the conservative Muslim lobby leading, in turn, to protests from liberal groups – and the Hindu nationalists.

Hindu nationalists were able to present themselves as protectors of India's liberal and secular polity which was alleged to be endangered by the 'pseudo-secular' INC, whose commitment to secularism was alleged to be limited to 'minority appeasement.' The question of the treatment of religious minorities in India transcends standard positions on modernisation and liberalism: The need to protect minorities, including protection from assimilation may interfere with the protection of individuals within the minority community. In the Shah Bano case an unlikely coalition of communists, liberals and Hindu nationalists positioned themselves as protectors of individual liberties, while the INC defended the need to protect the minority from assimilation by granting privileges.

The BJP position on the Shah Bano case itself and on the larger question of implementing a unified civil code cannot by any means be interpreted as a radical position. It is shared among a large part of the progressive spectrum of Indian civil society. However, the issue possesses an inherent possibility to portray Muslims as reactionary, an obstacle in India's development as a modern society and provides opportunities to reinforce stereotypical images of the Muslim 'Other' without appearing to do so. These were used to great effect especially regarding the middle classes who, at the time, were instigating a paradigm shift in the Indian discourse on modernisation increasingly oriented at technological progress and the supremacy of 'merit' over community privileges.

The BJP found itself in a rare occasion were it could simultaneously represent liberal attitudes among modern middle class supporters and reactionary, communalist sentiments without exerting great efforts at prevarication in policy articulation.

Thus, in its 1991 general election manifesto – during the party's most radical phase – it was still possible for the BJP to limit its reference to the unified civil code to a very short and ostentatiously liberal passage: 'We will appoint a Law Commission to study various Civil Laws, ancient, medieval and modern, to evolve a Common Civil Law for the whole country to give our citizens a feeling of unity and brotherhood.'[4]

National cohesion, in turn, constituted one of the most important issues in the Indian political discourse during most of the 1980s. While the BJP had striven for a balanced stance regarding the *Khalistan* movement, it reacted in a less accommodative way to the escalation of the Kashmir conflict in the wake of the 1980s. It strongly emphasised Pakistan's involvement which in Hindu nationalist parlance is often used as a substitute for suspicions of Muslim disloyalty, and attempted to present the conflict mainly as a communalist attack on Hindus.

> The BJP views with concern the recent developments in the Kashmir valley. Widespread violence in the State has led to an anarchical situation. This has paralysed tourism, the backbone of the Kashmir economy. The Pakistan-inspired violence against Hindus has caused those Kashmiris to become refugees in their own land. The BJP will [w]eed out Pakistani elements from the valley; [h]old free and fair elections in the State as soon as conditions stabilize there; [h]ave separate Regional Development Councils for Jammu and Ladakh [areas of the state which do not have a Muslim majority]; [m]ake relief and rehabilitation facilities available to Kashmiri refugees [a reference to the Hindu Kashmiri Pandits], settling them in the hills of Pir Panjal Range; and [e]nd all uncertainty about the future status of the State by deleting Article 370 of the Constitution.
>
> (BJP election manifesto for the General Elections, 1991)

The larger issue of national cohesion was also advanced by the VHP whose *ekatmata yatra* (unity of the motherland) attempted to present the issue with strong quasi-religious connotations. De facto this constituted an effort to portray national cohesion as a communal issue (Jaffrelot 1996: 330–1).

While national cohesion and the treatment of minority communities provided opportunities for advancing a more radical agenda, during this phase the BJP still continued its efforts at integration into the political mainstream and, by and large, opted for policies and political strategies which are associated with political moderation. The large-scale *kisan* (farmer) movements in the late 1980s provided an opportunity to stress the party's commitment to rural India – often couched in a moral economy idiom despite reacting to specific organised interests. The agricultural policy of the BJP was often accompanied by excursions into the issue of cow protection, a part of the party's cultural identitarian agenda.

Overall, the BJP was placed in an awkward position vis-à-vis farmer demands as the major *kisan* movements highlighted an alleged urban bias in Indian development policies in their attempts to transcend class divisions in rural society. This challenged urban middle class perceptions on development strategies and, accordingly, the interests of one of the party's main support bases. The BJP by and large managed to overcome this dilemma[5] but simultaneously faced a similar one regarding demands for OBC reservations in the public sector, administration and educational institutions.

The party's efforts at re-alignment with the centre-left political spectrum were facilitated by an issue which centred around the interests of its key constituency – rising middle classes not yet fully incorporated into the rentier economy – while allowing its presentation in the moral idiom of the Hindu nationalist cultural identitarian agenda: the campaign against corruption.

In the wake of the evolving Bofors scandal, INC leader V. P. Singh split away from the Congress to emerge as a focal point of re-alignments among the opposition parties. Eventually, he was instrumental in founding the *Janata Dal* which entered into a series of formal and informal electoral alliances with other opposition parties, including the BJP. The unification of opposition forces helped to defeat the Congress under the leadership of Rajiv Gandhi and led to the formation of the National Front government which was provided outside support by both the communists and the BJP. The anti-corruption campaigns, apart from contributing to public and especially middle class disenchantment with the INC, served as a temporary kit within the alliance which, otherwise, was strongly divided on the issue of OBC reservations.

The radical phase: 1990 to 1993

The decision to engage significantly in the *Ramjanmabhumi* campaign with Advani embarking on the *rath yatra* denotes the symbolic turning point for the radicalisation of the BJP. The decision is, however, attributed to the coterminous escalation in the policy of extending reservations to OBC communities: the Mandal controversy (Basu 1996; Chhibber 1999).

This escalation followed the eventual implementation of the recommendations of the so-called Mandal Commission vis-à-vis the extension of affirmative action to the Other Backward Classes (OBC), a stipulation in the Indian constitution which previously had been neglected ostentatiously on the grounds of differences over the classification of social strata belonging to the OBC category. The Mandal Commission recommended caste over class as the criteria for inclusion in the OBC category, and (both past and present) social discrimination over economic under-development as the factor justifying measures of positive discrimination.[6] As such, the Mandal Commission Report provided the means to extend reservations to politically influential social strata, mostly accorded the status of *shudras* in the *varna* system, which had benefited to a significant extent from the transformation of the agrarian order in the wake of the land reforms and the Green Revolution (Hasan 1998: 130–2). The comparatively hasty implementation of the new reservation policy is further linked to a power struggle within the *Janata Dal* leadership. In the event, Jats – the main support base of one of the most important internal rivals of V. P. Singh – were excluded from the benefits of reservations. This issue is also related to the conflict over leadership within the *Lok Dal*, one of the largest constituents of the JD, between Jat- and Yadav-based political leaders, exemplified by the power struggle between Ajit Singh and Mulayam Singh Yadav after the death of Charan Singh in the second half of the 1980s (Hasan 1998).

It has been noted that the implementation of the Mandal Commission's recommendations hardly constituted a major challenge to upper caste dominance and social status since the implementation by the central government was restricted to the central level and, accordingly, did not involve a sufficient number of jobs (Weiner 2001: 203–4). The severity of upper caste reaction is then usually attributed to the symbolic importance of the policy. This argumentation neglects two aspects: (1) the importance of higher formal education for the maintenance of socio-economic status especially with the simultaneous shift to liberalisation which removed select highly paid economic sectors from political contest; and (2) the effects of OBC reservations in terms of class, not caste.

The former aspect has already been discussed. With regard to the latter, in caste terms the reservation regime provides employment and enhanced opportunities for higher education to previously disadvantaged social strata, although these will not necessarily be economically 'backward' anymore. In class terms, however, it has to be stressed that relatively well-paid employment even under the new reservation regime was still restricted to comparatively highly educated individuals who were by and large from the more prosperous (lower) middle class segment of OBC communities: a part of the newly rising middle classes. While lower class individuals from among the OBC communities tended to benefit from reservation policy, most benefits accrued to this social segment, not the lower classes. A trickle-down effect will certainly have to be taken into consideration but, by and large, the reservation regime functions as a means to ensure (usually lower) middle class status. The caste dimension should not, however, be neglected: The BJP reaction to the Mandal controversy is strongly related to the further restriction of large-scale benefits accruing from OBC reservations on the basis of caste.

The BJP and the INC were placed in a dilemma vis-à-vis the implementation of the Mandal Commission's recommendations since they received support from both sides of the controversy and were anyway reluctant to be portrayed as opposed to 'social justice.' Once again, the issue of electoral support is usually depicted in the Indian academic discourse in terms of caste blocks, despite the fact that OBC voting preferences were not homogenous (Chhibber 1999: 161). Correspondingly, Indian politics after the Mandal controversy were mostly reduced to an OBC-upper caste and the secular-Hindu nationalist cleavage. Barring a relatively short period in the early 1990s in Hindi heartland politics, there is no significant evidence for the constitution of a durable OBC-upper caste cleavage even at the state level. In fact, the Mandal controversy did not only divide Indian society as a whole or, at the least, upper castes and OBC, but neatly dissected the newly rising middle strata of society on the same lines.

The BJP dilemma in the face of the Mandal controversy is obvious: Upper caste party supporters from among the middle classes were more numerous than their OBC counter-parts. In addition, the movement was ideologically opposed to any attempts to divide the Hindu community on socio-economic lines which it perceived as a direct challenge to the concept of *hindutva*. Still, the party was being compelled by the ferocity of the controversy to position itself, thereby giving preference to one side over the other.

Disregarding the consequences in the longer term, the decision to implement the Mandal Commission's recommendation had been a major strategic success for V. P. Singh: It effectively removed internal rivals and settled the question of predominance within the *Lok Dal/Janata Dal* in terms of caste orientations of its leadership, and it placed the INC as the main rival of the JD in a position, where the party found itself unable to formulate a counter-strategy. The BJP, however, did react with a strategy of its own.

With regard to OBC reservations, the official party line welcomed the new policy. At the same time, party leaders began to express their reservations on the policy whenever faced with contexts where upper caste (and established middle class) reactions were sufficiently accentuated (Basu 1996), while still maintaining its outside support to the National Front government which had become increasingly pre-occupied with factional conflicts. The party (as well as the larger movement) were also increasingly portraying its commitment to OBC emancipation by ushering in a new line of second-level leadership from among OBC communities, in a way engaging in a process of social engineering (Jaffrelot 1998a). Several key leaders regarding later developments emerged during this phase, among them Kalyan Singh, Uma Bharati, Vinay Katiyar, and Shankersinh Vaghela. The BJP also highlighted its commitment to economic reforms, in this reaching out to middle class economic interests.

Having formulated this complex policy of double-speak, the party proceeded with diverting public attention from its fixation with the Mandal controversy and caste identity by entering the previously VHP-led Ayodhya campaign, effectively taking over the issue. The decision to launch the *rath yatra* in late 1990 served as a diversion, but also as a rallying call to anti-Muslim sentiments, and an attempt to 're-unite' the Hindu community under the leadership of the Hindu nationalist movement. Excerpts of the preamble to the BJP election manifesto for the general elections in 1991 serve to illustrate the way in which the complex BJP counter-strategy was formulated officially.

> The country stands today on a major cross-road of his history. A right turn – and the country would be well on its way to fulfillment. A wrong turn – and the country would be in serious trouble. [...] The country has been advancing at a snail's place when it has not actually been declining. Prices are rising and employment generation is falling. The foreign debt trap is closing on us. Communal violence has rocked several States. For the first time in his

history we had immolations by the frustrated flower of Indian youth. State-Centre relations are seriously strained. Opportunistic alliances have brought Democracy itself into disrepute. Secessionism has raised its ugly head in Punjab, Kashmir and Assam. [...] In the face of this challenge, other parties have gone casteist, communalist, or both. Different political parties exploited even the tragic Gulf War to carve out and corner communal vote banks. [...] The Bharatiya Janata Party as the party of Nationalism, Holism and Integral Humanism offers a complete, new and higher alternative to the current dismal scene. As the party of Swadesh and Swadharma, it is wedded to our country, our people and our culture. It believes in consensus and co-operation, and not in contrariety and conflict. It would uplift the poor and the downtrodden, without pitting caste against caste, without inciting class against class. As the party of law, order and justice, it would ensure the security of life, limb and honour of all citizens. It seeks the restoration of Ram Janmabhoomi in Ayodhya only by way of a symbolic righting of historic wrongs, so that the old unhappy chapter of acrimony could be ended, and a Grand National Reconciliation effected. Hindus and Muslims are blood-brothers. But on account of historical reasons their relationship has not been harmonious. It shall be the endeavour of BJP to make all Indians fraternal and friendly once again. BJP is no prisoner of dogmas. We will de-bureaucratise the Economy to maximise production. We will make even the Sarkari [public] sector productive and profitable by throwing open some of the public sector units to people's participation. The BJP will modernize the country on the basis of Science and Technology, even while strengthening the cultural roots of our national life.

(BJP election manifesto for the General Elections, 1991)

The comparatively hallowed tone adopted in the manifesto was accompanied by crudely formulated recourses to communal sentiments, often including more or less open incitements to violence, during the *rath yatra*. The choice of the official line, here, serves to illustrate the extent to which the BJP leadership at the time understood the linkages between not only 'Mandal' and '*mandir*,' the Ayodhya movement, but also between these issues and the rise of the middle classes, rent scarcity and liberalisation, all of which were summarised and linked – within the bounds of Hindu nationalist ideology – in the narrative of a crucial turning point in India's development cited above.

The Ayodhya campaign does not only mark the most radical phase in the party's evolution in terms of ideological stridency, but also its most militant phase. The campaign was accompanied by large-scale violence throughout most of India – the communal violence which had 'rocked several States' mentioned in the passage of the manifesto cited above. When the V. P. Singh government finally decided to react, with the JD chief minister of Bihar at the time, Lalu Prasad Yadav, arresting Advani, the BJP finally withdrew support to the National Front government, effectively toppling it. The newly formed government under Chandra Shekhar, heading a JD splinter group and supported from the outside by the INC, let the campaign resume.[7] The first attempt by the *yatra* to reach Ayodhya was stopped by the then UP chief minister Mulayam Singh Yadav who ordered the state police to open fire on the protesters leading, in turn, to the fall of his government.

With the INC deciding to withdraw support to the Chandra Shekhar government, the BJP used the incidence of violence against the *kar sevaks* to great effect in the elections at the centre and in UP. While the Congress managed to form a minority government at the centre led by Narasimha Rao after the assassination of Rajiv Gandhi during the electoral campaign, the BJP emerged as the single largest opposition party and won a majority of seats in the UP legislative assembly. The *Babri Masjid* in Ayodhya was eventually destroyed in the *rath yatra's* second attempt to reach Ayodhya, with the BJP state government 'failing' to protect law and order at the site (and elsewhere) and the INC-led central government unwilling to interfere in time. The anti-Muslim violence associated with the campaign climaxed once more during the Bombay riots in early 1993.

The Ayodhya campaign and especially the Bombay riots showed an increasing participation of the *Shiv Sena* in Hindu nationalist agitation and an increasing co-operation between the *Sena* and the *Sangh Parivar*. Co-operation in agitation between the BJP and the *Sena* was formalised in 1995 when the two parties entered into an electoral alliance for the elections to the legislative assembly of Maharashtra, with the *Shiv Sena* as the senior partner due to its stronger presence in the state. The electoral alliance led to the formation of a *Sena*-BJP coalition government. With the creation of the NDA, the *Shiv Sena* emerged as one of the most important partners of the BJP at the national level and was awarded with a number of ministries at the central level and, temporarily, the speaker's post in the *Lok Sabha*. The *Sena's* performance in governance was, by and large, moderately successful and did not lead to increasing radicalisation within the NDA government, despite the radical stances taken regularly by the party's Mumbai-based leadership. The electoral alliance between the two parties has so far been durable, although it is restricted to Maharashtra with the *Shiv Sena* occasionally (and without significant success) contesting elections outside of Maharashtra on its own.

The turn towards moderation: 1993 to 2004

The Ayodhya campaign proved to be enormously successful in electoral terms. As mentioned above, the BJP emerged as the single largest opposition party in the *Lok Sabha* in 1991. In 1996, it won more seats than the INC, though with a slightly smaller vote percentage. Its strong electoral performance was largely due to its dominance in large parts of northern and western India.

After the destruction of the *Babri Masjid* in December 1992, and the apparent complicity of the BJP state government in Uttar Pradesh, the central government belatedly reacted and deposed all BJP state governments. The BJP was thus unable to translate its electoral successes into the formation of state govern-

Table 5.1 Vote percentages of the BJP in elections to the *Lok Sabha*

1984	1989	1991	1996	1998	1999	2004	2009
7.74	11.36	20.11	20.29	25.59	23.75	22.16	18.80

Source: Election Commission of India.

ments. The party was faced with a situation where it had to overcome its almost total political isolation. In addition, the communalist excesses during the early 1990s had, after a time, led to public disenchantment with the party. In 1993, an electoral alliance between the *Samajwadi Party* (SP), a JD splinter group, and the newly rising Dalit-based *Bahujan Samaj Party* (BSP) managed to form the government in UP despite the BJP emerging as the single largest party. The process of government formation in UP showed that the centre-left spectrum of Indian politics had re-grouped, and still possessed large electoral appeal, in contrast to the INC whose simultaneous decline in many parts of India, especially parts of the Hindi heartland significantly weakened the party (Hasan 1998; Pai 2000).

While Advani had returned to the post of party president in 1992, succeeding Murli Manohar Joshi, his strong association with the Ayodhya campaign increasingly became a liability vis-à-vis public perception of the party. Along with several other BJP leaders, he was charged with a number of criminal offences for his role in the campaign. His later attempts to publicly apologise for the excesses during the *rath yatra* – including a description of the destruction of the *Babri Masjid* as the 'saddest day' of his life – were perceived by large parts of the public as half-hearted and insincere.[8] Effectively, the party's presentation in public soon passed to Vajpayee who had maintained a relatively low profile during the Ayodhya campaign. In the subsequent electoral campaigns for the general elections, Vajpayee was designated as the party's prime ministerial candidate, while Advani remained party president until 1998 and continued to dominate the party organisation even afterwards. The BJP consciously attempted to follow a course of political moderation, enhancing its appeal especially among the middle classes and gradually overcoming its political isolation.

Economic de-regulation and divestment of the public sector had been propagated by the party before, but were increasingly emphasised after 1992. At the same time, the BJP strongly protested against the misuse of power by the INC central government, a recurring feature during the government of Narasimha Rao exemplified by the so-called JMM case and the repeated misuse of gubernatorial authority. Frequent corruption scandals involving the INC provided an opportunity to place renewed emphasis on anti-corruption campaigns where the BJP once again found itself on the same side as the centre-left spectrum.

The BJP in the mid-1990s began to participate in campaigns for the creation of new states, an effort which culminated in the creation of Jharkhand, Uttarakhand (formerly Uttaranchal), and Chhattisgarh, respectively carved out of the states of Bihar, Uttar Pradesh, and Madhya Pradesh. Its demand for the creation of smaller states marked a significant change from early *Jan Sangh* policies which had, by and large, favoured large administrative units to ensure national cohesion. The new policy on smaller states enabled the party to reach out to new support bases in the regions concerned, especially Adivasis in Jharkhand and Chhattisgarh, and contributed to its decreasing political isolation in the wake of the 1990s. The *Jharkhand Mukti Morcha* (JMM) which led the campaign in Jharkhand temporarily joined the BJP-led alliance system in the late 1990s.

In 1995, the BJP utilised the rapidly deteriorating relations between SP and BSP to show-case its claims of concern for the lower strata of society, in this case Dalits, by offering outside support to the BSP in government formation in UP. Thereby it enabled the latter to topple the UP government despite aggressive *Samajwadi* attempts to split the BSP and form a government of its own. Apart from further reducing its political isolation, the BJP strategy in UP temporarily weakened the SP, its main regional rival at the time. The BJP–BSP alliance broke down within the year, but was summarily revived twice, in 1997 and 2001. The BSP also provided outside support to the NDA government at the centre at a crucial time following the Gujarat pogrom in 2002. BSP support in parliament at the time enabled the BJP to avert a breakdown of the NDA coalition government when several NDA constituents and supporting parties, notably the *Telugu Desam*, where initiating moves to bring down the government.[9] The alliances with the BSP had significant long-term consequences for the BJP in Uttar Pradesh which will be discussed further below.

After the 1996 general elections, the Indian president as per political custom appointed Vajpayee as Prime Minister as the leader of the largest legislative party in the *Lok Sabha*. Due to the party's continued isolation the BJP found itself unable to gather sufficient support to form a coalition government, and Vajpayee resigned before having to prove his majority in parliament. Instead, the new government was formed by a post-electoral alliance between the JD, JD splinter groups and regional parties – the United Front (UF) – with the INC providing outside support. The process of government formation in 1996 constitutes one of the rare instances in the history of independent India where the secular-Hindu nationalist cleavage actually affected the strategic positioning of political parties to a significant extent. The UF leadership successfully averted attempts by the BJP to gain support among its constituents and, subsequently, forced a reluctant Congress to offer outside support in view of the parties' common commitment to secularism. The INC systematically went on to destabilise the United Front, though, toppling both the first UF government led by Deve Gowda in 1997 and the second UF government under I. K. Gujral shortly afterwards.

In the event, INC political strategy in the mid-1990s demolished any chances for the establishment of a unified secular nationalist block against the BJP. The apparent impossibility to ensure the stability of such an arrangement, supplemented by emerging conflicts between several UF constituents, resulted in the collapse of the UF alliance and the return of an anti-Congress coalition, this time under BJP leadership: the National Democratic Alliance (NDA).

A rudimentary alliance had been in place already prior to the 1998 general elections, with the BJP forming pre-electoral alliances with a number of political parties outside the United Front alliance. The collapse of the United Front during 1998 presented an opportunity to enlarge the alliance, incorporating a number of centre-left or regional parties. Factional conflicts within the *Janata Dal* which had already led to the emergence of the SP in Uttar Pradesh and the *Samata Party* and later the *Rashtriya Janata Dal* (RJD) in Bihar resulted in the final break-up of the party which split into the *Janata Dal (United)* and *Janata Dal (Secular)*, the latter restricted effectively to Karnataka, the former to Bihar and Karnataka.

The JD(U) joined the NDA prior to the 1999 elections and eventually merged with the *Samata*. The JD(S) remained apart from the NDA but formed a temporary alliance with the BJP between 2006 and 2007. The collapse of the first NDA government in 1999 after the *All India Anna Dravida Munnetra Kazhagam* (AIADMK) withdrew its support led to the incorporation into the NDA of its main rival in Tamil Nadu, the *Dravida Munnetra Kazhagam* (DMK) which, in turn, left the NDA prior to the 2004 general elections, resulting in a rapprochement between BJP and AIADMK, although this relationship remained less formal and subsequently broke down. In Orissa, the BJP formed an alliance with the *Biju Janata Dal* (BJD), originally a Congress splinter group. Another prominent former UF constituent, the *Asom Gana Parishad* (AGP) also became part of the NDA. The AGP left the NDA subsequently, but has recently re-aligned with the BJP. The most important change in the BJP-led alliance system between 1998 and 1999 was the state-level pre-electoral alliance between the BJP and *Telugu Desam*. The latter stayed out of the NDA and neither joined the central government nor depended on BJP support in Andhra Pradesh to form the state government, but provided crucial outside support to the NDA government between 1999 and 2004. The *Telugu Desam* stayed apart from the NDA after 2004.

While the narrative of the various parties' alignments with the BJP gives an impression of instability – an impression which would be reinforced if the relations with smaller NDA constituents were taken into account as well – in fact, the major features of the BJP alliance system between 1999 and 2004 remained relatively stable. Typically, the BJP has found allies since the late 1990s in regions where it is relatively weak, especially in southern and eastern India. The party offers its regional allies the prospect of a small but potentially crucial increase in terms of vote percentages, apart from its often limited electoral presence in the respective states due to its relatively committed cadre base and civil society and media linkages. The regional ally then is designed as the senior partner in the respective state while participating, if possible, in the central government or else receiving equivalent benefits from supporting the BJP at the centre. In the cases of Bihar and Maharashtra where the BJP has been close in influence to its respective alliance partners, a similar design is followed (Heath 2002).

The first NDA government invited harsh criticism by left and mainstream observers as well as in the west by overturning the countries policy on nuclear armament by conducting the second Indian nuclear tests in 1998 at Pokhran, leading to subsequent Pakistani nuclear tests shortly afterwards and western sanctions against both countries which, however, failed to have a significant impact on the Indian economy. The nuclear tests proved immensely popular especially among the Indian middle classes where they were often perceived as a sign of India's emergence as a great power in the global system. Critics of the government interpreted the decision to conduct nuclear tests as an outcome of BJP radicalism, although it has been doubted by other observers whether a secular nationalist government would have reacted differently, especially since the nuclear tests clearly had already been an option which had been considered by the previous Indian governments (Garver 2002: 18). In terms of national security vis-à-vis Pakistan, the tests led to approximate nuclear parity, and thus reduced the importance of India's conventional military superiority. Its fall-out regarding low intensity conflicts with Pakistan became evident in 1999 during the Kargil conflict. This result was not openly admitted by the BJP or the government. Instead, the policy was justified by stressing its importance for India's position in the world, or as an attempt to achieve strategic parity with China (Garver 2002: 21).

The NDA government reacted to criticism regarding its allegedly confrontational foreign policy by continuing, even reinforcing, the UF governments' attempts to normalise relations with Pakistan. In early 1999, this led to a summit between Vajpayee and Pakistan's Prime Minister Nawaz Sharif in Lahore, and the so-called Lahore Declaration. Rapprochement between the two states received a temporary setback soon after the Lahore summit due to Pakistan's involvement in the Kargil conflict in the summer of 1999. The BJP used this 'betrayal' by Pakistan to fabricate a wave of nationalist sentiment highlighting the 'heroism' of the Indian *jawan* and the efficacy of the Indian military – despite severe losses inflicted on the Indian military by mostly irregular Pakistani forces (Swami 1999). Nationalist sentiment played a significant role in assuring the re-election of the NDA in 1999, although the enlargement of alliance arrangements might have been even more important in this.

The wave of nationalist sentiment also served to temporarily placate the RSS and the *Sangh Parivar* which had become increasingly disenchanted with BJP performance in government on a number of issues, including the emphasis on economic liberalisation and the apparent unwillingness to stridently advance the Hindu nationalist cultural identitarian agenda. The relatively 'normal' conduct of governance during the NDA period and open efforts by the BJP leadership to resist RSS and VHP interference regarding government policies gradually allayed fears of a radical turn of the BJP while in government among parts of the public.

The BJP attempted to reform the political system in the direction of an increasingly presidential system. This attempt was due both to the perceived popularity of Vajpayee who in surveys continued to be way ahead of the leader of opposition, Sonia Gandhi, and to a desire to institutionalise the bipolar appearing structure of the Indian party system by increasing the reliance of centre-left and regional parties (who have regularly been gaining large electoral support) on one of the two large national parties. Contrary to its self-depiction as a party which emphasises collective leadership and abhors personality cults, the leadership figure of Vajpayee was increasingly portrayed by the party and the government in a larger-than-life image, culminating in the 2004 general election campaign.

The second NDA government prided itself on its perceived achievements in development policy, especially regarding infrastructure. It reinforced divestment and liberalisation policies in general and celebrated the rates of economic growth achieved between 1999 and 2004 just as well as increases in the Sensex, the most important index of the Mumbai stock exchange. The NDA manifesto for the 2004 general elections strongly emphasised economic policy and provides an illustration of its public articulation.

The government, at the same time, became increasingly criticised on its alleged neglect of poverty alleviation and – worse with regard to its depiction in the Indian media – of giving preference to the interests of large industrialists, or 'corporate India,' over middle class welfare. This is exemplified by the near collapse of the Unit Trust of India (UTI) funds in 2001 which was mostly made up of savings of the salaried middle classes and led to increasing middle class disenchantment.[10] Already in late 1998, steep price rises in essential commodities had led to a temporary resurgence of the INC. The NDA alliance incrementally lost political influence by losing several state elections. In the state elections to the legislative assemblies of Rajasthan, Madhya Pradesh and Delhi in late 2003, the BJP further emphasised its commitment to the development of infrastructure by coining a new campaign slogan: *bijli, sadak, pani* (electricity, roads, water) which was abbreviated BSP in view of yet another media hype over the electoral performance of the *Bahujan Samaj Party* which had, by now, withdrawn its support to the NDA.

The subsequent electoral performance of the BJP in Rajasthan and Madhya Pradesh was used to create a media hype in the run-up to the general elections 2004 which were advanced by half a year in order to increase NDA chances to win the elections. Despite its earlier gradual decline throughout much of India, the BJP managed to convince both itself and public opinion on the alleged inevitability of its return to power (Jaffrelot 2005c). The NDA electoral campaign was almost exclusively based on the government's performance in economic development and summarised under the slogan *bharat uday* (rising India) which was translated for the English language media as 'Shining India.' The media hype on the expected performance of the NDA meant that the party was relatively unprepared for the new political context after the Congress-led United Progressive Alliance formed a government with outside support from the communist parties.

The 'normalisation' of the BJP

During its turns as the leading party in government, public perception of the BJP shifted notably. Media coverage of the party increasingly focussed on the portrayal of the BJP as a 'normal' political party – not always in positive ways: the 'party with a difference' was increasingly perceived to be less different from other political parties, especially the INC, than previously anticipated. The image of the 'party with a difference' was constructed around six aspects where the party allegedly stood out in comparison with its rivals:

1   the discipline of party cadres which ensured party cohesion;
2   internal democratic processes, notably the emphasis on collective leadership over personality cults and the 'dynastic' principles of leadership in the INC and other rival parties and the involvement of cadres in decision-making;
3   morality in politics, which found its expression in a refusal to indulge in corrupt practices and the simple life-styles of even higher level leaders who did not succumb to the temptations to partake in the glitz and glamour of high society;
4   an acceptance of democratic norms which prevented the abuse of institutional and constitutional powers to further the party's position vis-à-vis its rivals;
5   a refusal to co-operate with alleged criminals in order to benefit in elections from their capacities for intimidation which was supplemented by the argument that criminal cases against BJP leaders were restricted to their participation in political agitation and, hence, were justified as an expression of commitment to a cause;
6   the commitment of BJP cadres and leaders to a stringent ideology and the causes of nationalism and patriotism which prevented political opportunism.

In the academic literature, the problems the BJP is facing in maintaining its *Sonderstellung* is generally attributed to the rapid extension of both its cadre base and electoral support which brought into the party people not socialised in the RSS-dominated milieu of Hindu nationalism, and to the party's integration into the institutional structure of Indian politics with its corresponding temptations for accumulating wealth and enhancing publicly visible social status. The factional infighting which led to party splits emerged as a significant factor for the BJP. Factional infighting is amplified as a problem for maintaining party cohesion by defections. Individual or groups of legislators in India are, at times, provided with significant incentives to switch their political loyalties, either forming new parties or being received into existing rival parties. This is used by political parties to increase stability of coalition arrangements, foment parliamentary majorities in case of 'hung assemblies,' or topple elected governments.[11] The BJP after the 1990s used defections in this fashion in several instances, exemplified by the development of the party in Uttar Pradesh which will be discussed below. It also was at the receiving end of rival party-induced defections in several instances. Especially in smaller states where the respective regional party systems are less institutionalised, defections and even multiple defections with legislators switching party loyalties back and forth constitute a common feature of the political process.

Defections and party splits at the state level are often associated with factional infighting and power struggles within the leadership. At the central level of political organisation, the leadership structure in the BJP remained relatively stable since its founding: By and large, the party was dominated by Advani and Vajpayee. The second line of leadership was groomed consciously by both politicians – the BJP has prided itself on the high number of publicly visible 'second generation' leaders – but the elevated position of Advani and Vajpayee could not be contested by the second level leadership before 2004.

The duumvirate of Advani and Vajpayee was never free from friction but, in contrast to occasional media reportage, functioned comparatively harmoniously after 1992. Advani enforced his elevation from a 'mere' home minister to deputy prime minister in 2002, a position normally reserved – if at all existing – to important leaders from allied parties in coalition arrangements. At the same time, the choice of Vajpayee as prime minister was not contested by Advani. The choice of party presidents after Advani stepped down from this post in 1998 was portrayed in the Indian media as contested between the Advani- and Vajpayee-led groups, especially the selection of Bangaru Laxman as party president between 2000 and 2001 which was perceived to illustrate the increasing assertion of authority within the party organisation by Vajpayee.[12]

The authority of Vajpayee and Advani over BJP strategy and policy damaged the self-depiction of the party on collective leadership. The perception of factional organisation at the top level of party leadership, whether correct or not, supplemented defections and factional infighting at the state level to weaken the public image of a disciplined party aloof from the 'petty squabbling' between political leaders of rival parties. The problem of defections reached the central level – the BJP legislative party in the *Lok Sabha* – during the confidence vote of the UPA government in July 2008 when several BJP legislators defied the party whip to remain absent, abstain, or vote with the treasury benches, with implications by the BJP itself that the defectors had been induced by large payments from the ruling alliance.[13] While the party attempted to assume a moral high ground because of the alleged abuses of the ruling alliance, the incidence also indicated that even BJP MPs could be susceptible to bribery.

Worse for the party's image than the problems of discipline were recurring corruption scandals involving both the BJP and the NDA partners which severely affected the public image of the party. Already in the mid-1990s the so-called *hawala* (money laundering) scandal affected BJP members with even Advani himself being temporarily implicated in the scandal, although the charges could not be substantiated. In 2001, a sting operation conducted by the media outlet *Tehelka* managed to record a faked bribery attempt involving BJP party president Bangaru Laxman on film. Laxman was forced to resign subsequently and kept a low profile for some time before being reinvested with less visible positions of authority in the party apparatus.[14] Allegations that the Defence Ministry had been involved in the purchase of coffins for the 'martyrs' of the Kargil conflict at vastly inflated prices, implicating corruption, could not be linked directly to the BJP, since the ministry was led by *Samata Party* leader George Fernandes.

The incidence still significantly affected the BJP's public image, especially because of its sensitive nature for a party which tends to highlight its commitment to patriotism and led the commemorative campaign on the 'martyrdom' of Indian soldiers during the conflict.[15] In 2005, another sting operation showed that MPs across party lines but including the BJP were susceptible to accept money in order to raise specific (in some cases even ludicrous) questions during Question Hour in parliament.[16]

The BJP which had consistently opposed the misuse of gubernatorial authority associated with the constitutional provision of president's rule under Article 356 – a provision which enables the central government to take over governance in states in emergency cases[17] – attempted to impose president's rule in Bihar after the its main regional rival RJD had won a highly contested state election. The decisive role of speakers in the legislative assemblies (and the *Lok Sabha*) in the event of defections and party splits – and correspondingly in the fabrication of defections to weaken rival parties – forms another recurring feature of the abuse of constitutional authority in the history of independent India. The BJP during its terms in power at the centre and in the state did not differ significantly in this respect from its rivals, exemplified by the speaker's role in the UP legislative assembly since the mid-1990s which will be discussed below.

The *Tehelka* scandal included relatively overt attempts to silence party critics in the media. The media outlet was temporarily closed after allegedly fabricated charges were levelled against it and some of its employees.[18] Interference with the functioning of the media did not only involve legal procedures and investigations as in the *Tehelka* case: In the run-up to the general elections in 2004, the NDA government was compelled by opposition charges to disclose that a significant part of the funding for the 'Shining India' advertisement campaign – the centre-piece of the NDA electoral campaign – came from central government resources, under the guise of highlighting the successes of Indian development policy to improve the investment climate.[19]

The loss of the image as a clean alternative to the secular nationalist parties significantly weakened the BJP's electoral appeal. It also created friction within the Hindu nationalist movement and among the party's cadre base. Apart from the gradual loss of a moral high ground, the factors underlying the 'normalisation' of the BJP indicate its subjection to the typical rules which shape the rise and fall of political parties in India. In Indian parlance, these are often summarised under the term of anti-incumbency.

Anti-incumbency – the negative effect of running governments on public perception – in the Indian case constitutes a euphemism for the centrifugal forces associated with the reliance on rent allocation for political legitimacy.[20] Rent scarcity prevents the allocation of sufficient benefits which would ensure the continued co-optation of all supporters of a ruling party or alliance. Party organisation around factions and the linkage of factions with caste groups at the local and regional level serve to facilitate this distribution of benefits. Under conditions of rent scarcity the higher levels of party leadership cannot durably ensure the accommodation of all groups which leads to friction both within the party organisation and among the party's networks of social support. These factors culminate at the state level of Indian politics which is one of the most important reasons for the regionalisation of Indian politics. Opposition parties do not face the negative impact of these developments to an equal extent compared to ruling parties if the perceived likelihood of gaining access to state resources in the near future is sufficiently high, since the contest over access to benefits among their supporters is postponed. The increasing susceptibility of the BJP to factional infighting, party splits and rival party-induced defections as well as the exit of caste groups from its social constituency which is discussed below in the context of UP politics, are part of the 'normalisation' of the party due to its increasing involvement in governance, especially at the state level.

While the BJP won the general elections in 1998 and 1999, at the state level its influence gradually declined, most notably in Uttar Pradesh which elected almost a third of the BJP MPs in the *Lok Sabha* in 1998, but incrementally also in many other parts of India. This process was halted in Gujarat, Rajasthan and Madhya Pradesh in 2002 and 2003 but the series of reverses at the state level had accumulated to such an extent towards the end of the term that the likelihood of the party being able to maintain its presence in parliament in terms of seats was relatively low, barring a significant and unanticipated wave of support in its favour. In essence, the 'Shining India' campaign which constituted the culmination of the strategy of political moderation in the party's public self-depiction can be interpreted as an attempt to manufacture precisely this wave of electoral support.

Contested moderation: the BJP between 1998 and 2008

The turn towards political moderation had been contested from the hard line cultural identitarian wing among the BJP and some of its sister organisations within the *Sangh Parivar* from the outset. With the apparent electoral and political dividends arising out of the strategy in the 1996 and 1998 general elections, the shift in the party's strategy could not, however, be effectively challenged. In the mid-1990s, moderation as a political strategy was far more effective than radicalisation. The VHP, as an example, attempted to carry on with the mode of agitation used during the Ayodhya campaign but failed to evoke a significant public response (Schwecke 2009). Representatives of the hard line cultural identitarian wing of the party kept a low profile while Advani, the chief architect of the party's prior turn towards radicalism, undertook efforts to shed his hard line image.

Directly after the success in the 1998 general elections, tensions between the two wings in the party (and the larger movement) became publicly visible. Govindacharya, one of the chief ideologues of the BJP, had publicly described Vajpayee as the 'mask' (*mukhota*) of hard line Hindu nationalists which was needed to come to power. This reinforced earlier fears by secular nationalists that the moderation of the BJP constituted merely a tactical ploy and, once in government, the BJP would attempt to implement the radical agenda of Hindu nationalism. When perceived as part of a contest between the two wings on the direction of BJP politics, the controversy can be interpreted as an attempt to curtail the authority of Vajpayee as the most important representative of the moderate wing. In fact, Vajpayee during his time as prime minister continuously oscillated between expressing his commitment to Hindu nationalist ideology and showcasing his image as a centrist national leader, committed to carrying along all sections of society. In the immediate context of the *mukhota* controversy, Govindacharya had apparently overstepped. He later denied having made the remark and subsequently refrained from participating in everyday politics, ostentatiously to gain time to study the effects of globalisation.[21]

The first NDA government acted in a context of continuing attempts by the RSS and, to a lesser extent, the VHP to interfere in governance. Altogether the moderate wing of the BJP under the leadership of Vajpayee had, at the time, been able to deflect this interference, often by the argument that this would threaten the stability of the coalition arrangement. The BJP leadership also strongly implied that the BJP – while following the Hindu nationalist agenda as well as it could – was a separate entity with its own compulsions, especially when leading a coalition government. This led to a gradual and partial disassociation of the NDA government (and correspondingly the BJP) from parts of the larger Hindu nationalist movement. The gist of the argument was that Hindu nationalist ideology did not pertain only to the cultural identitarian agenda and the BJP had to ensure the implementation of the parts which would receive support of its alliance partners – namely economic policies which would reinforce India's development and lead to the country's emergence as a great power.

The argument that the BJP would have to do what it could, first, and then – after the general public had been swayed by its successes in governance to provide the party with an absolute majority – could go on to implement the rest of its agenda was also used successfully to legitimate the shift towards economic policy to party cadres. Interviewed BJP cadres in Aligarh were not necessarily content with the direction of policy during the two terms in power at the central level, but almost universally accepted this argument and repeated it during the interviews in similar ways.

> 'When the BJP was in power at the centre, the government was formed with a combination of 28 other parties and the agendas of all these parties had to be left out. A common minimum programme came into existence to form and run the government. Because of these limitations we could not implement our own agenda.'

> 'The people of India include a great percentage of illiterate people. They could not understand our limitations and thought that the BJP had left its agenda and wanted to come to power by any way. Even our brother organisations like VHP, Hindu [*sic!*] Jagran Manch criticized us.'

> 'We will have to go to the public, explaining to them the achievements of the NDA, good governance of the NDA, and ask them about the anti-people workings of the Congress-led central government.'

'At present, in Indian politics no party is in a position to form the government on its own. It is a time of coalition governments. If we come to power with the help of a coalition, we will have to make compromises with our own agenda. And if the BJP gets an absolute majority, then the old agendas shall be implemented. This is the hope of the workers.'

(Excerpts from an interview with Satyendra Sharma, 30 March 2006, Aligarh)[22]

The contest over the turn towards centrist political positions after 1999 increasingly shifted from open attempts at interference by the sister organisations and power struggles within the BJP to attempts to implement hard line cultural identitarian policies in ministries controlled by hard liners. Joshi's Ministry of Human Resources Development emerged as a focal point for attempts to implement hard line cultural identitarian policies, as mentioned above. Since these efforts met little resistance from the NDA allies, the above mentioned argument of the moderates remained ineffective, here.

The linkage between Islamism and terrorism which was increasingly created in the western world, especially after the terrorist attacks in New York in September 2001, served to reinforce the old Hindu nationalist allegations of Muslim disloyalty to the Indian nation and the image of Muslims as a violent 'Other' in significant parts of the Indian public even outside the Hindu nationalist movement.[23] Terrorist attacks conducted by Muslims in India heightened this perception. The terrorist attack on the Indian parliament in December 2001 was taken as a pretext for disengagement from the policy of rapprochement with Pakistan. Subsequently, large contingents of the Indian military were re-deployed at the international border with Pakistan in a show of strength.

While the moderate wing of the BJP had publicly prided itself on the claim that no communal riots had taken place under BJP rule, the Gujarat pogrom between February and May 2002,[24] and the corresponding emergence of Gujarat chief minister Narendra Modi as a focal point for the radical wing of the party and, temporarily, the larger movement constituted the most important challenge to the dominance of the moderate wing. In fact, the pogrom and the political events surrounding it provide an illustration of the contest over the direction of BJP policies.

In February 2002, the VHP had called for agitation on the Ayodhya issue in Uttar Pradesh which, in contrast to similar campaigns after 1993, was comparatively successful in terms of mass attendance. The BJP, at the time, was strongly divided over the VHP campaign.

The BJP, for its part, is deeply divided by the VHP's new provocations. Undoubtedly there is a section which believes that having achieved power the party should not abandon the cause that propelled it to the forefront of national attention. Others seem dearly to wish that Ayodhya would just vanish as an issue, leaving the BJP at liberty to enjoy the benefits of wielding power, if in uneasy coalition with a diversity of other parties. The price of attracting this broad-ranging support, they argue, was the consignment of Ayodhya as an issue to the lower orders in the party's list of priorities. And as long as the cohabitation continues, it should not be endangered by issues that have a tendency to disrupt the newfound solidarities.

(Sukumar Muralidharan. 'Ayodhya Offensive,' Frontline 19 (4), 16 February–1 March 2002)

The VHP had decided to go ahead with the construction of a Ram temple at the site of the *Babri Masjid*, initially by the consecration of columns and related ritual processions, and had gradually gathered a large number of cadres at its local campaign headquarters Karsevakpuram near Ayodhya. The central leadership of the BJP, in the event, decided to maintain both law and order and to accept its constitutional duty to maintain the status quo at the site. This led to increasing tensions between BJP and VHP. The VHP cadres burned to death at Godhra on 27 February 2002 had been returning from Ayodhya to Gujarat, although the agitation in Uttar Pradesh continued simultaneously to the pogrom in Gujarat which followed the incidence at Godhra. In the event, the non-accommodative stance of the central government towards the VHP on the Ayodhya issue prevented the escalation of the latter organisation's campaign. The VHP resumed its campaign one and half years later by attempting to organise a *sankalp sabha* (congregation for a show of determination) at the disputed site in Ayodhya in October 2003. By the time, a new government under SP leader Mulayam Singh Yadav had been formed in UP. The state government and the central government effectively co-operated efforts to prevent the VHP campaign's success, with the Advani-led home ministry providing sufficient central police forces to supplement the state government's efforts to prevent VHP activists from reaching Ayodhya.[25]

The central BJP leadership's handling of the Gujarat pogrom can be strongly contrasted to its handling of the VHP campaigns in Uttar Pradesh. Initially, both Advani and Vajpayee called for calm and insisted on the state government's duty to maintain law and order, even in relation to the anticipated 'spontaneous' reaction by the Hindu nationalist movement in Gujarat.[26] Vajpayee even went so far as to describe the violence as a 'black mark on the nation's forehead.'[27] Action taken by the Indian police seemed to have been successful initially, with the violence abating after a few days,[28] though incidences of violence continued to take place until May 2002.

Advani gradually began to shift his stance, at first dismissing opposition demands for the resignation of Gujarat chief minister Narendra Modi and lauding police efforts in quelling violence.[29] Government inaction over a VHP plan to launch processions carrying the ashes of victims of the Godhra incidence throughout India led to open protest from the NDA allies of the BJP.[30] Vajpayee once again deplored the violence in Gujarat a few days later.[31] The government proceeded to gain parliament's approval of the highly controversial Prevention of Terrorism Ordinance (POTO), which was criticised among other reasons on its alleged bias in practice against Muslims.[32] After a meeting between Vajpayee and Modi, the former hinted at his displeasure over the continuing violence in Gujarat, but remarked that a change of leadership in Gujarat was not sought by him.[33] Vajpayee visited Gujarat more than a month after the outbreak of violence to repeat his criticism of the violence as a 'blot' on Indian history.[34] Shortly afterwards, the BJP officially rejected Modi's offer to resign.[35] Advani emphasised that the BJP should not be apologetic about Hindu nationalist ideology.[36] Vajpayee went on to issue a warning to the NDA allies on withdrawing support.[37]

The latter three pronouncements were made at the National Executive Meeting of the BJP in Panaji. In the run-up to the meeting, the division within the BJP on the Gujarat pogrom had become increasingly obvious: BJP president Jana Krishnamurthy had rejected demands for the removal of Modi as chief minister and openly criticised Telugu Desam leader Chandrababu Naidu for demanding Modi's resignation. Vajpayee, in contrast, had hinted (if obliquely) at the possibility of Modi's removal and had used his visit to refugee camps in Gujarat to issue veiled warnings to Modi, including the observation that Modi should hold up *rajdharma* (morality in governance). Senior BJP leader and law minister Arun Jaitley had visited Ahmedabad prior to the National Executive Meeting in Panaji. The visit was interpreted by observers as an effort to prepare the ground for an eventual resignation of Modi on behalf of Vajpayee. In his opening speech at the National Executive Meeting, however, Vajpayee reversed his stance: He argued that the violence in Gujarat constituted a reaction to the Godhra incident, thereby obliquely suggesting that it had been justified, and went on to note the allegedly aggressive character of Islam which supposedly prevented social harmony where Muslims formed a minority community.[38]

The comparison of the BJP leadership's reactions to the Ayodhya agitation by the VHP in 2002 and 2003 and the Gujarat pogrom in 2002, respectively, provides an illustration of the contest over the course of political moderation. In case of the Ayodhya agitation in 2002, the moderate wing of the BJP prevailed over its rivals within the BJP and among its sister organisations. Advani's support to the moderate position in this case is especially notable because he showed an inclination to support the radical wing in the case of the Gujarat pogrom. In contrast, representatives of the moderate wing of the party – especially Vajpayee – oscillated between criticism and attempts at justification vis-à-vis the Gujarat pogrom. These shifting stances apart, the central government did not interfere sufficiently to prevent an escalation of the violence in Gujarat, in essence providing sufficient time for the management of the violence which was brought down due to police measures after the initial period, but continued until May 2002 and has been estimated as having led to more than 1,000 deaths by the Concerned Citizens' Tribunal.[39] The central government did not show any inclination to make adequate efforts to legally pursue the perpetrators of the violence and, eventually, resisted demands for the resignation of the Modi government by the opposition and some allied parties. The rejection of the NDA allies' demands is all the more notable, since it endangered the stability of the coalition government.

Government inaction over the violence in Gujarat and subsequent investigation and the oscillating stances of moderate BJP leaders illustrate the strong pressure exerted by representatives of the radical wing among the party and the larger movement to refrain from efforts to pursue a moderate line and maintain law and order. The contest over the direction of BJP politics was apparently significantly higher in the case of the Gujarat pogrom than in the case of the VHP agitation in Uttar Pradesh. The Gujarat pogrom clearly marked a re-assertion of the radical wing vis-à-vis the moderates which, nevertheless, remained incapable of comprehensively challenging the moderates' dominance, as can be seen in the reaction of the central government to the coterminous VHP agitation in UP.

After April 2002, the BJP progressed with a simultaneous advancement of the two conflicting agendas: Narendra Modi, who had emerged as a mascot of hard line Hindu nationalism, strongly emphasised the radical line in his re-election campaign until 2003, and sporadically even afterwards. Modi's subsequent estrangement from the RSS and VHP leadership contributed to his gradual readjustment in line with the emphasis on development policy in the run-up to the 2004 general elections. In contrast, the moderate wing advanced this emphasis on development and economic policy in the electoral campaigns for the state elections in late 2003 and the 2004 general election, as mentioned above.

The defeat in the 2004 general elections partially overturned established hierarchical structures within the party and their respective linkage to the divisions between the radical and moderate groups in the BJP. Vajpayee kept an increasingly low profile after 2004, though he continued to intervene at times in party affairs in the fashion of an 'elder statesman.' Advani took over the party presidency, and undertook fresh efforts to emerge as a leader of the moderate wing as well, in this way attempting to inherit the legacy of Vajpayee. With electoral prospects appearing relatively low at the time, Advani's position as the undisputed leader of the party became increasingly precarious. In fact, tensions within the second-level leadership of the BJP soon took on some characteristics of strategic manoeuvres to emerge as viable contenders for Advani's eventual succession.[40]

The BJP leadership appeared confused on the reasons for the party's electoral performance, with the various stances, once again, linked to the contest over the turn towards moderation. Hard liners openly linked the poor electoral performance to the NDA government's inaction on the cultural identitarian agenda and the resulting estrangement of the party from the larger movement and apathy among party cadres. Moderates linked the electoral performance to a variety of factors including the government's incapacity to communicate its successes in development policy to the electorate, over-confidence in the face of the media hype over BJP electoral prospects and a lack of balance within the communication of economic policy which had contributed to a public perception of preference given to 'Corporate India' over 'the common man.'[41]

Advani's attempt to take over Vajpayee's position as a leader of the moderate wing of the BJP and, correspondingly, emerge as a viable prime ministerial candidate due to his anticipated greater acceptability among the NDA allies and the general public, led to increasing strains with the RSS and VHP who wanted to use the electoral defeat to effect a course correction. These attempts culminated in the so-called Jinnah controversy. In mid-2005, Advani accepted an invitation to visit Pakistan, where he emphasised the secular outlook of Pakistan's founding leader.[42] The speeches were strongly resented by leaders and cadres among the Hindu nationalist movement, for whom Jinnah and the Muslim League due to their role in the partition of British India remained anathema. After his return to India, Advani undertook efforts to control the damage in his relations with the *Sangh Parivar* but, at the same time, refused to backtrack on the central features of his speech which, he claimed, were in accordance with both historical facts and the ideological premises of Hindu nationalism: In Advani's view, his speeches emphasised the distinction between Jinnah's personal preferences and his role in the partitioning of British India.[43]

The reaction to Advani's remarks by large parts of the *Sangh Parivar* resulted in the resignation of Advani's private secretary, Sudheendra Kulkarni, shortly after the controversy broke.[44] Kulkarni had played an important role in crafting Advani's attempts to effect a public reinterpretation of his political positioning, which still was heavily linked to his leadership of the Ayodhya campaign. Advani offered to resign as party president, only to be 'persuaded' by the second-line leadership to withdraw this offer soon afterwards. Eventually, Advani resigned as party president in late 2005.

Advani used his presidential address during the national executive committee meeting to openly express criticism of the *Sangh Parivar's* interference in BJP affairs, citing political necessities to which the BJP had to adapt which, he alleged, differed from those of the party's sister organisations.[45] The selection of his successor had been intensely contested prior to the meeting, with several contenders among the second line leadership temporarily emerging as aspirants and the RSS leadership, Advani and (to a lesser extent) Vajpayee interfering. In the end, Rajnath Singh – an upper caste leader from the ailing party unit of Uttar Pradesh who was considered to possess sufficient skills in strategic planning, administration and mediation and had kept a low profile during the contest over Advani's succession, but lacked a strong support base at the central level of party organisation – was elected more or less as a consensus candidate. Advani's influence on the party was curbed by the Jinnah episode and his subsequent resignation, but not sufficiently to qualify as a comprehensive change of the leadership structure.

In fact, Advani soon began to reassert his position within the BJP. His eventual designation as the party's prime ministerial candidate for the general elections in 2009 marked the culmination of his efforts to maintain his position of primacy within the party. After his resignation, Advani undertook efforts to show-case his commitment to Hindu nationalist ideology, in this way placating the RSS leadership without, however, advocating a comprehensive shift towards radicalisation. Instead, an amalgamation of the two approaches was increasingly projected in public. The emergence of a number of issues in the Indian political discourse which were easily linked to the party's cultural identitarian agenda facilitated this positioning.

These included the controversy over the Sethusamudram project[46] and the remarks by Prime Minister Manmohan Singh on the need to ensure socio-economic development of minority communities which indicated a preferential allocation of funds in this respect,[47] and the controversy over the allocation of land to the Amarnath Shrine in Jammu and Kashmir. Repeated instances of terrorist attacks in India after 2005 provided an opportunity to stress law and order and also could be used to imply suspicions of Muslim disloyalty to the Indian nation. At the same time, severe inflation in the prices of essential commodities facilitated a continuing emphasis on economic policy. In terms of the maintenance of the system of alliances, the NDA had lost several key constituents before and after the 2004 general elections and had become increasingly invisible as an entity in its own right in the first years of the UPA central government. The BJP partially managed to overcome the disintegration of the NDA.

The Jinnah episode and Advani's subsequent resignation as BJP president were interpreted in significant parts of the Indian media as a sign of RSS reassertion in the affairs of the BJP. Embedded in the larger development of BJP politics and the internal power structure of the party, the episode, on the contrary, serves to illustrate the limits of RSS control over the BJP: Strong (and public) pressure by the RSS leadership could enforce a change in the party's leadership and 'punish' Advani's transgression from the ideological line imparted by the RSS. This distinguishes the Jinnah episode from similar attempts at interference during the BJP's terms in power at the centre where Vajpayee and Advani – barring the Gujarat pogrom – had resisted RSS pressure together. Nevertheless, it could not prevent Advani's reassertion as the most powerful BJP leader, let alone a comprehensive re-orientation of BJP policies. The RSS could influence the selection of Advani's successor as party president, but not sufficiently to effect the selection of a real hard liner, and its influence on BJP affairs alone remained insufficient to prevent the new party president's position from being successfully challenged by his predecessor whose resignation the RSS had ensured.

RSS pressure had resulted in a greater emphasis on cultural identitarian issues, at least temporarily, although it is difficult to conceive that the BJP would have missed to highlight its commitment to this agenda, given the opportunity, in other circumstances. Policy-wise, open interference by the RSS effected changes which, by and large, were cosmetic in character. Given the amount of pressure exerted by the RSS leadership and the high political costs involved in sustained open criticism of the party leadership in terms of BJP electoral appeal, the undermining of established leadership structures in the party and the possible evolution of dissent over the strategy within the RSS itself, the results of RSS interference remained meagre, and do not qualify for an interpretation of events as a sign of a radical turn in the BJP's political orientation. In early 2009 K. S. Sudarshan stepped down as RSS *sarsanghchalak* and was replaced by Mohan Bhagwat.

The RSS leadership under Bhagwat renewed its pressure on the BJP to effect a generational change in its national leadership after the party's defeat in the

2009 general elections. The RSS strongly conveyed its preference for a successor to BJP president Rajnath Singh when the latter's term ended in late 2009. In the event, Nitin Gadkari was elected BJP president with strong RSS backing and Advani stepped down as Leader of Opposition. At the same time, however, Advani was elected working chairman of the NDA, while two BJP top leaders considered close to Advani, Sushma Swaraj and Arun Jaitley, were appointed as leaders of opposition in the lower and upper house, respectively. The relatively open and direct interference by the RSS in BJP affairs in late 2009 was perceived by many observers as a sign of renewed RSS control over the BJP, although the changes in the national leadership of the party may also be characterised as a compromise formula. So far, a significant change in BJP policy preferences cannot be ascertained. In fact, the BJP under its new leadership strongly emphasised economic policy issues, especially inflation, in the 2010 budget session of the Indian parliament.

In essence, the RSS remained restricted to ensuring the party's conformity with the ideology of Hindu nationalism more or less in the same fashion as it had done before – by providing 'moral guidance' and ensuring that some key positions in the party's decision-making process were occupied by leaders dependent on RSS support for political power within the BJP. Overall, the BJP's turn towards political moderation remains contested from within the party and the larger movement. The challenges to this direction of BJP politics have, at the same time, not been able to overcome its predominance as a strategy to achieve political success, leading instead to temporarily limited reassertions of BJP hard liners and, at irregular intervals, to a strategy of the latter's accommodation by the mainstream within the BJP leadership on select issues.

6 The BJP at the regional and at the local level

Uttar Pradesh and Aligarh

Politics in Uttar Pradesh today [...] is somewhat strange.
(Kalyan Singh, cited in Frontline 14 (23), 1997)

The BJP in Uttar Pradesh

Studies on Indian political parties and the Indian party system have increasingly focussed on the state level, on the grounds that political competition at the state level in the absence of the electoral waves which characterised the 1970s and 1980s has become decisive for electoral success (Sridharan 2002). In short, the national party system in India can be characterised increasingly as the sum of the various party systems at the regional level. The main distinction regarding the political process between the state and the national level in India is constituted by the comparatively open influence of economic interests, often articulated in terms of social justice by communities, on electoral mobilisation. The decentralisation of control over the system of rent allocation means that the distribution of benefits on the basis of political influence in India mostly takes place at the local and the district level. Similarly, caste and religious community which form two of the most important linkages between organised political interests and society in India, are most influential at this level of politics (Chhibber 1999: 53).

Political contest necessitates a focus on a higher level for the aggregation of these interests. Usually this is the state level, since the national level is too far removed from both decentralised control over rent allocation and the factors underlying community-centric political mobilisation. Moreover, the maintenance of large aggregations of diverse interests becomes increasingly difficult to achieve at the higher levels of Indian politics. Durable aggregation of diverse economic interests at the national level is increasingly impossible. The most notable exception to this rule is constituted by liberalisation policies which, however, form the antithesis to the above mentioned factors underlying the emergence of the state level as the decisive level for electoral mobilisation.

Politics in Uttar Pradesh, India's largest state by far, has been selected here to exemplify BJP state level politics – largely for two reasons: (1) The socio-economic factors shaping state level party politics in India, especially the impact of increasing rent scarcity on Indian politics, are highly visible in Uttar Pradesh, necessitating the party's adaptation to openly articulated politically organised socio-economic interests. (2) the BJP's evolution in Uttar Pradesh includes a highly successful phase from the late 1980s to the late 1990s, but also its severe decline afterwards. The factors underlying the rise and subsequent decline of the BJP in Uttar Pradesh serve to illustrate the challenges the party faces at the state level.

Party politics in Uttar Pradesh

Politics in Uttar Pradesh has often served as a prime example of the various developments in Indian politics which perceptibly have gone wrong. The state has had a fair share of communalist and caste violence, defections and party splits, governmental instability which necessitated frequent elections, corruption scandals, politicians involved in criminal cases including charges of rape and murder, and a range of other abuses of political power.[1] UP is lagging in terms of economic development, especially industrialisation,[2] and successful poverty alleviation. The state government, instead, has been in a state of financial crisis for a long time, largely on account of a highly over-inflated state administration whose efficiency is questionable and continues to be further reduced by the various state governments' insistence on ensuring the bureaucracy's political loyalty to the respective ruling coalition or party by effecting increasingly frequent mass transfers of civil servants (Pai 2002a: 1334–41).[3]

Congress dominance in Uttar Pradesh remained largely unchallenged until the late 1960s, although frequent factional rivalry within the INC state unit ensured a high level of governmental instability even at that time (Brass 1965; Hasan 1998). In 1967, the INC in Uttar Pradesh split, with former Congress leader Charan Singh forming the *Bharatiya Lok Dal* which emerged as the leading constituent of the centre-left political spectrum and the focal point of the various non-Congress governments in the state. The *Lok Dal* played a decisive role in the formation (and demise) of the *Janata Party* and, after Charan Singh's death, in the formation of the *Janata Dal*. The series of splits and mergers in the centre-left political spectrum of the state eventually led to the establishment of the *Samajwadi Party* (SP) in 1992, which has remained one of the most important political parties in UP since. Another major inheritor of the *Lok Dal* legacy in UP is the *Rashtriya Lok Dal* (RLD), a sub-regional party led by Charan Singh's son Ajit Singh which has a significant presence in western UP.

In 1989, a JD-led electoral alliance managed to form the state government, thereby initiating a new phase of non-Congress governments in the state. Congress decline in UP in the following years was sufficiently pronounced that the party has failed to be a viable contender for political power in the state since 1993. The decision by the Mulayam Singh Yadav government to stop the first attempt by the *rath yatra* to reach Ayodhya led to the withdrawal of support by the BJP at the state level as well. In the ensuing state elections in 1991, the BJP won an absolute majority. The Kalyan Singh government was removed by the imposition of President's Rule in UP after the destruction of the *Babri Masjid*. After the 1993 state elections, an alliance between SP and BSP managed to form the government, with Mulayam Singh becoming chief minister once again, though the BJP remained the single largest party. The alliance fell apart in 1995, and the BJP supported a BSP minority government led by Mayawati, before withdrawing support less than half a year later.

The 1996 state elections resulted in a hung assembly. With no party or alliance managing a parliamentary majority, President's Rule was imposed, once again, and later extended. The imposition of President's Rule benefited the SP which, at the time, was the leading constituent of the United Front central government from UP. To avoid fresh elections, BJP and BSP decided to form another coalition government in 1997 with both parties alternating in providing the chief minister. The chief minister's post accordingly passed from Mayawati to Kalyan Singh in late 1997. The latter then proceeded to split the BSP (and other parties with the major exception of the SP) in order to form a BJP government not dependent on BSP support. Factional infighting within the BJP resulted in 1999 in the replacement of Kalyan Singh by Ramprakash Gupta, a Vajpayee loyalist without a significant support base in the BJP state unit. Kalyan Singh instead formed his own party, the *Rashtriya Kranti Dal* (RKD). Continued factional conflict and Gupta's apparent inability to improve the party's position in UP led to his replacement by Rajnath Singh in 2000.

The 2001 state elections, once again, resulted in a hung assembly though this time the *Samajwadi Party* emerged as the single largest party. The prospect of an SP-led state government led to a realignment of forces, with the BJP and its NDA allies in Uttar Pradesh (mainly the RLD) supporting another Mayawati-led BSP government. In turn, the BSP provided valuable outside support to the NDA at the centre. The arrangement broke in mid-2003: The SP in alliance with Kalyan Singh's RKD and the RLD which, by the time, had withdrawn support to the BSP government had been reported to be close to engineering a split in the BJP state unit which had been increasingly disenchanted with the coalition arrangement.[4] The BJP, instead, moved to facilitate efforts by the SP-led alliance to split the BSP, leading to the establishment of the third Mulayam Singh government. The government remained relatively stable for the rest of the term, despite the dissolution of the RKD after Kalyan Singh's return to the BJP before the 2004 general elections, but lost the state elections in 2007, in which the BSP won an absolute majority, with Mayawati becoming chief minister for the fourth time.

With the decline of the Congress party, the BJP emerged as the largest political party in Uttar Pradesh without, however, managing to establish dominance. The BJP's position was constantly challenged by the two main regional parties, the *Samajwadi Party* and the BSP. BJP efforts to use the BSP to weaken the *Samajwadi*, especially in the 1990s, constituted a high risk strategy which eventually failed. Instead, SP influence on state politics was consolidated, while the strategy helped the BSP at several times to overcome SP efforts to weaken the BSP. The Congress after 1993 attempted to reclaim its former position of influence in Uttar Pradesh but, by and large, without any apparent long-term strategy and, so far, without durable success.[5] Instead of focussing on re-building the party organisation or establishing linkages with society, the INC mainly attempted to utilise its influence at the central level to destabilise the regional parties in UP.

The gradual decline of the BJP commenced during the late 1990s, despite the party's impressive electoral performance in UP in the 1998 general elections. After 2002, the political process in Uttar Pradesh was comprehensively dominated by the two regional parties. The BJP and, even more so, the Congress were increasingly reduced to supporting one of the two regional parties or else to remain decreasingly significant opposition parties.

There are several structural characteristics which distinguish the party system and party politics in Uttar Pradesh from other states, among them the lack of stringently defined regional identity as a political factor. Uttar Pradesh, as the core area of the Hindi heartland and the largest and politically most influential state by far, has never developed a movement mobilising on the basis of regional identity encompassing the whole state. Sub-regional movements have developed in Uttarakhand, leading to the creation of a new Indian state in 2001, and in western Uttar Pradesh, although the RLD demand for the creation of Harit Pradesh has, by and large, been mostly strategic and based more on economic considerations. The rise of the two main regional parties is not linked to regional identity – both have attempted to enlarge their area of influence to other parts of India and aspire for the status of national parties[6] – but to the structural problems of maintaining political influence in other states outlined above. The dominance of rent allocation in the political process of Uttar Pradesh is accentuated in comparison with other states, especially those outside the Hindi heartland.

One outstanding feature of the two regional parties in UP is their reliance on relatively low levels of electoral support to ensure their predominance over rivals: Neither the BSP nor the SP (together with their respective alliance partners) have been able to gain significantly more than 30 per cent of votes in elections even after 2002 when the two emerged as the largest political parties in the state. In fact, UP election results show a strong tendency for the optimisation of societal support for political parties: Electoral turnout is low in comparison to other Indian states indicating the prevalence of politically highly organised social groups over voters who are not as closely associated with specific political parties and who, accordingly, do not show strong tendencies for strategic voting. Indicators of party strengths in UP also show a clear tendency for the optimisation of highly organised electoral support by the two regional parties which constitute the main beneficiaries of these developments: The effective number of political parties has significantly increased between 1993 and 2002, while the average vote percentage of winning candidates in the constituencies has decreased correspondingly.

The average vote shares of winning candidates had by 2002 come down to a level which in an SMSP electoral system is highly abnormal. It is equally significant to note that this decrease is not due to increased competition from second

Table 6.1 Average vote percentages of candidates in elections in Uttar Pradesh, 1996–2002[1]

	Winning candidate	Runner-up	3rd placed candidate	Others
1996	40.56	30.61	20.91	7.92
1998	39.68	31.28	20.03	9.01
1999	36.55	29.26	19.87	14.32
2002	35.01	27.10	18.35	19.54

Note

1 Calculations based on Statistical Reports of the Election Commission of India for the state assembly elections in Uttar Pradesh, 1996 and 2002, and the general elections to the *Lok Sabha* in Uttar Pradesh, 1998 and 1999. Figures for the 2007 state elections have not been calculated but similar results can be expected, since BSP and SP together won a vast majority (303 out of 403) of assembly seats with a vote percentage of 30.43 per cent and 25.43 per cent, respectively, without any significant alliances.

or even third placed candidates which would indicate a higher level of political polarisation. In fact, the average vote percentages of second and third placed candidates decrease similarly to those of winning candidates. Accordingly, political success in Uttar Pradesh has been based increasingly on mobilising an optimal amount of social support: the least possible amount of votes which would allow viability in the electoral contest. Since the two regional parties' emergence as increasingly dominant actors in the political process in UP took place in synchronicity with the optimisation of electoral support by political parties in UP, it is to be expected that their rise is linked to their respective ability to operate in this context. Accordingly, the decline of the BJP would be linked to its corresponding inability to adapt to these changes.

The surprising evolution of the UP party system and party politics since 1993 can be explained by the dominant role assumed by rent allocation in UP politics, and increasing rent scarcity. Access to the system of rent allocation forms one of the most decisive factors for the voting behaviour of the highly politically organised social groups which dominate the political process in UP. Increasing rent scarcity has resulted in an inability of the main political parties to aggregate large social coalitions. Instead, political parties increasingly focus on articulating the interests of highly organised social groups over large social coalitions.

As a side-effect this creates a safeguard against negative public perception, for example due to corruption scandals or the involvement of alleged criminals with political parties: The politically highly organised social sections which are crucial to electoral success do not have an incentive to switch political allegiances on the grounds of corrupt practices linked to rent allocation.

Competition among the politically highly organised social sections is intensifying according to the decreasing capacity of the state government to provide access to rents. This to some degree explains the increase in intensity in UP politics since the late 1980s. Improved access to the system of rent allocation forms one of the most important factors affecting the political strategies of both politicians and politically organised social sections. It can lead to defections and to flexible adaptations by social sections to changing contexts, including their exit from the social coalitions which determine a party's support base in the state. The imperative of participating in governance, or at least the prospect of participating in governance in the near future, in order to have access to rent allocation which, in turn, provides the means for future political success reinforces this flexibility regarding political allegiances. Accordingly, the process of government formation in UP has regularly involved the engineering of defections from rival parties.

The rise and decline of the BJP in Uttar Pradesh

The rise of the BJP in Uttar Pradesh partially preceded the Ayodhya campaign.[7] In the 1989 state elections, the party contested with partial seat adjustments with the JD and gained 11.61 per cent of votes, and 18.11 per cent of votes in the 275 seats contested by the BJP.[8] In 1991, the party contested 415 of the 425 constituencies in UP and gained 31.45 per cent of votes, winning an absolute majority of seats.[9] The party's positioning vis-à-vis the Mandal controversy and economic liberalisation combined with the integration of select OBC communities and the electoral fallout of the Ayodhya campaign had resulted in a substantial further increase in the party's presence in the state. The political isolation of the BJP after 1992 prevented its continuance in power at the state level between 1993 and 1997, although the party successfully prevented the establishment of a durable SP-led government in 1995 by effecting a realignment of political actors in UP. At the same time, the decision to provide support to BSP-led governments meant that the BJP had to forsake political power at the state level, and instead was providing crucial help to another rival. The offers of support to the BSP, especially after 1996, were highly contested within the state party unit and had significant implications for the party's later evolution in UP.

The BJP vote shares in Uttar Pradesh remained high until the late 1990s, culminating in its electoral performance in the 1998 general elections to the *Lok Sabha*. BJP vote shares decreased drastically after 1998, partially due to factional infighting. In the run-up to the 1999 general elections, BJP chief minister Kalyan Singh had eschewed campaigning after having been denied a dominant role in candidate selection and future rapprochement with the BSP – which Kalyan Singh rejected – had not been ruled out by the central party leadership.

Table 6.2 BJP electoral performance in Uttar Pradesh, assembly elections 1989–2007

Year	1989	1991	1993	1996	2002	2007
Vote Share	11.61	31.45	33.30	32.52	20.08	16.97

Source: Election Commission of India.

Table 6.3 BJP electoral performance in Uttar Pradesh, *Lok Sabha* elections 1989–2004

Year	1989	1991	1996	1998	1999	2004
Vote Share	7.58*	32.82	33.44	36.49	27.64	22.17

Source: Election Commission of India.

Note
* The BJP contested 31 of 85 constituencies in UP in the 1989 general elections to the *Lok Sabha*.

Instead, one of his loyalists began to actively campaign for non-BJP OBC candidates, especially from the *Samajwadi Party*. This was interpreted at the time as a covert attempt by Kalyan Singh to damage the position of rival BJP leaders in UP and an indication of his incipient removal as chief minister.[10] Kalyan Singh was replaced by Ramprakash Gupta shortly after the elections.

The factional infighting which led to the removal of Kalyan Singh as chief minister and his exit from the BJP was interpreted in the Indian media as the outcome of caste-based conflicts within the party. Kalyan Singh had been the most influential OBC leader of the party in UP, while his main detractors in the state party unit – Rajnath Singh, Lalji Tandon, and Kalraj Mishra – were representatives of influential upper castes, Thakurs and Brahmins. In this interpretation of events, the expansion of the BJP in the early 1990s which had brought substantial OBC support to the party had been possible only by curtailing the traditional upper caste hegemony in the party's state unit in favour of promoting an OBC chief minister. Kalyan Singh had attempted to safeguard his position by promoting other OBC political leaders in the party's state unit and, accordingly, had attempted to reduce the influence of the powerful upper caste-dominated factions further. His replacement was, then, the consequence of an upper caste backlash which resulted in upper caste reassertion within the BJP in Uttar Pradesh. Kalyan Singh's subsequent defection from the BJP foreshadowed the exit of OBC communities from the party's support base in UP which, in turn, explains the decreasing vote shares of the party after 1998.

This interpretation of the factional conflicts within the BJP state unit in the second half of the 1990s ignores some factors underlying the polarisation between OBC and upper caste-led factions, especially concerning the importance of the contest over future alignments with the BSP.[11] In the run-up to the 1999 general elections, an alignment with the BSP was not a viable option for the BJP: The BSP had not attempted to become part of the NDA at the central level. At the state level, the BJP had manufactured a significant split in the BSP less than two years ago, and headed a government which depended on a motley group of coalition partners, mostly defectors from rival parties, but which nevertheless had remained relatively stable. Moreover, assembly elections in UP were due in late 2001 or early 2002, and the BJP had won a large majority of constituencies in UP in 1998 without alliances. The outcome of curtailing the influence of Kalyan Singh could have been anticipated by BJP leaders at both the central and the state level. The decision to risk a weakening of the BJP state unit at least partially on the question of an eventual realignment with the BSP appears strange.

The rationale behind the factional conflicts, and the central leadership's reaction to it, has to include a larger perspective. For the central leadership, the rationale behind the decision is relatively clear: The central leadership had tried to project the decision to support the BSP in government formation in UP in 1995 and 1997 not as a strategy to contain the spreading influence of the *Samajwadi Party*, but as a sign of the party's commitment to the emancipation and development of Dalits, or the poor in general. This was done partially in view of extending the party's support base in UP but, most importantly, in view of spreading the party's influence among Dalits outside Uttar Pradesh. Notwithstanding the fact that the strategic aim of SP containment very probably constituted the overriding reason behind the decision, the positioning of the party vis-à-vis Dalits remains a credible, if partial, motive.

With regard to the state leadership and the various factional leaders in the BJP state unit, the motive behind the decision and the importance attributed to it are more complex. The initial move, in 1995, can easily be explained by its strategic importance and was far less contested within the state unit: The alliance between SP and BSP in 1993 had been hailed in the Indian media as a signal of the emergence of a socio-economic realignment, in which the poorer sections of society – OBC, Muslims, and Dalits – were organised against the alleged traditional dominance of upper castes in Indian politics. Moreover, the alliance had checked the rise of the BJP despite the latter's strong electoral performance. It could be seen as the embodiment of all the various factors which had gained centre-stage in the Indian political discourse during the Mandal controversy, the coalescence of which the BJP had averted with the help of the Ayodhya campaign. The utilisation of the rift between its two rivals to prevent the establishment of a viable contender for political power in UP (and possibly in other states as well) by the BJP state leadership is hardly surprising. In addition, the BJP state leadership in 1995 had at least hoped that its association with the BSP would – in the long term – force the latter to depend on the BJP and eventually become a junior partner, or that a break-up of the BSP could, at some time, be engineered. In fact, media reports in late 1995 speculated on precisely this, with allegations of differences between chief minister Mayawati and BSP founder Kanshi Ram which indicated that the former was propagating a closer association with the BJP. The sudden withdrawal of support to the state government by the BJP in late 1995 can be interpreted as an admission of failure in this respect (Hasan 1998).

The impasse in government formation after the 1996 assembly elections was used by some BJP leaders to call for realignment with the BSP. Initially, this was rejected by the dominant faction around Kalyan Singh, despite the fact that a prolonged period of President's Rule in UP de facto equalled SP control over governance in UP. When continued extension of President's Rule in UP had become politically untenable for the United Front government in late 1996 and early 1997, the BJP reversed its prior stance to avoid fresh assembly elections.

The acquiescence of Kalyan Singh to these developments in 1997 was partially due to the fact that under the coalition arrangement he would become chief minister again later in the year. The sudden deterioration in relations between the BJP and the BSP after the transfer of the chief minister's post to Kalyan Singh, which culminated in the split of the BSP legislative party in UP, indicates that the new coalition was also perceived as a second opportunity to prevent the coalescence of another viable contender for political power at the state level. The polarisation in the BJP state unit over the question of relations with the BSP intensified only after the break-up of the coalition arrangement in late 1997 to the level where it threatened BJP cohesion in the state, and was only then mixed with the conflicting interests of OBC and upper caste-dominated factions.

While Kalyan Singh had contested upper caste assertion in the state unit before, polarisation between OBC and upper caste leaders in the state unit had not accentuated to a similar degree before 1998. In fact, the fabrication of the split in the BSP legislative party in late 1997 has been attributed to joint efforts by Kalyan Singh and Rajnath Singh, at the time speaker of the UP assembly. Realignment with the BSP might have damaged the standing of Kalyan Singh, since the BSP would have demanded chief ministership at least for some time, but it would not necessarily have damaged Kalyan Singh's standing within the BJP state unit. To understand the importance attributed to the question of a future alliance, its effects on the state government's capacity to ensure rent allocation to the core constituents of its social support base has to be taken into account.

The expansion of the BJP in Uttar Pradesh to include sections of the OBC social strata had significantly impacted the amount of rents available for allocation to the upper castes, whose dominance in the BJP state unit had previously been relatively unchallenged. The efforts at reassertion of upper caste-dominated factions, in turn, threatened the basis for the integration of OBC communities into the party's support base. BJP efforts to integrate the BSP into the system of rent allocation in the state, or at least the acquiescence to the BSP's establishment as a partner in governance, would have upset the balance of power within the BJP state unit. Since the influence of OBC-dominated factions within the state unit was precarious compared to that of the established upper caste factions, either a BJP–BSP alliance or the further extension of the party's social support to include Dalits would have significantly reduced the position of OBC-led factions and political leaders. For the upper caste-dominated factions, the rationale behind realignments with the BSP was the replacement of OBC support by Dalit support and, accordingly, the termination of the perceived threat to upper caste dominance in the party by OBC-led factions.

The BJP, at the time, had achieved to gain electoral support above 35 per cent. The extension of the party's support base to this level under conditions of severe rent scarcity in UP and in the context of a system of party politics heavily dependent on the reciprocal exchange of rents for electoral support was simply not viable. In short, the BJP in Uttar Pradesh had over-extended its electoral support base. This over-extension resulted in the incremental exit of politically highly organised social groups, a development which reinforced itself in a downward spiral after the exit of social constituents impacted electoral results – and which is reminiscent of the decline of the INC in Uttar Pradesh earlier. In caste terms, the defection of Kalyan Singh was accompanied by the exit of the two most important OBC communities which had been associated with the BJP in UP, Lodhs and Kurmis.

The removal of Kalyan Singh did not arrest the factional infighting which shifted from upper caste – OBC polarisation to infighting between Thakur- and Brahmin-dominated factions. The incipient exit of Thakurs from the BJP's social support base which became apparent in the local elections in the state in 2000 and 2001 led to the replacement of Ramprakash Gupta, a Brahmin, by Rajnath Singh, the highest profile Thakur leader in the state unit. By this time, even the ascension of a Thakur leader to the chief minister's post was not anymore sufficient to arrest the exit of this community durably. The SP commenced wooing other communities which had previously been close to the BJP, among them Banias, with at least partial success, before the 2002 assembly elections. The BSP strategy in 2007 to co-opt Brahmins into its support base has been partially successful as well. It is important to note that these attempts by the regional parties to extend their support has not led to a similar over-extension so far, with both parties being unable to raise their electoral support significantly over 30 per cent.

The factors underlying the rise and decline of the BJP in Uttar Pradesh illustrates the importance of rent allocation especially at the state level and also the extent to which the BJP has been able to adapt to the main characteristics of mainstream politics in India. At this level of politics, the BJP functions in a manner which is very much reminiscent of its main secular nationalist rivals. Factionalism and 'casteism,' the two main features of state level political organisation associated with the prevalence of rent allocation in Indian politics, have been key elements in the evolution of the BJP state unit once it emerged as a viable contender for political power in Uttar Pradesh. The 'normalisation' of the BJP, its adaptation to the 'standards' of Indian politics in general, is even more accentuated at this level of politics than at the national level. An equivalent development is apparent when observing the functioning of the BJP at the local level, although here the increased linkage with civil society and accordingly the larger Hindu nationalist movement serves to set the party apart from its rivals in this respect.

The BJP in Aligarh

The political context of Aligarh, its evolution after independence and the emergence of the BJP as one of the major political forces in both the city and the district have been summarised in detail by Brass (2003). The focus in this work is on recent developments in the local unit of the BJP and its relationship with the direction of BJP politics, so that only a brief outline of the context of politics in Aligarh will be provided here. A distinction between the structural features of local politics has to be made between Aligarh district and Aligarh city. Emphasis here will largely be placed on the latter.

Aligarh city is situated in the Ganga-Yamuna *doab*[12] in the state of Uttar Pradesh, approximately 130 km south-east of Delhi. The city and the area around it are influenced to a significant extent by the socio-economic development of the Greater Delhi area, the National Capital Region (NCR), but still possess the main characteristics of a semi-urban area in the Indian hinterland with the city of Aligarh as its only major urban conglomeration. Politics in Aligarh district can be dissected from politics in Aligarh city in that it is based largely on agrarian interests and in that different social groups predominate: In the district – as in most areas of the upper Doab – the largely agrarian Jats wield a significant political influence. The most significant OBC groups in the larger area, Yadavs and Lodhs, are far less represented in Aligarh city than in the surrounding district. Among upper castes, Thakurs have a presence in the city, but their political influence is due more to their socio-economic clout than their numerical presence. In the rural areas of Aligarh district, however, Thakurs form a major part of the established social and political elite. The most numerous Dalit group in both district and city, as in most of Uttar Pradesh, are Jatavs. A major difference between city and district is the respective presence of Muslims who constitute about 40 per cent of the population in the city, but have a significantly lesser presence in the district.[13]

With strong linkages between the above mentioned social groups and the major parties in the area, it is hardly surprising that major differences in the relative strengths of parties (and their positioning vis-à-vis their respective core constituencies) exist between the city and the district. Politically highly organised social groups in Uttar Pradesh tend to have a relatively homogenous voting behaviour, at least at the constituency and district level. A large presence of certain communities often corresponds with an increased presence of political parties, although these communities can shift their allegiances in between elections or even between candidates from different parties in distinct electoral constituencies in the same elections, depending on the candidates' positioning vis-à-vis the respective community. Less influential communities often show similarly homogenous voting behaviour at the local level but not at higher levels of politics, since they often become part of informal alliance systems dominated by the highly organised and influential communities. Homogenous voting behaviour of communities in Uttar Pradesh can signify a common preference for candidates of 80 per cent or higher, although it is usually less accentuated.

By and large, Jats in western Uttar Pradesh are associated with the *Rashtriya Lok Dal*. The RLD, accordingly, has a significant presence in Aligarh district, but not in Aligarh city. The association of Jats with the RLD in Aligarh district is less accentuated than in other districts of western UP, partially due to their relatively lesser presence in Aligarh district. Jats in Aligarh district have oscillated between supporting the RLD and other political parties, especially the BJP, SP, and INC. Longstanding animosities and conflicts of interest between Jats and Jatavs have so far prevented a BSP presence among the Jat community. While

Jatavs (and other less numerous Dalit groups) have a significant presence in both district and city, this presence is less accentuated than in many other parts of Uttar Pradesh. The association between Jatavs and a single political party, in this case the BSP, is possibly the strongest in state politics. The BSP has a strong presence in both city and district, though it is less influential in the city, but has so far not been able to turn this presence into successful electoral performances.

The *Samajwadi Party* has a strong support base in both city and district and has been one of the most important contenders for political power in both. At the same time, the socio-economic profile of the SP differs markedly between city and district: In the larger district, it relies heavily on Yadav support while also, at times, receiving support from Muslims, Jats, and Thakurs among the politically highly organised communities. The large concentration of Muslims in Aligarh city and the comparatively small number of Yadavs there result in a marked reliance on Muslim support in the city, which has tended to oscillate between SP and Congress. This has led to significant fluctuations in the party's electoral performance in Aligarh city and, though to much lesser degree, in the larger district.

Congress influence in the area suffered from Muslim disenchantment with the party already in the 1960s, much earlier than in most of Uttar Pradesh, due to the party's involvement in anti-Muslim communal violence (Brass 2003: 44). In recent years, temporary shifts in Muslim voting patterns have resulted on occasion in strong electoral performances. This is exemplified by the 2002 assembly and 2004 *Lok Sabha* elections where the INC managed to win in both the Aligarh assembly and Aligarh *Lok Sabha* constituencies. These electoral performances were, however, at least partially due to the local standing of the respective candidates. The party organisation in the area is not sufficient to ensure a permanent strong presence, and the Congress party, especially in Aligarh city, is even more reliant on the shifting Muslim voting preferences than the SP.[14]

Apart from the BJP, whose presence in the area is discussed below, no other parties have a significant presence in either Aligarh city or Aligarh district. Electoral contests in Aligarh city since the early 1990s have been won, effectively, only by the BJP or either the *Samajwadi* or the Congress due to high political polarisation. Vote shares in state elections serve to illustrate the essentially two-sided political contest in the city despite the presence of other major parties.

Economically, Aligarh city relies heavily on its educational facilities and small-scale industry. Aligarh is home to the Aligarh Muslim University (AMU), one of the most renowned academic institutions in India. While the AMU is open to Hindu students, Muslims constitute a large majority of students. Economically, AMU serves as the employer of a significant part of the Muslim upper middle class in Aligarh, a fact which has occasionally been resented in conversations with (lower) middle class supporters of the BJP who are generally private sector oriented. A number of local degree colleges exist in Aligarh, often dominated by Hindu students and teachers and generally restricted to serve the local population's needs for higher formal education. Hindu nationalist influence

Table 6.4 Vote shares in Aligarh (assembly constituency), 1993–2007[1]

	BJP	BSP	INC	SP	Others
1993	40.84	39.42	7.12	–	12.62
1996	31.54	12.45	–	53.10	2.91
2002	20.46	7.79	41.87	6.25	23.63
2007	30.28	9.68	19.04	36.76	4.24

Source: Election Commission of India.

Note
1 In 1993, BSP and SP contested the state elections jointly, with the BSP contesting in Aligarh. The high vote percentage of the BSP in 1993 is, accordingly, not necessarily an indication of its political influence. The Congress did not contest the 1996 state elections in Aligarh, having formed an alliance with the BSP. The RLD (or its various predecessors) has not contested assembly elections in Aligarh between 1993 and 2002. In 2007, the party gained a mere 0.97 per cent of votes.

in some of these institutions is relatively strong (Brass 2003: 78). Some local degree colleges are affiliated with Agra University, the closest major state government funded academic institution in Uttar Pradesh. A large number of private coaching centres provide employment in the educational sector outside the publicly funded institutions.

The city has traditionally been home to a large part of India's lock (and metal appliances) production which still continues to form the backbone of industry in Aligarh. This branch has been subject to a tendency of concentration recently which led to the establishment of larger manufactories, although small home-based manufactories still continue to dominate the old city. Recently, attempts to situate other industries in the area have led to increased diversification, but the lock industry remains the most important industrial branch.

Aligarh is gradually being drawn into the area influenced by the rapid economic growth in the National Capital Region. The NCR has increasingly become a destination for migrating labour, especially for young people with a relatively high level of formal education who can find employment in services and industry. Apart from Delhi itself, a substantial part of these young people find employment in the sprawling urban conglomerations which surround Delhi. Given their vicinity to Aligarh, Ghaziabad, Noida and Greater Noida have emerged as major destinations for migrating labour in relatively well-paid professions. Remittances from these migrants contribute to the further development of Aligarh which can clearly be seen in the continuing construction of shopping malls and similar complexes in a style reminiscent of the NCR in the more prosperous areas of Aligarh.

The increased need for higher level formal education for young upwardly mobile people to gain well-paid employment in the NCR is adding to the resentment among Hindu youths in Aligarh – who are mostly restricted to the local degree colleges for acquiring higher education – against the AMU which is substantially more prestigious, but only provides limited education opportunities to local (Hindu) youths. In conversations with young BJP supporters, resentment was mixed with aspirations to join either AMU or similar non-minority educational institutions in UP or Delhi in order to be able to fully participate in the opportunities provided by the rapid economic development of the National Capital Region. Resentment was not expressed in openly communal terms but, instead, was couched in a discourse on merit. In this way, resentment of the AMU was to a lesser degree presented as due to its character as a minority institution, but as due to its perceived provision of privileges to select (and mostly Muslim) contenders for employment opportunities, since the institution's prestige was perceived to override merit.

While overt communalist sentiments were missing to a surprising extent among young, educated BJP supporters, the city of Aligarh still shows a strong polarisation on communal lines: The city can be divided on religious lines in mostly Hindu, mostly Muslim, and mixed *mohalle* (neighbourhoods). This division is similar in both upper (and upper middle) and lower class quarters. The sense of social tension which is prevalent among many north Indian towns and smaller cities is present throughout Aligarh, but is becoming accentuated as one enters a mixed quarter of town.

The rise of the BJP in Aligarh city is closely linked to incidences of communal violence. It has to be noted, however, that outbreaks of communal violence in the city precede the rise of the BJP. Brass (2003: 44) notes that Aligarh had been notorious for communal violence even in the early decades after independence when it was still politically dominated by the INC and the various locally influential centre-left political parties. Interviewed BJP cadres or local leaders obviously tend to downplay the role of communal violence in the rise of the BJP (as did interviewees close to the BJP who were not party members.) If communal violence was mentioned at all, BJP cadres were often portrayed as victims, or the violence was interpreted as the result of self-defence by Hindus against either organised attacks or politically motivated acts of provocation by elements of the Muslim community. The latter were portrayed in a fashion reminiscent of political entrepreneurs who possessed a stake in fostering violence for their individual benefit and were able to carry along the Muslim 'masses' against their interests.

The involvement of the Muslim 'masses' in these incidences was often alleged to be due to the compulsions of communal identity, but also to a general tendency for fanaticism among Muslims and/or a lack of education. The last remark constitutes a recurring feature in interviews with relatively moderate BJP supporters when commenting on the possibilities to overcome the spectre of communal violence, which was often perceived possible only after the Muslim community's level of education had increased. In this perspective, as long as the Muslim community remained underdeveloped in terms of education, the Muslim 'masses' would allegedly remain open to incitement by political entrepreneurs which were associated either with the party's main secular nationalist rivals, the INC and the SP, or with select persons or indistinct groups from the AMU faculty and AMU student politics who were obliquely alleged to possess links to organised crime.

If communal violence was admitted to have played a role in the rise of the BJP in Aligarh, this was usually traced to its unifying effects on the Hindu community in the city, and general resentment among the Hindu community over alleged 'minority appeasement,' i.e. alleged discriminations against Hindus which were perceived to be due to the secular nationalist parties' reliance on Muslim votes. Violence was never openly justified in the interviews conducted, but instead – unless incidences of violence were clearly resented by the interviewee himself – was often linked to the need for self-defence against provocation or even attacks by the party's rivals. This interpretation has gained weight because BJP cadres and local party leaders in Aligarh have, at times, been at the receiving end of political violence, especially after the decline of the BJP state unit in Uttar Pradesh in recent years significantly affected BJP influence on the local security apparatus. These instances were presented in communal terms by some BJP supporters while others presented it in terms of their rivals' linkages with organised crime.

While the interviewed leaders from the BJP's rivals clearly indicated the role played by communal violence in the rise of the BJP, the general picture of responsibility for violence and the way in which incidences of violence have evolved given by these leaders shows several similarities to the interpretation of events by supporters of the BJP associated with the party's moderate wing. An indictment of the local BJP leadership was provided by INC leader Vivek Bansal who, however, qualified his remarks subsequently:

SCHWECKE: 'Do you think that the BJP instigates violence against Muslims in Aligarh?'

BANSAL: 'They are on the lookout for an opportunity. Not that the minority communities don't do it also. They also. There is a section in both the communities which thrives on it, on flaring these communal passions. But these BJP people, they also thrive on it. Inciting and planning. No, it is not clear if they are planning it. Communal passions, that is it.'

(Interview with Vivek Bansal, 30 January 2007, Aligarh)

A more comprehensive interpretation of the role of violence in politics in Aligarh was provided by local SP leader O. P. Agrawal who outrightly denied that the local leadership of the BJP played a role in instigating communal violence, despite the fact that he thought the BJP benefited from it. While Agrawal would not rule out an involvement of some BJP cadres in instigating violence, he agreed to Bansal's remarks that 'some sections among both communities' were thriving on and fomenting communal violence. Agrawal continued to give accounts of the role of political entrepreneurs in fomenting communal violence, and the shared responsibility of these entrepreneurs from both communities for communal violence. The denial of direct responsibility for violence of local BJP leaders was strongest when asked to comment on high profile leaders which had been indicted on their role in major incidences of violence by academic and civil society observers.

Brass has provided a partial explanation for the refusal even by political rivals to directly implicate the BJP in fomenting communal violence as a part of the efforts to reinterpret events in order to fit into official narratives on communal violence (Brass 2003). Still, the denial of direct responsibility of local BJP leaders for the instigation and conduct of communal violence has to be taken into account, especially since the argumentation emphasised the role of militant elements, political entrepreneurs, among the two communities. It is obvious that contacts exist between political parties and political entrepreneurs involved in communal violence. Political parties benefit from communal violence in certain circumstances and will, accordingly, utilise their contacts with these entrepreneurs in order to maximise their own gains while, at the same time, limiting the risks of indulging in violence by allowing the establishment of a division of labour in which political entrepreneurs can be accorded direct responsibility in case of negative fall-outs of the violence. Parts of the local leadership and the cadres of the BJP and possibly its rivals may be involved directly in instigating and conducting violence at times, but this need not be typical.

Already in 1967, the BJS had emerged as a viable contender in elections in Aligarh when its candidate Indrapal Singh defeated the INC candidate Ravindra Yusuf Khwaja. The BJS lost the elections in 1969 to the INC, but Indrapal Singh again won the elections in 1974. Political polarisation in the wake of the emergency regime created a seemingly bizarre situation: the successful *Janata Party* candidate in the assembly elections, Mozziz Ali Beg, a Muslim and reader at AMU came from the *Jan Sangh* quota within the JP, and received support both from the Muslim community in Aligarh and supporters of the Hindu nationalist movement. In 1980, a *Lok Dal* candidate won the elections in Aligarh and in 1985 the constituency was once again won by the INC.[15]

The BJP consolidated its position in Aligarh after 1989 when its candidate Krishna Kumar Navman won in three consecutive elections in 1989, 1991, and 1993. Navman was eventually defeated by SP candidate Abdul Khalik in 1996 after political polarisation in the wake of the violence which accompanied the Ayodhya campaign had receded, and Navman's position in the BJP had increasingly been challenged.[16] In 2002, the constituency was won by the Congress candidate Vivek Bansal and in 2007 by the *Samajwadi Party*. The BJP had not been able to replicate its electoral performances of the late 1980s and early 1990s when it gained vote shares of more than 40 per cent since 1996. Barring the 2002 assembly elections when its vote shares plummeted to barely above 20 per cent, the party has still been able to maintain a strong presence in the Aligarh assembly constituency, winning above 30 per cent of votes in 1996 and 2007. It also performed strongly in local and mayoral elections after 1993.

The continuing relative strong electoral performance of the BJP in Aligarh – despite the overall setbacks in UP – is partially due to the constancy of factors influencing electoral results in the city: Socio-economic determinants of politics in Aligarh city have remained relatively unchanged. And many of the changes which are taking place are more beneficial to the BJP than to its rivals. In caste terms, the Hindu community in Aligarh is strongly dominated by two Bania caste groups – Agrawals and Varshneys – who are (by and large) aligned with the Brahmin community in Aligarh. So far there has not been any indication of a shift of Brahmin votes to the BSP in Aligarh, a development which has taken a prominent place in the discourse on UP politics recently despite the lack of substantive evidence for the proposition.[17] Bania dominance among the Hindu community in Aligarh has resulted in an increased reliance on Muslim votes for the electoral viability of the party's rivals. This, in turn, contributes to the institutionalisation of political polarisation on the lines of religious community membership, instead of caste or class. Non-Bania Hindu caste groups are not sufficiently influential in Aligarh politics to viably participate without aligning with either the Bania castes or the Muslim community.

The BSP which does not have significant presence among local Muslims or Banias has successfully mobilised Dalit groups in Aligarh for almost two decades, but has still been incapable of challenging the respective representatives of Bania or Muslim interests. Fluctuations in Muslim voting behaviour explain the shifting electoral performances of the Congress and the SP which, according to temporary preferences among the Muslim community, form the principle rivals of the BJP in local politics. Both these parties also mobilise support among Hindu caste groups including a small percentage of Banias, but have not been persistently capable of challenging the BJP's dominance among Hindus in Aligarh.

In class terms, the gradual rise of private sector-oriented (lower) middle classes in terms of social prestige and economic clout as well as in terms of their proportional share of the population is beneficial to the BJP in several respects: (1) It increases the capacity of the main constituents of these middle classes (primarily Banias) to selectively co-opt lower class groups dependent on employment in the private sector. (2) It strengthens linkages between non-Bania Hindu caste groups who constitute a part of the (lower) middle classes with the Banias who dominate this social segment, reinforcing political polarisation between the two religious communities. (3) It strengthens the position of private sector oriented social strata against public sector oriented social strata. Since the important educational sector in Aligarh is dominated by Muslims, this increases the influence of Hindus (and especially Banias) while reducing that of Muslim middle classes and elite social strata in local politics. The increasing linkage of Aligarh city with the NCR reinforces the cohesion of a larger middle class-dominated milieu which is highly compatible which Hindu nationalist ideology and political practice.

Another factor for the continued strong BJP presence in Aligarh city is the party's strong linkage with civil society (both formal associations and informal networks) among the Hindu community in Aligarh. The BJP has by and large emerged as the focal point of Hindu nationalist influenced or inspired civil society institutions or networks in the city. Both the RSS and the VHP have a presence in Aligarh, but in general it is the BJP which dominates the Hindu nationalist spectrum there. Many local BJP cadres are also RSS *swayamsevaks* or have at least taken part in RSS training activities and meetings. Nevertheless, a large majority of these cadres described themselves primarily as BJP cadres in interviews and informal conversations.

Instead of relying primarily on direct RSS or VHP involvement in civil society activities, the *Sangh Parivar* in Aligarh city is mainly constituted by the BJP and an assortment of local associations, institutions and networks covering education, religious practice, professional and caste associations and neighbourhood associations with various degrees of formalisation. Caste associations of the two main Bania castes, Varshneys and Agrawals, are highly influential in Aligarh and are, at least at the local level, closely associated with the BJP. Both the party and the civil society groups associated with it are well connected with parts of the local administration and the local media.

The importance of these civil society associations and networks for everyday life in Aligarh is immense and leads to the institutionalisation of milieus among the Hindu community in Aligarh which is comprehensively influenced by Hindu nationalist ideology, if usually in a relatively vague fashion. In conversations and interviews with young Hindu men from both the old city and the newer (and more prosperous) parts of town, the influence of Hindu nationalism in this relatively vague form on their worldview and general outlook on life was obvious, notwithstanding aspirations to migrate to the metropolises (or even western countries) and adapt as far as possible to partially westernised metropolitan upper middle class role models. Supporting the BJP was generally taken for granted, not only in their individual capacities but also as the (almost) exclusive political preference among friends, relatives and acquaintances.

Varshney (2002) has argued that the absence of civil society organisation across religious community membership at the local level is especially conducive to communal violence. The pervasive influence of Hindu nationalism on (Hindu) civil society in Aligarh certainly forms one of the reasons why communal violence has continued to take place in the city for several decades. The strong linkage of the BJP with civil society in Aligarh city does not, however, necessarily lead to a radicalisation. Violence is certainly facilitated, but overall the Hindu nationalist milieu in Aligarh covers the spectrum of Hindu nationalism, from its most radical extremes to the moderates, comprehensively.

The young Hindu men mentioned above – whose worldview was very much influenced by Hindu nationalist ideology – were very much part of the Indian mainstream and far from militancy or radicalism. Association with the BJP or the *Sangh Parivar* in general was taken for granted because of their everyday experiences in a milieu in which this association was commonplace. It also had its strategic rationale: To ensure an eventual fulfilment of their aspirations, these young men needed formal education and a network of contacts which facilitates information on employment opportunities in Aligarh (and the NCR), helps to gain employment through personal relationships, and provides a degree of social security for them and their families. The network of Hindu nationalist influenced civil society organisations in Aligarh is contributing to the spread of Hindu nationalist ideology in the area, but it is primarily designed to provide for these and similar socio-economic needs. In this, it does not differ fundamentally from civil society networks dominated by Muslims in Aligarh city.

The importance of association with the BJP in Aligarh for substantial segments of the city's population forms one of the main reasons for its strong presence in the city. It also helps to expand the party's support base to social sections which may be influenced by Hindu nationalist ideology, but remain primarily concerned about economic interest and social prestige, not ideology. Given the large spectrum of diverse interests and preferences covered by the party in Aligarh, tension and conflict within the local party unit and among the local Hindu nationalist movement are hardly surprising. State level factional conflicts affected the BJP and the larger movement in Aligarh to some degree in the 1990s due to the association of Kalyan Singh with the larger area. The city BJP unit being dominated by Banias and to a lesser extent Brahmins restricted Kalyan Singh's influence on politics in Aligarh city and the Aligarh assembly constituency, although he has had a strong influence in the neighbouring assembly constituencies. A certain degree of rivalry with parts of the local unit's leadership and the former BJP Member of Parliament from Aligarh, Sheila Gautam, had existed throughout the 1990s. The eventual defection of Kalyan Singh from the BJP in 1999 significantly impacted the BJP in the district and, to a lesser extent, in the city itself.

It is difficult to ascertain conflicts and tensions within the local party unit. In interviews and informal conversations, the cadres and the local leadership cannot be expected to comment upon internal problems, especially in a party which places a high level of importance on internal discipline and the 'organic' and 'family-like' character of internal hierarchical systems. Media reportage on events within a particular local party unit is almost non-existent. Nevertheless, it is clear that already in the mid-1990s tensions existed in the local party unit in Aligarh over the leadership of Krishna Kumar Navman, which contributed to his electoral defeat in 1996. Navman's association with the large-scale anti-Muslim violence in Aligarh during the early 1990s (Brass 2003: 91) came to be perceived increasingly as a liability for newly rising leaders who placed greater emphasis on economic policies, partially due to self-interest.

The party's rise to near-dominance in the early 1990s had helped to expand the social base of the party and had increasingly brought in people who perceived their position in the BJP to a larger extent as a tool to enhance their own socio-economic positions. The current mayor of Aligarh, Ashutosh Varshney, was described by some representatives of rival parties in interviews as 'the richest man in Aligarh.' While this may have been exaggerated (partially in order to substantiate allegations that Varshney's electoral performance in 2006 had been founded on 'money power,' a euphemism for political practices bordering on bribery), Varshney certainly is part of the city's economic elite.

Navman's position in the local party unit had already been undermined to a significant extent much earlier. Prior to interviewing him in early 2006, he was introduced to me – in accordance with his status as a former MLA and leader of the local BJP during its most militant phase – as 'the lion of Aligarh,' but already at the time the impression was of a political leader who had lost much of his former influence. In mid-2006, after an incidence of communal violence in the city, Navman was once again taken into custody. Earlier charges against him led to his subsequent detention under legal provisions covering incitement of communal violence.

Navman proceeded to defect from the BJP which – as he alleged – had left its Hindu nationalist agenda and become an increasingly 'normal' party. In the wake of his detention, Uma Bharati – the former national BJP leader who defected from the party to form the *Bharatiya Jan Shakti* ostentatiously on the issue of a return to the BJP's former hard line agenda – issued a statement protesting the detention which implied that the BJP leadership had not sufficiently intervened to protect Navman.[18] Navman joined the *Jan Shakti* and contested the ensuing mayoral elections from jail as the latter party's candidate, though without significant success. While the local BJP leadership was averse to comment about the issue in detail, it was relatively obvious that they perceived Navman's defection as the result of his defeat in a recent power struggle, notwithstanding possible resentment over the course of BJP policies.

This interpretation of events was further substantiated by a number of local BJP cadres and, significantly, by observers of local politics associated with the party's secular nationalist rivals. After the declaration of results for the mayoral elections, the mood of many local BJP cadres was jubilant, in some cases expressly because of the negligible impact of Navman's candidature on the BJP performance in the elections.

The example of local politics in Aligarh illustrates that the BJP was able to resist the decline which set in across many parts of Uttar Pradesh. In UP, the decline had been based to a large extent on the party's over-extension: the inability of political parties to distribute sufficient rents to its support base above a certain level of social support and the tensions which arose from the expansion to new social groups which brought in changes in the direction of the party's policies and new political leaders who attempted to challenge the established hierarchies within the party. While these factors are visible in the development of the local party unit in Aligarh, their impact was lessened there mainly because of the relative homogeneity of the BJP support base and the strong linkage with civil society.

The power struggles within the local party unit resulted in the assertion of a new group of local leaders who may – in specific circumstances – still revert to the 'old' agenda, including militancy, but who are by and large preoccupied with representing the socio-economic interests of large sections of the city's population and have increasingly become 'normal' in these respects. Challenges by parts of the previously established local leadership who wanted to place a greater emphasis on ideological stringency and – especially in the case of Navman – were strongly associated with political entrepreneurship and communal violence were contained. The party was able to safeguard its cohesion. Its dominant role in the larger Hindu nationalist movement at the local level prevented an escalation of tensions with the party's sister organisations which would have threatened the stability of the BJP's linkages with local civil society.

In effect, the BJP in Aligarh is increasingly being transformed into a mainstream representative of mainly middle class Hindu interests. The party's dominance among the Hindu community and political polarisation in the city, which still prevails if to a lesser extent than in the early 1990s, facilitates the co-optation of lower class segments of society into the middle class-dominated project of Hindu nationalism. While Hindu nationalism as an ideology is becoming more and more pervasive in the local Hindu community, the concept has broadened and has lost some of its stringency, especially among the party's newer supporters. While BJP supporters would not agree to this latter interpretation and instead would point out that recent policies were very much in accordance with the party's ideological heritage, the shift in emphasis has certainly been perceived by its main rivals.

SCHWECKE: 'Would you say that the BJP is turning towards moderation or is...'
BANSAL: 'Yes!'
SCHWECKE: '...it still a radical party?'
BANSAL: 'Their recent tenure at the central government shows that they realized that unless and until they moderate all their policies, all the time, they will not be able to form and run the government.'
SCHWECKE: 'But now, since Rajnath Singh is the party president there have also been some tendencies towards radical policies.'
BANSAL: 'No, that is only because elections are approaching, just to attract the hard liners and all. That is why.'
SCHWECKE: 'And in Aligarh they are also turning towards moderation?'
BANSAL: 'They realized that without that, they cannot be successful, despite whatever they may think.'

(Interview with Vivek Bansal, 30 January 2007, Aligarh)

7   The changing face of the BJP

The BJP and the larger *Sangh Parivar* have, at times, been interpreted as unchanging and monolithic entities. This interpretation is often based on the perception of a vast, if opaque threat the Hindu nationalist movement and the BJP as its principal political representative are alleged to pose to the Indian polity – or even the very fabric of Indian society. The reasons for this are manifold: The unifying tendency inherent in Hindu nationalist ideology clearly poses a contrasting image to the kaleidoscope of Indian society which may become devoid of many of the various shades and ambiguities that have enthralled so many observers – both Indians and foreigners – if implemented in the way it had been envisaged by the founding leaders of the movement. Political violence associated with Hindu nationalism obviously poses a direct threat to some of the minority communities in India and parts of the movement – at times including the BJP – have also challenged proponents of liberal lifestyles, especially in the arts and science. This is supplemented by preferences among Hindu nationalists to interpret the democratic political process in India as the rule of the majority, in the extreme case the rule of a predefined majority: the unified Hindu community.

In many ways, the homogenising influence the BJP and the *Sangh Parivar* have on Indian politics and society correspond to the ideational evolution of the Indian middle class and – as a result – to the middle class-dominated process of nation-building in India. In these respects, the BJP does not only represent middle class interests, it constitutes an embodiment of the aims and aspirations of a significant part of the Indian middle class. As such, the party has always been able to adapt to the context it is operating in, at least to the degree necessitated in order to function as a political project. In the process, it has shed some of its radicalism and fashioned itself increasingly in the way of the segments among Indian society which form its core constituency. This core constituency is too diverse in its socio-economic background, social milieus, and aims and aspirations to be characterised in monolithic terms. It forms a major part of what has been classified as the 'new middle class' by Fernandes (2000) and also forms a substantial part of the 'New India' propagated in Indian life-style magazines.

The BJP itself appears to be aware of the diversity of interests and aspirations it attempts to represent, but has so far been unable to agree openly on the key elements which form its social support base. Hindu nationalist ideology – originating from the first half of the twentieth century – is hardly sufficient to express all the aims and aspirations the party tries to subsume, except in diffuse forms which at times appear obsolete. In the run-up to the 2004 general elections, the BJP attempted to showcase its commitment to its core constituency by focussing on addressing 'New India,' coining the 'Shining India' and *'Bharat Uday'* slogans. The attempt failed to elicit sufficient electoral benefits as it was perceived to lean too heavily towards only a part of its electoral support, the mostly metropolitan upper middle class. After the electoral defeat by the United Progressive Alliance, sections within the party contested the validity of this perception of its core constituency. However, this process of introspection currently appears far from being concluded.

The BJP's conceptions of its core constituency

In Hindu nationalist ideology, the perception of who supports the Hindu nationalist movement is both clear and stringent: put simply, the movement's supporters are 'true' nationalists, those who profess their love of the Indian motherland and accept the cultural foundations of the Indian nation as projected by Hindu nationalist ideology. Since some religious minorities in India and those ostentatiously affected by foreign, usually western, influences are suspected by many Hindu nationalists to deviate from the very foundation of Indian nationality, the concept in practice emphasises a reformed and unified Hindu community selectively including non-Hindus but shorn of those suspected of disloyalty.

The perception of Hindu nationalist support in terms of community to some degree prevents an analysis of the movement's support base in terms of interests by the party. BJP supporters are depicted as 'true' nationalists and, correspondingly, as the good people. In turn, BJP detractors are then seen as either 'bad people' or those who have not been instilled with sufficient knowledge to accept the truth of Hindu nationalism. This perception is strongly prevalent still at all levels within the party. A highly educated local BJP leader with a very modern outlook on life in Aligarh put this sentiment in the following words when asked what the party should do to return to power:

> 'Our workers are very laborious and committed, having deep thoughts. There are intellectual workers, hardworking intellectual workers in the party since the Jan Sangh period. We should revert to our own agenda. We are hard workers and deep thinkers, so we will again form the government. The party is still known as one of the best in India, the number one in India.'
> (Interview with Dr Shivkumar Sharma, 28 March 2006, Aligarh)

Similar sentiments were expressed by a number of interviewees from the local BJP unit in Aligarh. The district president of the *Mahila Morcha* noted that the primary task of the BJP and all its cadres and leaders was education. In her view, the BJP was getting support from all sections of society and all castes, but even more so from educated people. In her opinion, the BJP already gained the votes of many Muslims, namely of nationalist and educated Muslims. She deplored the alleged lack of education among large parts of the Muslim community in India and stated that the next BJP government should prioritise educational campaigns for Muslims, who would also vote for the BJP after benefiting from increased possibilities for education.[1] The conception of the BJP's support base being constituted by good and educated people from all sections of society, irrespective of particularistic interests, is shared among many representatives of the party's national leadership.

In part, this perception is obviously based on political rhetoric and a refusal to admit to the influence of sectional interests on BJP policies. In this, it forms almost a mirror image of political rhetoric by secular nationalist politicians. Its expression by BJP leaders and cadres, however, includes a vehemence which has to be taken seriously: For many BJP supporters, the notion of political support being based on sectional interests remains inconceivable. As with the middle class-dominated Indian political discourse in general, policies benefiting the interests of some social sections always have to be expressed in terms of the progress of the whole country as a single entity. The BJP in this – similarly to the Congress party, its main rival for middle class votes – stands apart from the regional and lower caste based parties whose social justice idiom implicitly acknowledges preferences regarding sectional interests.

Accordingly, the BJP finds it difficult to engage in the idiom of social justice apart from references to 'the common man.' While the party uses caste as an instrument for electoral mobilisation, often to great effect, it can neither articulate policies in caste terms nor openly conceive its electoral support in this way. This is exemplified by interviewees' responses from Aligarh. Here, trends of caste-wise support to the BJP and its main rivals were known almost precisely by the overwhelming majority of interviewees. At the same time, if it was accepted at all that the BJP gained support mainly from specific castes, this was explained with reference to the relatively high level of formal education among these castes' members.

> 'All castes vote for the BJP. More high caste people vote for the BJP than low caste people, but low caste people vote for the BJP as well. Those who vote for the BJP are those who are educated. There are more educated people among the high castes, so we get support from those who are educated.'
> (Interview with Virendra Sharma, 30 March 2006, Aligarh)

Again, there are no substantial differences between the local and the national level. At the latter level, the inability or unwillingness to conceive electoral support in caste terms – apart from references to education and patriotism – is articulated also with regard to the inability to rely on caste as an instrument for electoral mobilisation at the higher levels of Indian politics. Sushma Swaraj articulated this line of argument in the following way:

'[T]he days are gone when BJP was known only as a party of middle class or party of traders. Now we have base in all these things and we are ruling on our own, without coalition in 5–6 major states of this country. [...] If you do not have support from all the classes, you cannot rule even a village panchayat. With one caste base, you cannot rule a village panchayat. So if we are in power in all these states that means we have support from everybody. If we are only a party of traders, then we will get only 10 per cent vote, or if we have support of the upper castes, at the most 15 per cent. Unless and until you gather the support from all the classes, how can you be in power?'

(Interview with Sushma Swaraj, 5 March 2007, Delhi)

Prakash Javadekar, national spokesperson of the BJP, used a similar argument to refute the hypothesis that the BJP was a middle class-based political party.

'[W]e are not restricted to one class of the Indian society. We are ruling in 8 states today which are basically identified as the poorest of the poor states. So the poor have responded to the BJP and become frustrated with Congress misrule, which gave the slogan of 'garibi hatao' [remove poverty], but did not succeed in their mission. And that is why for their overall development even the poorer sections of society now want the BJP.
[...]
[I]dealism is not restricted to one class or caste alone. If idealism persists in all classes, it's an attitude.'

(Interview with Prakash Javadekar, 7 March 2007, Delhi)[2]

The conception of substantial middle class support[3] is acknowledged in the party leadership, but without reservation it is mostly acknowledged by leaders associated with the party's economic policies. There, the link between the BJP and the middle class is expressed openly. While it is still stressed that the party does not exclusively rely on middle class support, the dominance of the middle class among party supporters and even more so among party members is clearly accepted. This is apparent from the following interview excerpts with representatives of this wing of the party, Jagdish Shettygar – the president of the BJP economic cell – and Seshadri Chari – at the time president of the BJP Party Worker Training Cell. Chari is openly noting the relationship between the middle classes, especially the emergence of new middle classes, and the BJP:

'There are two aspects: One is the emergence of the BJP and its movement towards the centre stage of Indian politics and the other aspect is the emergence of the middle class. Like the proverbial question of whose emergence comes first, think of the hen. So is it the middle class which emerged and then brought up a political course that is more or less conducive to its own growth? Or is it the BJP which grew and came to some stage and then it created its own vested interest. So this question can be looked at from these two aspects. But whatever way we look at it, the fact is that the emergence of the BJP and the emergence of the middle class seems to be correlated.'

(Interview with Seshadri Chari, 5 March 2007, Delhi)

Shettygar, in turn, emphasises the longstanding support the BJP received from the middle class:

'First of all let me make very clear that we are being a liberal party right from the beginning, even when we were known as the Jan Sangh, when the socialistic party pattern was the most accepted system. The liberal attitude was not encouraged at that time. [...] So even when [the Jan Sangh] became the BJP, we continued with the same programme. In fact many people think that in 1991 it was the Congress Party which initiated the reform measures but if you go through the election manifestos of the 1991 Lok Sabha elections – for most of the measures initiated by the Narasimha Rao government Manmohan Singh is getting the credit – you can find that most of these measures were in the BJP election manifesto, that is the 1991 election manifesto. But they came to power and they initiated the reforms and naturally they get the credit and today [Manmohan Singh] is considered as the "Father of Economic Reforms."'

(Interview with Jagdish Shettygar, 6 March 2007, Delhi)

Shettygar explicitly notes the importance of the middle class in the constitution of the party's cadre base. The latter part of the interview excerpt is of interest – apart from the inference on clientelism among some rival parties – in that it implies that other political parties which receive substantial middle class support would also have a middle class-dominated cadre base, if these parties' organisations would not be restricted to linkages with local notables which were activated during electoral campaigns:

'[A]s far as the party structure is concerned, by and large our structure, say the cadre comes basically from our support base. That is the middle class and all. But this does not mean that we do not have the cadre among the poorer section. There are many cases, actually. The people are coming from the poorer section but percentage-wise, their number may be comparatively small compared to say the Congress workers or maybe the Left Front. [...] But there are workers, like maybe the fishermen, or the weavers, or the poor farmers and all, there are many workers. But their percentage is small, compared to say that the Janata Dal or the Communists. The Congress does not have so many cadres. During election time they go to a particular locality and identify the leader. Of course, by experience they know who the leader of that locality is. And they make a deal, with the payment and through that it is a sort of workers who get engaged for a specific assignment for a specific period. Unlike, say, our party, we have got the cadre. Similarly the Left Front, they have got a cadre, the Congress does not have a cadre.'

(Interview with Jagdish Shettygar, 6 March 2007, Delhi)

On being asked to explain why the BJP at the national level used various cells and fronts (*morcha*) to appeal to various social sections but did not have a cell or front for the middle class, Shettygar reinforced his remarks that the BJP principally was a middle class party.

> 'We do not need a morcha because all our morchas work in the same sphere. Take the youth wing. Basically, they work in the same sphere, that is, in one segment of the middle class. And when you go to the Mahila Morcha [the women's front], naturally they approach this segment from the middle class. Then you have the Kisan Morcha, for the farmers. That is another segment of the middle class. Ultimately, all these morchas, they put together what you call the support base. That is the middle class.'
>
> (Interview with Jagdish Shettygar, 6 March 2007, Delhi)

The acknowledgment of middle class support was relatively strong among younger functionaries at the BJP headquarters in Delhi. In addition, the inclusion of middle class support into the idea of a 'New India' was much more direct. This is illustrated by the following interview excerpt with a youth wing leader:

> 'We view the middle class as an attitude, as the best attitude. The middle class attitude is the best for India. The economy's health is important, and the middle class has grown and benefited from it. Simultaneously, we are for hindutva. But with hindutva, we do not only mean Hindus.'
>
> (Interview with Vivek Thakur, 2 March 2007, Delhi)[4]

The clear acknowledgement of substantial middle class support which is apparent from the interview excerpts above is not shared by many party leaders associated with the cultural identitarian wing of the BJP. While the latter generally agree that the BJP receives support from the middle classes, they do not conceive this support as class-based support. In their perception, support to the BJP is based on idealism and on the public perception that the BJP is the most important nationalist party in India. Idealism and patriotism in this view transcend particularistic interests. A slogan which was repeated again and again in conversations with BJP members, both national leaders and local cadres, was: 'India first, the party second.' This view is illustrated by the responses of leaders from this wing of the party, exemplified by Prabhat Jha, a BJP secretary. Jha strongly refuted the argument that the BJP was especially attractive to the middle classes:

> 'It is not a question of attractiveness. [The support we get] is because of morality, because of moral duty. We want all the people of India to say that first is bharat mata [the Indian motherland], first is India. And without bharat mata, how can we say that we are Indian? It is a primary duty of every Indian to say bharat mata zindabad, bharat zindabad [Long live the Indian motherland, long live India]. […] We do not want to attract on the basis of

this national slogan, of nationality. The people and the youth of India – you want to know why they are attracted to the BJP? They are attracted because we are the only party that says that first, we want to save India, we want to improve India. We say that we are first an Indian and a nationalist party. (…) The people of India, the youth know the character of the BJP. Our character is not only a slogan.'

(Interview with Prabhat Jha, 5 March 2007, Delhi)

This notion of interest-transcending support to the party by people committed to idealism is strongly present at the local level as well. When asked directly who voted for the BJP, a large majority of cadres interviewed in Aligarh responded in a similar fashion. While occasionally this question was answered with direct references to religious community – Hindus or *hinduvaadis* – interviewees usually preferred to use the terms nationalists or patriots. This is exemplified by the response of a former president of the local BJP unit: 'Only nationalists, persons of all sections of society without any [distinction of] caste and breed.'[5] The current mayor of Aligarh, one of the most important local BJP leaders, included the issue of religious community membership into this conception of popular support:

> 'We receive the support of all communities, all castes. Muslims are by heart against the BJP, but we receive some support from them as well. The BJP talks to all people. There were BJP ministers [in the central government] from the Muslim community. Most votes are from the Hindu community.'
>
> (Interview with Ashutosh Varshney, 27 March 2006, Aligarh)[6]

When asked directly on the amount of support received from particular sections of the Hindu community, especially OBC or Dalit communities, it was usually conceded that many of these communities tended to support other parties. Nevertheless, significant emphasis was always put on the fact that the BJP received at least some support from these social groups. The underlying reasons for this were usually perceived to be the party's refusal to indulge in 'casteism.' The general secretary of the BJP youth wing of the local party unit expressed this clearly:

> 'The BJP is a big brotherhood. It is not a casteist party. It gets votes from all communities. It gets the votes of those people who are against casteism, all people who are nationalists. There are no class differences.'
>
> (Interview with Rajeev Bharti, 30 March 2006, Aligarh)

This conception of support to the BJP is contrary to the public perception even in Aligarh which strongly emphasised support by 'the business community.'[7] In fact, the interviewed cadres appeared aware that their party's support extended only to some sections of society, and was restricted even among the Hindu community. Yet they were either unable or unwilling – with rare exceptions – to conceive popular support to the BJP in terms of particularistic interests and, accordingly, did not acknowledge that caste or class could be more important for the decision to support the party than nationalist idealism. In their interpretation – as a rule – those social groups which did not support the BJP substantially were either misled by rival parties or interested only in their individual benefits. The former category most often included Muslims (apart from 'criminal' or 'anti-national' elements among the Muslim community) and Dalits who would be more inclined to support the BJP once the level of formal education among these communities was increased.

At the larger level, the perception of popular support based on idealism, not particularistic interests finds its expression in an interpretation of the concept of a 'New India' which supports the BJP not because of its middle class status, but because of its idealism. The 'New India' which, by accident, is dominated by the middle class, is returning to idealism and patriotism and, therefore, eschewing particularistic interests. A simultaneous fixation of this social segment with high levels of consumption is deplored as 'consumerism' which is nevertheless overlaid and at least partially overcome by idealism. Sushma Swaraj responded in the following way to a question on the role accorded to merit in Indian society:

'There has been a great change during last ten years. There is meritocracy now. All these middle class children, they are getting education, now they are getting jobs in these call centres or somewhere. So, and especially with this electronic media boom, there is an exposure [to western influence]. Still, with all these things, they want to build this New India; and they want to be participating in this. They want to participate in this growth. But you see, all these children having mobiles and having two television sets in their house, and all this new rich middle class consumerism, this is already set on in India. There is this influence. But still, I think, when a child goes abroad and studies there, he returns more Indian than before. (...) So they have become more culture oriented, the children have become more culture orientated, the new generation.'
(Interview with Sushma Swaraj, 5 March 2007, Delhi)

The excerpt of the interview with Swaraj illustrates the way in which the original and cultural identitarian thought of Hindu nationalism is being adapted within the BJP in order to enable the party to operate in the context of modern Indian politics without leaving the restrictions posed by Hindu nationalist ideological heritage. The 'New India' is deplored one the one hand as consumption oriented and influenced by western lifestyles, if not selfish, but it is on the other hand celebrated as a social strata which is returning to the cultural ethos of the Indian nation, as defined by Hindu nationalism. The vast gulf that separates the different conceptions of popular support in the views cited above is symptomatic of the two main strands of political thought within the BJP, the cultural identitarian and the economic wings.

The party's difficulties in conceiving the key constituency of the BJP reinforce tensions within the party, as shown by the party's discourse after the electoral defeat in 2004. They also form obstacles in clearly defining and communicating the party's role in Indian politics to its supporters and – equally crucial – to its cadres. On the positive side, they allow a certain degree of flexibility and enable party leaders to reach out to different social groups simultaneously and facilitate course corrections when and if necessary. The difficulties in conceiving popular support do not necessarily coincide with corresponding difficulties in identifying electoral support bases: From the time of its emergence as a viable contender for political power in India until the campaign to the 2004 general elections, the BJP appears to have been quite capable of identifying its social support, even to the extent of selective expansion of its popular appeal by strategic targeting specific social strata such as *Adivasis* in the tribal belt.

Profile of BJP cadres: the BJP party unit in Aligarh City

One respect in which the BJP is often portrayed to differ from many Indian political parties is the strong role accorded to its cadres. In this, the BJP is closer to the left spectrum of Indian party politics than to the Congress and many of the socialist and regional political parties. In turn, the higher emphasis placed on ideology in the internal discourse of both the BJP and the Left Front is clearly related to the importance of the cadre base for these parties. In the case of the BJP, the emphasis on ideological discourse is reinforced by the diffusion between party and movement: There is often no clear separation between activists in the Hindu nationalist movement and party cadres at the local level. Since the BJP relies heavily on the support of its cadres and the larger movement's activists for political mobilisation, shifts in policy or political strategy have to be communicated to the cadres and activists. While these shifts do not necessarily have to be approved of by a majority of cadres, the underlying compulsions have to be accepted by them and the shifts often have to be communicated in accordance with ideological heritage to gain this acceptance. Failure to do so can lead to apathy among the cadre base and tensions within the party and between the organisations which make up the larger movement and thus affect electoral results.

The importance of the party's cadre base for electoral success is strongly acknowledged by both local cadres and the national leadership. This is exemplified by responses to questions on the reasons for the BJP electoral defeat in the 2004 general elections. Other reasons played a significant role in the party's electoral performance – most notably the failure to arrest the disintegration of local electoral support bases which had been apparent in the gradual loss of political power in several major states between 1999 and 2003 and the loss of major allies. Still, apathy among the cadres expressed either directly or indirectly as over-confidence, is uniformly stressed as one of the most important factors contributing to the relatively poor electoral showing.

'The communication, from man to man, within the party must be improved. The party must link better. Usually, the party workers are quite devoted to the party but sometimes they feel bad about compromises. The party workers were not fully motivated [in 2004]. They did just a little less. The next time they should do a little more for the party. And the cadres were over-confident. We got less votes because of unawareness of our own situation.'

(Interview with Krishna Kumar Navman, 25 February 2006, Aligarh)[8]

'The BJP had neglected its party workers while forming the government. It neglected the feelings of the party workers. The leaders did not listen and care properly [to the party workers]. The party workers felt neglected and did not work as much as they could have. This had less to do with the neglect of our core agenda because the party workers know about coalition pressures. The common man did not understand these issues, and some of the party workers did not as well. But most did, and for these it was more the feeling of neglect which led to this state of apathy. Now, this situation has improved.'

(Interview with Prof Krishan Sahab Saxena, 27 March 2006, Aligarh)[9]

The perception among party workers that the electoral defeat was to a significant degree due to a failure to motivate the cadre is echoed by representatives of the national leadership. The high importance attributed to the continued motivation of the party's cadres by the leadership also finds its expression in the preference for modes of electoral mobilisation, especially *yatra*-style agitation, which in recent years have by and large failed to elicit significant popular support but were nevertheless continued, to a large extent in order to improve the level of motivation among the cadres (Schwecke 2009). The fact that these efforts proved relatively unsuccessful in boosting the party workers' morale does not impact the argument on the importance attributed to the cadres, it only illustrates an at least partial failure to understand the cadres' needs on the part of the national leadership.

As a result of this relatively strong reliance on party cadres, the BJP leadership faces significant constraints in its political strategy. Course corrections cannot always be justified, and often have to take place incrementally in order to carry along the cadre base, one of the most valuable assets of the party. The views and preferences of the BJP cadres, their *weltanschauung*, have to be considered in any analysis of the party's development. Given the enormity of this task, the analysis of BJP cadres here is restricted to one local unit of the party, the BJP in Aligarh city.

While this one local party unit is certainly not representative of the BJP cadres at the all-India level, the selection of the Aligarh party unit serves a number of purposes. The BJP in Aligarh has been strongly associated with communal violence in the past (and, if to a reduced extent, in the present as well), an association which has been highlighted by the work on communal violence in India of Paul Brass among others (Brass 1997; 2003). The party in Aligarh is also strongly dominated by its traditional key constituency – Brahmins and

Banias and small-scale traders and industrialists. In these respects, the local party unit constitutes a hard test case for the hypotheses of increasing moderation and normalcy of the BJP. As mentioned above in the discussion of the party's evolution in Aligarh, however, Aligarh city is gradually being drawn into the orbit of the National Capital Region. The local BJP unit, accordingly, presents an opportunity to analyse the operation and functioning of the party in a context in which the 'New India' – both in terms of objective socio-economic transformation and in terms of the ideological construct the BJP is aiming at – is present in an incipient stage of its evolution. In other words, Aligarh is not representative but it is highly informative for a study on the development of the BJP.

Field research in Aligarh was conducted between early 2006 and early 2007. Apart from informal conversations with BJP and *Sangh Parivar* activists, more than 10 per cent of the party's cadre base (according to estimates of party leaders) including a majority of local party leaders were formally interviewed in this period. In addition, two surveys were conducted: a cadre survey which covered approximately two thirds of the BJP activists in Aligarh city, conducted in co-operation with the Department of Economics, Shri Varshney College, Aligarh; and a household survey with a sample size of 450 in three pre-selected localities in Aligarh city, conducted in co-operation with the Department of Sociology and Social Work, Aligarh Muslim University. This was supplemented with interviews with various experts on local politics and leading representatives of the BJP's main rivals in Aligarh, the INC and the *Samajwadi Party*.

The BJP cadres in Aligarh City: socio-economic, demographic, and educational background

The *Bharatiya Janata Party*, both its leaders and the local activists, often prides itself on the extent to which the party can rely on a cadre base. In the BJP self-image as well as in much of the academic literature, the party is distinguished from many other parties – most notably the Congress – by its significant body of local, grassroots activists. The obvious starting point for a profile of the BJP cadre base in a locality, hence, is to identify the extent to which this cadre base actually exists on the ground. In this regard, the local BJP unit in Aligarh city provides an affirmative indication, although the survey findings obviously cannot be generalised for this aspect. BJP party workers in Aligarh were asked to indicate how much time they regularly spent in working for the party.

The results illustrate the extent to which the BJP can rely on the work of its cadres in a locality like Aligarh. While the cadre base certainly expands significantly during election campaigns (or similar programmes), a majority of respondents claimed to spend at least several hours per week on party affairs, and more than 20 per cent of the respondents claimed to be engaged in party-related work on a daily basis. While it has to be taken into consideration that the cadres' claims may have been exaggerated, the survey findings still reinforce the argument of the importance of the local cadres to the party.

Table 7.1 Profile of BJP cadres in Aligarh City, degree of activity in party-related work

Time spent in party-related activities	No. of responses	Percentage of responses
Only during election campaigns	89	44.5
Several hours per week	60	30.0
Several hours per day	23	11.5
Most of the day	19	9.5
No answer	9	4.5
Total	200	100.0

As mentioned above, popular support to the BJP in Aligarh city strongly corresponds to the party's original core constituency as described in much of the relevant literature on the party: the Brahmin-Bania-trader network. In fact, the trends among the cadre base are in many ways even more pronounced. Depicted in terms of class analysis, the party's cadre base is dominated to a large extent by the Hindu middle classes, especially the lower middle classes, and most notably by private sector-oriented small-scale and mid-level industrialists and manufacturers as well as traders. This is supplemented by a number of public sector-oriented typically middle and lower middle class professions, especially teachers and civil servants.

In caste terms, this corresponds to a strong predominance of the two major local Bania castes, Varshneys and Agrawals, but also includes much of the local Brahmin population and a majority among the comparatively small local Thakur community (Brass 2003: 48). Support from OBC and Dalit communities is small compared to the above mentioned upper caste communities and appears to be partially dependent on individual incorporation into the class structure outlined above. In demographic terms, the party has a strong appeal among the younger and mid-aged sections of society, although this appears to mirror the demographic set-up of Aligarh's society and, accordingly, does not significantly set the party apart from its rivals. Polarisation of neighbourhoods (*mohalle*) in Aligarh in religious terms and also in terms of the trend for public or private sector orientation of middle class professions – the two aspects overlap to a significant degree in Aligarh due to the strong impact of the Aligarh Muslim University on typical middle class professions for local Muslims – results in a corresponding spatial polarisation of the city on party lines with the BJP cadre base (and those of its main rivals) for all practical purposes being restricted to certain areas.

In terms of the educational background of BJP supporters, the BJP is strongly supported by social sections with a relatively high level of formal education, especially noticeable at the level of college graduates. Typically, the medium of education is Hindi, not English. With regard to education, the trend of support among relatively high levels of formal education is even more pronounced than with regard to its electoral support base in the city.

The following tables are based on the survey of BJP cadres in Aligarh city conducted between late 2006 and early 2007. Comprehensive representativeness of the sample in terms of the social background of respondents could not be ensured. However, the sample size (200 respondents) covers approximately two thirds of the party's cadre base in Aligarh according to reliable estimates by several local party leaders and critical observers of the local BJP, so that the survey can be expected to provide a fair approximation as a profile of the local cadre base of the BJP.

Apart from the general social background of BJP cadres in Aligarh city, as outlined above, the relatively low presence of women is noticeable. However, it

Table 7.2 Profile of BJP cadres in Aligarh City, age

Age group	Below 25	25–35	35–45	45–55	55–65	Above 65	Total
No. of responses	26	28	67	51	21	7	200
Percentage of responses	13.0	14.0	33.5	25.5	10.5	3.5	100.0

Table 7.3 Profile of BJP cadres in Aligarh City, religion

Religious community	Hindu	Other
No. of responses	200	0
Percentage of responses	100.0	0

Table 7.4 Profile of BJP cadres in Aligarh City, caste group

Caste group	Upper caste	OBC	SC	Total
No. of responses	173	18	9	200
Percentage of responses	86.5	9.0	4.5	100.0

Table 7.5 Profile of BJP cadres in Aligarh City, profession[1]

Profession	Civil service	Business	Teaching	Student	House wife	No answer	Total
No. of responses	49	76	34	17	20	4	200
Percentage of responses	24.5	38.0	17.0	8.5	10.0	2.0	100.0

Note
1 This question was posed open-ended. The responses were later grouped according to the categories listed in the table.

Table 7.6 Profile of BJP cadres in Aligarh City, residential area (neighbourhood/ Mohalla)[1]

Mohalla	Ramghat Road	G T Road	Agra Road	Civil Lines	Total
No. of responses	24	33	132	11	200
Percentage of responses	12.0	16.5	66.0	5.5	100.0

Note
1 This question was posed open-ended. The responses were later grouped according to the categories listed in the table.

Table 7.7 Profile of BJP cadres in Aligarh City, level of education

Level of education	Primary school	High school	Degree (college and above)	Total
No. of responses	10	30	160	200
Percentage of responses	5.0	15.0	80.0	100.0

Table 7.8 Profile of BJP cadres in Aligarh City, medium of education

Medium of education	Hindi	English	Total
No. of responses	189	11	200
Percentage of responses	94.5	5.5	100.0

Table 7.9 Profile of BJP cadres in Aligarh City, gender

Gender	Male	Female	No answer	Total
No. of responses	166	32	2	200
Percentage of responses	83.0	16.0	1.0	100.0

has to be noted that in comparison to rival parties the level of political participation of women in the BJP as depicted in the survey findings (16.0 per cent), especially in the Hindi heartland states, is relatively high, though not outstandingly so.

Respondents were also queried on when they joined the BJP. The survey findings here are highly interesting as they show three general trends: (1) Party workers who joined the party before 1992 still form a majority. This indicates a strong trend of continuity within the local BJP cadre base. (2) A relatively small number of respondents joined the BJP between 1992 and 1997, i.e. after the termination of the Ayodhya campaign and before the formation of the first NDA government at the centre. This indicates that the BJP during much of the

Table 7.10 Profile of BJP cadres in Aligarh City, time period of joining the BJP

Membership since	Before 1992	1992–1997	1998–2006	No answer	Total
No. of responses	110	25	53	12	200
Percentage of responses	55.0	12.5	26.5	6.0	100.0

1990s had reached a plateau with regard to its support among society. (3) A significant number of respondents joined the BJP after the party came to power at the centre in 1998. This indicates a gradual shift within the cadre base from 'long-time' party workers who were recruited by the party while in opposition and while it was relatively isolated within the Indian party system to 'new' party workers who did not experience the party as a mostly oppositional political force and may partially have been attracted by the prospect of joining a ruling party.

The survey findings on the social background of BJP cadres in Aligarh show that these in many ways reflect the composition of the party's electoral support base, though the general trends among the party's social constituency are even more pronounced with regard to the cadres in many respects. While the BJP cadre base in Aligarh at first glance appears to show the continuation (in this locality) of the party's traditional core constituency, the large presence of relatively young activists within the local party unit – coupled with the general socio-economic trends in Aligarh – illustrates the adaptation even of a solidly traditional local party unit to the developments associated with post-liberalisation India. The high number of cadres recruited after 1998, when contrasted to the relative low number of newly recruited cadres between 1992 and 1997, indicates that the party increasingly appeals to prospective members as a potential ruling party, and less as an opposition movement.

The local party unit in Aligarh still demonstrates the prevalence of a strong social polarisation, but the BJP in Aligarh has certainly been able to maintain a broad-based acceptance among the Hindu middle classes. Given the strong position of private sector oriented middle class professions within the BJP, the party's acceptance among civil servants and other public sector oriented professions in the locality is noteworthy as it partially overturns the tendency of predominance of administrative and public sector oriented middle class professions within many Indian political parties. The changing face of the BJP, its emergence as a mass-based middle class dominated party – though restricted by religious community membership – and a party relying to a significant extent on a social constituency which favours economic liberalisation is apparent from the social background of its cadres, even in a locality which has strongly been associated with the radical and militant faces of the Hindu nationalist movement. This development is equally apparent in the survey findings on the views and perceptions of BJP cadres in Aligarh.

A profile of views and perceptions of BJP cadres in Aligarh City

The survey among BJP cadres in Aligarh city was conducted primarily in order to ascertain whether or not perceptions were noticeable among the cadres which could reinforce the argument that a gradual process of political moderation was taking hold even in a traditional hard line local party unit. To this end, questions were formulated in order to determine the cadres' perceptions and views on the party's position within the Indian political system, the differences between the BJP and rival political parties, the policy priorities the party should adopt, and the interpretation of the BJP cultural identitarian heritage. Moreover, questions were asked in order to identify the cadres' perceptions on their own role within the party and, subsequently, to ascertain their preferences vis-à-vis types of political activity which typically would indicate either the political behaviour of social movements or of political parties. Lastly, it was assumed that the overall course correction towards a gradual political moderation by the central party leadership would be resented at least by parts of the party's cadre base, especially in a locality like Aligarh. Questions were posed in order to elicit the extent of strains between the local cadre base and the central leadership and the cadres' interpretations of the underlying reasons for these strains.

While politics in Aligarh remains highly polarised along community membership lines, the question of whether or not the BJP cadres perceive their party to be integrated or excluded within Indian politics also depends on the behaviour of rival parties towards the BJP and on the role of non-party social and political organisations in fomenting co-operation outside party competition. Vestiges of a sense of strict polarisation were relatively few among the responses. When asked on the number of important political rivals of the BJP in Aligarh and Uttar Pradesh, a surprisingly high percentage of respondents – 43.5 and 50.5 per cent respectively – answered that there was only one major rival. The responses are surprising since politics in Uttar Pradesh is patently multi-polar, more so than in Aligarh which, however, was actually perceived to be multi-polar by a larger number of respondents. Partially, this can be explained by the context in which the survey was conducted, i.e. in the run-up to state elections which saw no major political alliances, yet was strongly characterised at the discursive level by the campaigns of opposition parties against the ruling *Samajwadi Party*. Still, the results point towards a continued perception of polarisation: Being factually incorrect, they indicate a tendency to perceive rival parties as united in their opposition to the BJP.

Responses to other questions in the survey tended to indicate a stronger perception of the party being integrated in the Indian political system. When asked who voted for the major rival parties – with possible responses grouped according to religious membership to elicit whether the respondents perceived the electoral contest to be based on communal issues – the results indicate a very low agreement with the idea of polarisation on communal lines. Instead, most respondents perceived support to rival parties to transcend community membership and a significant number admitted that popular support to rival parties came largely from Hindu communities.

Table 7.11 Aligarh BJP cadres' perceptions on the composition of electoral support to rival parties in Aligarh and Uttar Pradesh

Main electoral support of rival parties by community	Aligarh %	Uttar Pradesh %
Hindus	12.0	12.0
Muslims	28.0	15.0
All communities	52.5	65.5
No answer	7.5	7.5
Total	100.0	100.0

Similarly, when asked whether the main rivals of the BJP were working together against it, a surprisingly high percentage of respondents (21.5 per cent) comprehensively rejected this idea, though a larger percentage (37.0 per cent) responded affirmatively. 38.5 per cent of respondents perceived rival parties to be working together against the BJP occasionally. This response is interpreted as an indication of the party's continued integration into the political system here as it does not indicate a systemic opposition to the BJP. When asked whether rival political parties were interested in working together with the BJP, 7.0 per cent of respondents were outright affirmative, while 24.5 per cent agreed that rival parties were interested in co-operation occasionally. A large majority (65.0 per cent) did not perceive any interest in co-operation with the BJP on the part of its rivals. Apparently, while a majority of surveyed party workers did not have a sense of polarisation between the BJP on the one side and its rivals on the other, co-operation between rival parties was not perceived to take place to a signific-ant degree. It should be noted, however, that co-operation between political parties in India rarely takes place at the local level, being largely restricted to seat sharing agreements (which often do not involve joint canvassing) and parlia-mentary work even in the case of formal alliances, and may not have been part of the local cadres' own political experience.

At the time the survey was conducted, intra-party conflicts had been an important nuisance for the BJP and had been highlighted in the Indian media reportage on the party. In the neighbouring constituencies, the BJP had suffered from the formation of the *Rashtriya Kranti Party* by Kalyan Singh (despite his return to the party in 2004), while several other party leaders, most notably Uma Bharati, had left the party between 2004 and the conduct of the survey in late 2006 and early 2007. In order to ascertain the reaction of the BJP cadres on leaders who had defied the party line and in some cases even formed rival parties – whether these leaders were perceived as traitors to the cause or simply as poli-ticians whose defections were deplorable but did not form obstacles to their reintegration in the larger interest of the party – respondents were asked whether the BJP should make efforts to bring these leaders back into the party fold. A large majority of respondents (82.0 per cent) answered affirmatively, while only 12.0 per cent rejected the idea. The responses imply a strong perception of the

BJP as a 'normal' political party, instead of an ideological project in which transgressions from the common cause would have had to be punished.[10]

BJP cadres in Aligarh were participating to a great extent in programmes organised by other political and civil society organisations. Among the respondents to the survey, only 35.5 per cent did not participate in other civil society organisations or declined to respond to this question. 20.0 per cent participated regularly in the programmes of one other organisation, while 44.5 per cent participated regularly in the programmes of more than one other organisation. These obviously included the party's local sister organisations, but also caste, professional, and neighbourhood associations which may be influenced by Hindu nationalist ideology, but not exclusively so and which can be expected to provide a platform of interaction with activists from outside the Hindu nationalist political spectrum.

Similarly, the cadres' perceptions of the party's treatment in the Indian media can be used as an indication of their views on the party's exclusion or integration into the mainstream of Indian politics. National and state level leaders of the BJP have often been complaining of the party's alleged unfair treatment in the media. In contrast, the cadres' perceptions on the party's relations with the media are surprisingly positive.

In order to identify the stances taken by the cadres on the party's integration into the mainstream Indian political system, two issues – efforts to increase the party's acceptability among Muslim voters and the treatment of the party's three 'core issues' in coalitional arrangements at the national level – can be considered to be highly informative. In both cases, the issues directly relate both to symbolically magnified aspects of traditional Hindu nationalist ideological heritage and to the pragmatic adaptation of the party to the compulsions of Indian politics. This is most pronounced in Aligarh with regard to efforts to increase the party's acceptability among Muslims, since the local cadres' own political experiences are shaped to a large extent by the Hindu–Muslim polarisation in the locality itself. The responses on these two issues, unsurprisingly, show a significant divide between two wings in the local party unit.

The relatively high importance attributed to the cultural identitarian agenda of the BJP by the cadres can be shown in the responses to the question on whether the BJP should make efforts to protect Indian culture against westernisation. An

Table 7.12 Aligarh BJP cadres' perceptions on media behaviour towards the BJP

Media behaviour towards the BJP	No. of responses	Percentage of responses
Very good	30	15.0
Good	108	54.0
Not good	52	26.0
Very bad	2	1.0
No answer	8	4.0
Total	200	100.0

Table 7.13 Aligarh BJP cadres' responses on whether the BJP should increase efforts to raise the party's acceptability among Muslims

	No. of responses	*Percentage of responses*
Yes	74	37.0
No	124	62.0
No answer	2	1.0
Total	200	100.0

Table 7.14 Aligarh BJP cadres' responses on whether the BJP should offer not to pursue its three 'core issues' (Article 370, Common Civil Code, Ram Temple in Ayodhya) in order to form coalitional arrangements

	No. of responses	*Percentage of responses*
Yes	113	56.5
No	75	37.5
No answer	12	6.0
Total	200	100.0

overwhelming 91.0 per cent of respondents answered affirmatively, while only 4.0 per cent rejected the idea. However, the results have to be seen in combination with responses to the same question asked during the interviews conducted in Aligarh. There, the notion that it was necessary for the BJP to protect Indian culture against western cultural influence was held up, unsurprisingly, but responses were generally formulated in a much more moderate fashion which implied that western cultural influence should be resisted only where it was perceived to be threatening alleged Indian or Hindu core values.

BJP cadres in Aligarh did not see the perceived threat to the Indian cultural ethos by westernisation as something connected to foreign policy at all. When asked about the most important foreign policies of a prospective new BJP-led government, a majority (51.0 per cent) declined to answer. In itself, this is hardly surprising, since foreign policy rarely plays an important role in India in mobilising the electorate. For a local BJP activist, foreign policy cannot be assumed to form an area of special interest. However, what is noteworthy is the reaction of the respondents who opted to answer the question which was asked open-ended. All respondents who chose to respond to the question (49.0 per cent) answered that the most important foreign policy goal of a new BJP-led government should be to further Indian business interests abroad. Similarly, a significant majority of BJP cadres in Aligarh expressed their wish that the BJP, if voted to power at the national level in the coming elections, should strive to increase the level of foreign direct investment (FDI) in India.

Table 7.15 Aligarh BJP cadres' responses on whether a new BJP-led government should make efforts to increase FDI in India

	No. of responses	*Percentage of responses*
Yes	116	58.0
No	64	32.0
No answer	20	10.0
Total	200	100.0

At the time the survey was conducted, there had been a prominent debate in the Indian public discourse on the tilt towards enhanced integration of India into the global economy, initiated mostly by reservations of the Left Front parties which provided outside support to the Manmohan Singh-led central government. The RSS had relatively openly positioned itself as a defender of Indian autonomy, both in foreign and foreign economic policy, i.e. as a defender of *swaraj* and *swadeshi*. In view of this debate, the respondents to the survey were asked whether they perceived the Congress-led UPA government as compromising Indian autonomy (both in terms of *swaraj* and *swadeshi*) by allowing western nations greater influence in Indian affairs. While a relative majority of respondents answered affirmatively, the percentage of affirmative answers is surprisingly low considering that the question provided an opportunity for the cadres to criticise the party's main rival at the national level for a lack of nationalist fervour.

In contrast, the reaction of BJP cadres in Aligarh when provided with an opportunity to criticise the Congress-led central government on its economic policy was on expected lines, especially concerning the effects of the UPA government's economic policy on the 'common man,' the most important electoral plank of the Congress in the 2004 general elections. 77.0 per cent of respondents described the effects as 'bad,' with only 15.5 per cent having a positive view of UPA economic policies towards the general public. When asked to comment upon the effects of UPA economic policies on other specific target groups, the results were by and large similar, with the notable exception of foreign businesses.

Table 7.16 Aligarh BJP cadres' responses on whether the UPA government compromised Indian national autonomy by allowing increased Western influence on Indian affairs

	No. of responses	*Percentage of responses*
Yes	93	46.5
No	61	30.5
Don't know	32	16.0
No answer	14	7.0
Total	200	100.0

Table 7.17 Aligarh BJP cadres' perceptions on the effects of the UPA government's economic policies for specific target groups, percentages

	For the 'common man'	*For Indian businesses*	*For foreign businesses*	*For the development of India*	*In general*
Good	15.5	20.0	67.0	21.5	13.0
Bad	77.0	69.5	20.0	64.0	65.0
No answer	7.5	10.5	13.0	14.5	22.0
Total	100.0	100.0	100.0	100.0	100.0

The exceptional results for the target group of foreign businesses are notable, since they appear to contradict the survey findings depicted in table 7.16 on whether the UPA had compromised national autonomy. Apparently, however, the surveyed BJP cadres in Aligarh distinguished between the perceived trend in economic policy favouring foreign business and the nationalist credentials of a central government led by its main rival and refused to interpret the central government's policies according to the traditional idiom of nationalist discourse in India.

Despite the BJP cadres' criticism of UPA economic policies, the survey results illustrate the general tendency within the party, even at the level of its local cadres, to see economic policy within the paradigm of economic liberalisation. Given the relatively strong backing of liberalisation policies by the respondents to the survey, the criticism of the UPA economic policies – apart from the obvious theme of criticising a rival's policies – appears to be based more on the policies' implementation than on a general disagreement with the direction of economic policy under the UPA government.

All in all, economic policy was accorded a surprisingly high importance by the local BJP activists. This is apparent from the responses to two questions in the survey – how important is economic policy for winning elections in India, and what are the main policy changes if the BJP should win the next general elections compared to the UPA government?

Table 7.18 Aligarh BJP cadres' perceptions on whether the BJP on coming to power at the centre should continue divestment and deregulation policies

	No. of responses	*Percentage of responses*
Yes	72	36.0
Yes, with modifications	41	20.5
No	29	14.5
Don't know	30	15.0
No answer	28	14.0
Total	200	100.0

Table 7.19 Aligarh BJP cadres' perceptions on the importance of economic policy for winning elections in India

	No. of responses	Percentage of responses
Very important	85	42.5
Important, but other factors are even more important	92	46.0
Not important	9	4.5
No answer	14	7.0
Total	200	100.0

Table 7.20 Aligarh BJP cadres' perceptions on most important policy changes if the BJP would form the next central government[1]

	No. of responses	Percentage of responses
Good governance	140	70.0
Better employment generation	6	3.0
Greater emphasis on cultural policies	14	7.0
No answer	40	20.0
Total	200	100.0

Note
1 This question was asked open-ended. The answers were grouped according to the classifications listed in the table afterwards.

Lastly, respondents to the survey were asked to identify their perceptions on what they considered to be the most important activities the BJP party workers engaged in and which should be accorded the greatest emphasis by the party leadership. This question was primarily intended to ascertain the degree to which the BJP cadres perceive themselves to be part of either a social movement – especially a movement whose main aim was formed by opposition to the established political order – or a political party whose main task was electoral mobilisation of voters in order to form governments. The question also provided an opportunity to test for two aspects which could not have been directly posed with any hope of eliciting correct answers: militancy and clientelism. It was perceived to be necessary, still, to test for these two aspects in a relatively opaque way which diminishes the analytical utility of the survey results in this regard, although it was anticipated that it would at the least provide some information on general trends.

To this effect, respondents were asked to identify the most important activities for a BJP party worker among four options: (1) face-to-face interaction with voters in the locality in order to communicate the party's policies and agenda; (2) social work in the neighbourhoods (*mohalle*) in order to handle directly problems faced by individual voters; (3) protection of party meetings and areas where the BJP was relatively strong against activists from rival political organisations;

and (4) to participate in party campaigns organised at the supra-local level in order to reach out to the public at the national level.

A general preference for option 1 was interpreted as an indication of a preference for political party-style activities. Option 2 was included to test the extent to which BJP party workers in Aligarh expected gains for the party from activities which have an inherent potential for being used to exploit clientelist mechanisms in Indian politics. Option 3 was included to test for the willingness of BJP party workers to engage in violent behaviour. It was formulated in this way since BJP cadres interviewed before the conduct of the survey had tended to emphasise violence by rival political organisations directed against the BJP. A preference for option 4 was interpreted as a sign of a preference for social movement-style activities associated especially with a political organisation in opposition. Altogether, preferences for options 1 and 2 would indicate political pragmatism and moderation to a larger extent than options 3 and 4.

The low percentage of responses favouring option 3 should not be over-emphasised in the way that the survey results in this regard would provide a fair indication of the overall potential for violence within the local party unit of the BJP. It is hardly surprising that most party workers would have preferred one of the other options. Nevertheless, it provides a rough indication of the percentage of cadres who are highly willing to use violent means. It has to be noted that most BJP cadres have a middle class background and are less likely to participate directly in violence unless in exceptional circumstances.

While the relatively low level of responses favouring option 3 was anticipated before the survey, the similarly low preference for option 4 is much more surprising, since one of the activities a number of national party leaders engaged in after the electoral defeat in 2004 was to embark on especially these kinds of campaigns, most publicly visible in the form of the Advani-led *yatras*. These did not serve any clear electoral purpose and, accordingly, can only have aimed at re-consolidating the cadre base (apart from playing a role, if only a limited one, in intra-party power struggles.) The reaction of BJP cadres in Aligarh towards

Table 7.21 Aligarh BJP cadres' perceptions on what constitutes the most important area of work for BJP cadres

Most important activity for BJP party workers	*No. of responses*	*Percentage of responses*
1 Face-to-face interaction with voters	155	77.5
2 Social work in the neighbourhoods	35	17.5
3 Protection of party meetings against violence by rival organisations	3	1.5
4 Participation in supra-local campaigns	3	1.5
No answer	4	2.0
Total	200	100.0

these attempts when asked in informal interactions was, understandably, less than favourable (Schwecke 2009). Option 4 – even more than option 3 which could not have been expected to be the choice of a large part of the cadres – stands for the movement character of the BJP which was most visible during the party's radical phase in the early 1990s. The almost negligible response in favour of option 4 thus indicates the consolidation of the BJP as an increasingly mainstream political party. With respect to options 1 and 2, it was similarly anticipated that responses would by and large favour option 1.

While clientelism is shown in the survey findings to play a significant role, the most important trend is the preference by a large majority of cadres for electoral mobilisation via face-to-face interaction with the public in order to communicate the party's policies and agenda. This result is reinforced by answers of interviewed BJP cadres in Aligarh on the reasons for the party's electoral defeat in 2004 and its decline in Uttar Pradesh. The cadres in Aligarh appear to be aware that in order to be more successful, the BJP should focus on its role as a political party (which in India includes a partial reliance on clientelist practices.) The argument that the BJP should return to movement-style politics reminiscent of its radical phase in order to come to power again is clearly rejected.

The results of the cadre survey in Aligarh show a pervasive ambiguity towards the turn towards political moderation, indicative of a party in transition. While a substantial number of BJP cadres highlighted traditional interpretations of the party's agenda, as was expected in a local party unit traditionally associated with hard line Hindu nationalism, a surprisingly high number of respondents to the survey showed opinions which are much more in accordance with the process of political moderation. Among the moderate wing of the BJP national leadership, these developments appear to be known, as can be discerned from the following statement by Seshadri Chari:

QUESTION: 'Are the party workers responsive to these new pragmatic policies?'
CHARI: 'Certainly. The party workers do realize that we are also addressing their interests. In the last couple of decades, the cadre base of the party was expanded. We have new members and these new members are from different strata of society, but most of them have in some way or other benefitted from the economic policies of the NDA government. They are the new recruits. So we see that we are able to attract new voters who are marginally different from the existing vote base. They relate faster to some of the economic policies than to those policies which are bereft of any economic trappings.'

(Interview with Seshadri Chari, 5 March 2007, Delhi)

Tensions between cadres and national leadership as an illustration of difficulties arising from the changing face of the BJP

As mentioned above, the high importance accorded to the party's cadre base means that changes in the policy directions and strategies followed by the national leadership of the BJP must be communicated to the cadres. Failure to communicate these changes can lead to disenchantment among the cadres which can be expected to lead to apathy among the cadres and in this way damage the party's electoral prospects. Since a part of the cadre base remains committed to hard line interpretations of the BJP agenda, to a greater extent than the pragmatic and increasingly moderate wing dominating the national leadership, a failure to communicate these changes within the bounds of the traditional ideological heritage of the Hindu nationalist movement can be expected to lead to strains between the cadres and the national leadership.

Effective communication establishes trust and confidence in the national leadership among the majority of the cadres, especially in a party like the BJP which takes pride in its 'discipline' and 'value-based' politics. Even hard line cadres in the BJP would normally tend to trust moderate leaders of the party to act in good faith according to their interpretations of the party's ideological heritage and, hence, 'in the interest of the Indian nation.' The increasing contestation of the turn towards political moderation after the formation of the first NDA government within the party could have been expected to result in a deterioration of relations between hard line cadres and moderate leaders. However, no such indication was forthcoming in the interviews and informal interactions with the cadres in Aligarh. Instead, the general sentiment can be summed by the following interview excerpts:

> 'We should have complete faith in our leaders, whoever he or she is. But we should also be able to solve the problems of the small party worker, so that they know that the leaders are with them. There was some trouble there.'
> (Interview with Savitri Varshney, 30 March 2006, Aligarh)[11]

> 'Our leaders should come to the doorsteps of the party workers and thus strengthen internal democracy. Our leaders should make efforts to remove the grievances of the party workers at the proper forums. When they do that, then the party workers should feel satisfied.'
> (Interview with Satyendra Sharma, 30 March 2006, Aligarh)[12]

The general trust in the national leadership is also reflected in the findings of the cadre survey conducted in Aligarh. On being asked whether the local or the national leadership (or both) were more important for their faith in the party, only a relatively small fraction of the respondents opted for the local leadership.

Tensions between the cadres and the national leadership were less the result of the course correction in itself than of the problems of communicating these in a way which was perceived by the cadres as including them and their views in the decision-making process in a meaningful way. The cadres by and large accepted the turn towards moderation even among the hard line wing of the party, since they believed it to be necessary. They resented the way in which it was done, though, in effect resenting being taken for granted by the national leadership. Many cadres were reluctant to talk about this openly, at least in

Table 7.22 Aligarh BJP cadres' perceptions on the importance of the national and the local party leadership for their faith in the party

	No. of responses	*Percentage of responses*
Local party leaders	17	8.5
National party leaders	79	39.5
Both	89	44.5
Don't know	7	3.5
No answer	8	4.0
Total	200	100.0

formal contexts, since open disagreement with the leadership was perceived to compromise the image of a disciplined party. Still, the cadre survey conducted in Aligarh provides a clear indication of the strains between cadres and the leadership.

The cadres in Aligarh were certainly aware that course corrections towards an increasingly mainstream positioning of the party had taken place. These were partially resented among the hard liners, but generally accepted as necessary, and surprisingly often perceived as a good development. Once again, many BJP party workers were reluctant to admit openly that changes had occurred. Instead, they preferred to emphasise that all policies and political strategies followed by the party were compatible with its ideological heritage and the BJP was only shifting its emphasis on policies within its original agenda. This line of argumentation was even followed by many cadres who openly agreed with the course corrections. These cadres mostly resented the implication in the term 'change' that the BJP was straying from its original agenda, but not the view that the party was emphasising different policies than it did earlier. Considering this reluctance to admit to change (as opposed to the relative weight of policies followed by the party), the acceptance that the party's policies had actually changed in the last two decades is surprisingly high.

Similarly to the reluctance to talk openly about changes in BJP policies, BJP party workers in Aligarh often did not talk about strains between the cadres and the national leadership in formal situations, lest their remarks be misinterpreted

Table 7.23 Aligarh BJP cadres' perceptions on whether BJP policies had changed significantly in the last 20 years

Change in BJP policies during the last 20 years	*No. of responses*	*Percentage of responses*
Yes	130	65.0
No	61	30.5
No answer	9	4.5
Total	200	100.0

to question intra-party discipline and party cohesion. When talking informally, reservations against the national leadership were presented much more forcefully. The importance of the topic in informal interactions gradually receded towards the end of 2006 as the level of motivation among the cadres increased after the party performed well in the local elections in Aligarh and had won a number of state-level elections outside Uttar Pradesh. Both the general reluctance to express direct criticism of the leadership in formal situations and the improvement in the general mood at the time the survey was conducted have to be kept in mind in the analysis of the survey results. The prevalence of strains between the cadres and the leadership still is apparent in the cadres' responses. When asked directly on the relationship between cadres and the national leadership, a majority of respondents chose to indicate criticism of the leadership, though for the most part in a toned-down fashion.

The sense of strains in the relationship between the cadres and the national leadership was even more pronounced when the question was put less directly. On being asked whether there was an improvement in relations after the selection of Rajnath Singh as party president – a national leader with a relatively strong backing among the cadres whose inauguration as the party president ended a period of open friction between the BJP leadership under L. K. Advani and the RSS – a clear majority (55.5 per cent) responded affirmatively. 6.0 per cent answered that relations had become worse afterwards and 28.0 per cent of respondents saw no change in the relationship. The last option, of course, can include both satisfied and dissatisfied party workers. The response to this question reinforces the sense of decreasing tensions within the party which became apparent in the interviews and informal interactions with local party activists during the period of field research in Aligarh.

In the interviews, many cadres had expressed a feeling of being neglected by the national leadership especially after the party came to power in 1998. This dissatisfaction with their own treatment by the national leadership is also reflected in the survey where the respondents were asked to clarify whether the behaviour of the national leaders towards the cadres was better when the party was out of power.

Table 7.24 Aligarh BJP cadres' perceptions on the relationship between the party workers and the national leadership

	No. of responses	*Percentage of responses*
Good; there are no problems	76	38.0
Some leaders have to meet the cadres more frequently	43	21.5
The relationship used to be better	45	22.5
Not good	30	15.0
No answer	6	3.0
Total	200	100.0

Table 7.25 Aligarh BJP cadres' perceptions on whether they were treated better by the national leadership when the BJP was not in power

	No. of responses	*Percentage of responses*
Yes, the leadership's treatment of party workers is better when the BJP is not in power	106	53.0
No, the leadership's treatment of party workers is worse when the BJP is not in power	27	13.5
There is no difference	48	24.0
Don't know	13	6.5
No answer	6	3.0
Total	200	100.0

The visible tensions between the BJP cadre base and the party's national leadership have been interpreted as a direct outcome of the increasing contest over the turn towards political moderation, in essence pitting hard line cadres (supported by the BJP sister organisations) against the national leadership which increasingly had become dominated by the moderate wing of the party. With regard to frictions between the BJP and its sister organisations, as part of the contest over the turn towards moderation, the survey results in Aligarh do not provide a clear indication of the cadres' perceptions. When asked whether relations between the BJP, on the one side, and the RSS and VHP, on the other, had deteriorated, the respondents split into three large groups.

The field research results from Aligarh do not give any indication that the contestation of the turn towards moderation was taking place on these lines. Instead, political moderation was by and large accepted, and the strains between the cadres and the leadership were mostly due to a sentiment of neglect and disrespect in the treatment of the cadres by the national leadership. These tensions still serve to illustrate the changing face of the BJP since the party increasingly

Table 7.26 Aligarh BJP cadres' perceptions on changes in the relationship of the party with the RSS and VHP in the last ten years

Changes in relationship between BJP and RSS/ VHP	*Relations with RSS*		*Relations with VHP*	
	No. of responses	*Percentage of responses*	*No. of responses*	*Percentage of responses*
Improvement	76	38.0	55	27.5
Remained unchanged	66	33.0	85	42.5
Deterioration	52	26.0	53	26.5
No answer	6	3.0	7	3.5
Total	200	100.0	200	100.0

loses its originally relatively strong movement character. In doing so, the relationship between the local activists and the higher level leadership changes in
character.

While the BJP will certainly not give up its ideological agenda, membership
and activism in the party will increasingly become based on other considerations, chiefly the prospects of the party to form governments which, in turn, is
likely to lead to a re-interpretation of its ideological heritage and increased
emphasis on pragmatic adaptation to the Indian political mainstream. The
national leadership will certainly attempt to maintain the cadre base of the party
and to keep up its motivation, but it is likely to do this increasingly in order to
keep an asset, less to increase nationalist sentiment among the Indian population
according to the aims of the Hindu nationalist movement. The contest over the
direction of party politics for the most part appears to take place at the level of
the party leadership whereas the cadre base has been surprisingly capable of
adapting to the turn towards moderation and appears to be more concerned with
the loss of the party's original social movement characteristics concerning the
relationship between cadres and the leadership, though not with regard to the
preferred political strategies of the party.

The contest over the turn towards moderation within the BJP national leadership

> 'Economic thinking had been there both within the Jan Sangh and the BJP
> right from the beginning. But, you see, it is a question of emphasis from
> time to time. [...] So we are trying to emphasize these aspects again.'
>
> (Interview with Seshadri Chari, 5 March 2007, Delhi)

The field research on BJP cadres in Aligarh city was supplemented by interviews
with several representatives of the national party leadership, covering both high-
ranking political leaders and lower ranking functionaries of the national party
organisation. The interviews were conducted in spring 2007. At the time, the
BJP perceived itself to be on an upswing again after or in the run-up to a number
of relatively good electoral performances at the state level which were perceived
by party leaders to reverse the declining fortunes of the party after 2004, but
before the relatively poor electoral showing of the BJP in the Uttar Pradesh
assembly elections in 2007.

Observers after the end of the Ayodhya campaign have often divided the BJP
national leadership into two groups, moderates and hard liners. The division was
reinforced in public view by the 'division of labour' among the duumvirate of
Vajpayee and Advani which tended to dominate the party leadership and the
consequent classification of second-rung leaders as either Advani or Vajpayee
loyalists. During the two terms of the NDA government, this division was supplemented by a distinction between the leading government figures and the party
organisation, notwithstanding the fact that both incorporated moderates and hard
liners. In public view, the contest over the turn towards political moderation was

often interpreted as a challenge to the primacy of Vajpayee as Prime Minister by the party apparatus, the latter strengthened by support from the RSS and the party's sister organisations. In this interpretation, after initial setbacks in this challenge to the moderates' dominance especially in 1998, the pogrom in Gujarat and the subsequent emergence of Narendra Modi as the publicly most visible face among the BJP hard liners served to effect a change in power equations within the party. Following the electoral setback in 2004 and Vajpayee's withdrawal from the party leadership, the contest over the turn towards moderation was perceived to have reached a climax, culminating in the replacement of Advani as party president by Rajnath Singh under intense RSS pressure. In this narrative, the latter then represents a more hard line face of the party vis-à-vis Advani who had attempted to take over the position of Vajpayee as the leader of the moderate wing of the BJP.

There are a number of problems within the narrative described above. These can be exemplified by the evident consensus between Advani and Vajpayee over the course correction after the end of the Ayodhya campaign, the co-existence of hard line and moderate policies during the NDA tenures, and Modi's emergence as one of the most strident proponents of a middle class-based economic policy and his problematic relationship with the RSS and VHP leadership. All in all, these problems tend to be related to an over-simplification of the underlying characteristics of the turn towards moderation and the internal contestation of this course. While there certainly are unambiguous representatives of either hard line or moderate policies within the BJP, a large part of the national leadership cannot easily be classified as comprehensively moderate or radical.

To understand the dynamics within the party, it is necessary to start from three main assumptions: (1) The contest over the turn towards moderation is interlaced with intra-party conflicts arising from conflicting personal ambitions of party leaders; (2) national party leaders often transcend the clear division between hard liners and moderates and often move between the two 'camps' relatively freely depending on policy preferences and strategic aims; (3) the key characteristic of the contest over the turn towards moderation is constituted by a conflict over emphasis on either economic or cultural identitarian policies which, however, can be enacted simultaneously in many cases. While several BJP leaders can be identified for analytical purposes as being close to moderate or hard line positions, decision-making in the BJP is strongly dependent on the preferences of the centrist group which transcends the division into moderates and hard liners. The contest over the turn towards moderation accordingly depends on these centrist leaders' perceptions on the necessity to include issues associated with either moderate or hard line positions.

In essence, the underlying dynamic of the turn towards moderation stems from the necessity faced by its proponents to formulate the rationale of their policy preferences within the bounds of Hindu nationalist ideology. The general vagueness of this ideology in many respects leaves a discursive space for the proponents of moderation to stress aspects which are much more compatible with the mainstream Indian political discourse in order to follow an agenda based strongly on the interests of their core constituency, a major part of the Indian middle class. In accumulation, the emphasis on these aspects tends to shift the discourse of the party away from ideological stringency but it does not preclude arrangements with cultural identitarian policies or proponents of ideo-logical stringency, especially on specific issues. This fluidity is compounded by the emergence of younger leaders among the lower ranks of the national leader-ship hierarchy who were not part to the decisions to turn towards radicality in the early 1990s and towards moderation in the mid-1990s and thus often defy attempts to classify them according to the hard line – moderate divide.

In order to analyse the dynamics of the turn towards moderation and its implications for the future development of the BJP it is necessary to depict the positioning of national leaders within the two main policy discourses in the party, the economic and the cultural identitarian agenda. This analysis does not need to encompass all the various shadings within the national leadership but will, instead, attempt to include leaders who exemplify the general trends of positioning.

The positioning of national leaders on the economic agenda

The economic agenda of the BJP constitutes the discursive space in which the divide between hard liners and moderates is most apparent. While BJP leaders will always tend to express economic policy in terms of the party's commitment to nationalism, there are two distinct aspects which separate the two groups: (1) the detail of elaboration of the economic programme; and (2) the underlying assumptions with respect to development policy. Evidently, the two groups also differ in the emphasis placed on economic vis-à-vis cultural identitarian policies which partially explains the difference in elaboration of economic thought.

Among the hard line group, the positioning within the economic policy dis-course can be summed up in the following way: Given the primacy accorded to nationalism, economic policy should strive to improve the welfare of all Indians which, in turn, will strengthen the position of India in the world. Since national identity transcends sectional interests, the party should adapt its policies to the various regional demands and act both flexibly and pragmatically to ensure the maximum benefit to all sections of society. However, in India emphasis would have to be laid on addressing the problems faced by the common people, espe-cially farmers and artisans who form the majority of the population but also small traders, manufacturers and employees in the urban areas. Since both urban and rural areas have different demands on economic policy and the party would strive to adapt to these different contexts, collisions of different interests do not take place to a significant degree. Social justice is enacted when the interests of all are taken care of. Economic policies favouring sectional interests, especially policies favouring large-scale businesses, are not precluded by this agenda, but are perceived to contain inherent dangers both to the idea of nationalism and to the mass of the Indian people who may not benefit from these policies. Globally, there is no danger in integration into the world market, but the world market is perceived as distorted by western dominance, so that India will have to strive towards the implementation of fairness in the system of world trade.

The hard liners' positioning within the economic policy discourse as described above can be discerned from excerpts of an interview with Vinay Katiyar:

> 'Our ideology, the BJP's ideology, is a holistic way of thinking. When we think about the economy, we also have to think about all the rest. The BJP is always trying to include all the other aspects as well and to develop its economic thinking according to the changing contexts. [...] On the economic question, on social justice, we think that if we do not come up with solutions, the whole fabric of the country will break down [...] We are thinking that development should cover everything, it should cover both the villages and the cities. [...] So what we think of as the most important task is to increase employment and get rid of unemployment. But nowadays employment is not [sufficiently] generated. [...] There has been too much which was done for the big companies. If we continue this in India, the country will get weakened. We have no problems with the big companies, but we have to think about the mutual harmony of the whole society. If we give too much land to the big industrial companies, they will produce everything that is needed, yes. But they will create big malls and sell the products there, and in the villages and small towns the farmers, the traders and the small shopkeepers, they will all get unemployed. In this context, the BJP says there cannot be big industries on all the agricultural land. And even today, if we can generate employment somewhere, it is in agriculture. And now, you see, America is giving subsidies to its agriculture, but they say to India that we should not give subsidies to our farmers. [...] We say to America that this is not right.'
>
> (Interview with Vinay Katiyar, 1 March 2007, Delhi)[13]

Katiyar's remarks constitute the most comprehensive explanation of the hard liners' positioning within the economic discourse among several interviewees from this group.

The moderates' positioning within the economic discourse of the party differs both with respect to the detail of elaboration and with regard to the sources of their economic thought. In essence, positions deriving largely from the tradition of Gandhian socialism which are pervasive in the hard liners' discourse on economic policy are largely replaced by economic liberalism. The moderates' emphasis on the economy in contrast to the hard liners' pre-occupation with cultural identity encourages detailed elaboration, as does their dominance within the party's decision-making processes on economic policy. The relatively low level of elaboration of economic thought among many party leaders actually causes problems for those leaders engaged in formulating the party's economic policies, as was readily admitted by Jagdish Shettygar on the issue of allowing foreign direct investment in the Indian insurance sector:

'But then again, if you are talking about these tensions, sometimes they did occur and whenever possible we try to carry forward and sometimes you are able to convince others. They also co-operate. I mean, in a couple of situations and in certain cases, of course, with what you would call the experience in the governments, we learned something and we changed our views. [...] I will give you one concrete example: For instance, until we came to power, we were totally opposed to foreign investment in the insurance sector. [...] But when we were in power, in government, we learnt that in infrastructure – because the NDA government was giving emphasis on infrastructural growth – when we were in government we learned that throughout the world the finance for infrastructure projects was mobilized through the insurance sector. Normally, the conventional funding agencies, they support only projects with a short-term gestation period, about a three or four years gestation period, whereas in infrastructure projects the gestation period is more than eight to ten years. So the banking sector is not in a position to fund these infrastructure projects whereas the insurance sector, because their funds get locked in for 15 or 20 years depending on the policy, that is why they are in a position to fund the infrastructure projects. So since we are all giving support to infrastructural development we thought that the best method of mobilising the funds would be strengthening the insurance sector. [...] So that is why we brought in the reforms in the insurance sector. At the time there was a misunderstanding, what you call tensions.'

(Interview with Jagdish Shettygar, 6 March 2007, Delhi)

Shettygar went on to imply that the various positions on economic policy represented in the party had beneficial effects on the BJP, at least as long as the moderates' dominance over the articulation of economic policy was not effectively challenged.[14] On being asked to comment on the opposition of two of the BJP sister organisations associated with disagreement over the direction of BJP economic policy – the *Swadeshi Jagran Manch* and the *Bharatiya Mazdoor Sangh* – he responded in the following way:

'See, these [organisations] have their own constituencies. And through that, of course, they try to mobilise the support of those sections. But, as a centrist political party, we have to take a balanced approach. Ultimately, that is beneficial to us. But they are articulating the issue in such a way that it is beneficial to one particular section of society. It is similar with the Bharatiya Mazdoor Sangh. They are appealing to the working class. But again, when it comes to the political benefit, it gets translated into our votes, ultimately. Now, the BMS cannot support the labour reforms, amending certain sections of the Labour Act, allowing the closure of sick [public sector] units. How can they? They are a trade union. They will loose support, and the workers who are with them will go to some other union. But being in government, or now being the major opposition party expecting to come back to power, we have to say that in the larger interest of the economy, labour reform is required.'

(Interview with Jagdish Shettygar, 6 March 2007, Delhi)

Seshadri Chari attempted to incorporate the moderates' advocation of economic reform into the larger Hindu nationalist debate on economic policy. As mentioned above, this constitutes a necessity for the moderate group in order to carry the party along on liberalisation policies. In this way, Chari provides a comprehensive overview of the moderates' positioning within the party's economic discourse which merits citation in full.

'The economic policy of the Jan Sangh was not very different from the economic ideas expressed by Mahatma Gandhi. [...] So one of the ideologues of Jan Sangh, Pandit Deendayal Upadhyaya, he lifted some of these ideas and paraphrased them into slogans. And he developed the economic policy of Jan Sangh, in which he said: 'We should adopt a decentralized economy.' Centralised political structure with decentralised economic structure; this was his idea. Because when the centre becomes too weak politically the whole country disintegrates. [...] And another thing that he stressed was that we are an agricultural economy, so there should be stress on agriculture. We need not go for huge production centres, like the Russians have done. So, instead have smaller production centres; as many production centres as possible. Use the local resources, use the local market, use the local production techniques, do not import production techniques from an outside world, which does not suit your country; this is what he advocated. [...] If the agricultural production goes up, people get employment and people get money; when people have money, they spend; then the economy is galvanised. [...] We carried this economic package with us, but moved into the fast track of Indian politics. And that is how we could come to political power along with our economic ideas, which was neither a state controlled socialism, nor uncontrolled laissez-faire. So we adopted a new path. So this is how the Bharatiya Janata Party came to accept a certain amount of economic liberalisation. But what happened was, it should have been the fitness of things to liberalise the economy first, then globalise it. Unfortunately we became the members of WTO when we were not in power. [...] So we had to globalise the economy first, then liberalise it. It should have been done [in] reverse. Therefore, when the BJP led coalition came to power, the BJP started dismantling the state structures of economy slowly. But there were a lot of pressures of globalisation also. So we had to balance between the pressures of globalisation, the pressures of conditionalities of WTO and also the demand, internal demand for a liberal economy. Luckily we were able to manage both. So whatever contradictions you see, these contradictions are more on the pressures of globalisation than on the pressures of liberalisation. So: liberalisation yes, globalisation no. [...] This created a contradiction among the [party] workers also. And this was interpreted as swadeshi economy versus videshi [foreign] economy. The economic policies have always been important for us. We did recognise the fact that however unique and ancient your culture may be, if your people are poor and unfed today; that would constitute a great threat to your very existence. What we are trying to achieve is to dispel the impression that the idea of nationalism and the idea of hindutva is not in any way an anathema to the idea of a prosperous country economically.'

(Interview with Seshadri Chari, 5 March 2007, Delhi)

In this way, Chari presents the BJP economic agenda in a fashion which would be acceptable to its intra-party opponents, while leaving the general direction of the party's economic policies in favour of economic reform and middle class interests intact. Other interviewed leaders from the moderate party spectrum expressed very similar justifications of the economic agenda within the bounds of the Hindu nationalist ideological discourse. Altogether, the moderate group within the party is giving a strong impression of unanimity in both the actual programme and the discursive justification of the agenda.

In the way the economic agenda is presented by the moderate group, it is easier to extend the moderates' sway to those leaders not associated strongly with either group. For instance, Sushma Swaraj – an important party leader not strongly associated with the moderates' positioning on economic policy – emphatically expressed her agreement with Chari's assumption that economic liberalism and Hindu nationalism not only did not preclude each other but actually complemented each other.

'Our economic policies are not in contradiction with our cultural policies. If I say I am a good Hindu, why can I not be a liberal economist? Rather, they are complementary to each other. Because Hindu ideology, Hindu cultural identity was never, never for command economy. It always advocated entrepreneurship. [...] So with all these cultural issues, I say, the more you are a Hindu, the more liberal you are economy-wise.'

(Interview with Sushma Swaraj, 5 March 2007, Delhi)

The growing acceptance of the importance of the economic agenda among leaders not directly associated with the moderate wing of the party for winning elections amplifies the moderates' attempt to build a broader consensus on economic policy based on liberal economics instead of Gandhian socialism, but articulated in a way which incorporates the Hindu nationalist ideological discourse. The growing acceptance of the importance of economic policies for winning elections among other political leaders can be shown in the following remarks by Prakash Javadekar:

'In Indian politics, the voters' behaviour is very different from state to state. Normally, he votes on certain emotional issues, not on physical issues. But of late, right from Bihar to other areas, there is a growing section among our society which is clamouring for overall development. This is called bijli –

sadak – pani [electricity, roads, water]. And people, they don't vote on these issues the way you people do. In Europe or America, there are certain definite issues. Here, it's a different perception among different sections of society, but the clamouring for overall development certainly is growing.'

(Interview with Prakash Javadekar, 7 March 2007, Delhi)

The economic agenda of the BJP serves as an illustration of the party's turn towards moderation. Here, the moderates' dominance is most clearly visible. The factors which reinforce this dominance can be summarised shortly:

- There is a clear unanimity among the moderate group on the direction of economic policy which includes the continuance and even augmentation of liberalisation policies.
- The moderate group within the party is benefiting from its far greater understanding of economic policy complexities vis-à-vis their rivals which enables them to dominate day-to-day decision-making processes concerned with economic policy.
- The relative vagueness of Hindu nationalist ideology on economic issues and the primacy of cultural identitarian issues and nationalism in general within the ideological discourse enable the moderates to present their views within the bounds of Hindu nationalist ideology without losing their commitment to liberalisation.
- While the strand of Gandhian socialism in Hindu nationalist economic thought provides the potential of an elaborate alternative to liberal economics, the lack of concern among the hard liners for elaborating this alternative, and often even the failure to rise above platitudes within the economic discourse diminishes the challenge by Gandhian socialist to liberal economics within the party.
- The general preference among BJP supporters and activists for private entrepreneurship prevents the emergence of a principled opposition against the direction of the party's economic policy and increases the likelihood of enhanced acceptance of these policies among leaders not strongly associated with either group.

Essentially, as long as the linkage of liberal economics with nationalism via the claim of increased national development can be maintained by the moderates in the party's discourse, the moderates' dominance on the economic agenda is highly unlikely to be challenged effectively by their rivals. Instead, the contest over the turn towards political moderation is increasingly removed from the discourse on the economic agenda where the moderates' predominance has largely been established. Given the increasing importance attributed to economic issues by party leaders even outside the economic policy wing, and the decision by the hard liners, for the most part, to base their challenge to the turn towards moderation on the cultural identitarian agenda, the hard liners' position of influence within the party is already compromised to a significant degree.

The positioning of national leaders on the cultural identitarian agenda

As stated above, the validity of the cultural identitarian agenda and its linkage to the party's interpretation of the concept of nationalism remains unchallenged within the BJP. There is, for all practical purposes, no visible attempt by the proponents of political moderation to challenge the conception of cultural identity, nor would such an attempt be feasible within a party like the BJP. The authority of the ideological legacy of Hindu nationalism simply cannot be contested. The turn towards political moderation of the BJP, instead, has to be understood as a series of efforts to emphasise issues whose linkage with the cultural identitarian agenda is vague. Cumulatively, these efforts serve to de-link the party from the cultural identitarian agenda in its radical interpretation but not from its adherence to an increasingly vague concept of nationalism based on cultural identity as such. The scope for such a reconsideration of the relative importance accorded to hard line and moderate interpretations of Hindu nationalist ideology within the boundaries of Hindu nationalist ideological discourse is actually quite large, since the ideology was originally conceived with a view to encompass large and diverse, though not necessarily all, parts of the Indian public.

The contest over the turn towards political moderation on the cultural identitarian agenda can essentially be characterised as an attempt by the hard liners to resist the reinterpretation of the party's agenda within the bounds of Hindu nationalist ideology. This serves to illustrate one of the most important characteristics of the contest over political moderation: The hard liners' challenge, mostly, is restricted to a refusal to adapt. Though the hard liners' potential for disturbing the turn towards moderation is much greater within the cultural identitarian discourse, their principal aim is to limit the scope for innovative interpretations. In political practice, this often corresponds to a consistent propagation of earlier policies and political strategies, some of which have lost to a significant degree their electoral utility for the party.

For obvious reasons, the principally reactive stances taken by the hard liners on the cultural identitarian agenda – their refusal to adapt to innovative interpretations – is not directly admitted. Instead, the positioning can be discerned by the hard liners' tendency in interviews to highlight issues taken up by the party earlier and, on a more general basis, to indulge in historiographic narratives in order to explain the party's policies. In contrast, the moderates' line of argumentation in interviews, except when attempting to present the party's policies in line with its ideological tradition as an assurance of their continued commitment to Hindu nationalist thought, strongly emphasises present and future policies and issues.

In the hard liners' cultural identitarian discourse there are two distinct characteristics – the tendency to highlight issues propagated by the party earlier and the tendency to embed the response into historiographical narratives. This is also evident in the hard liners' continued propagation of the party's three 'core issues,' which undoubtedly have a strong emotive appeal to BJP cadres and leaders but whose electoral utility in recent times has diminished significantly and which the BJP has been compelled to play down after 1998 in order to remove one of the major obstacles in alliance formation.

The diminishing electoral significance of these three 'core issues' is most pronounced with respect to the demand for the abrogation of Article 370 of the Indian constitution which grants a special status for the state of Jammu and Kashmir within the Indian Union. With regard to its electoral strategy, the BJP – both as a right wing and a centre-right wing political party – is generally comfortable with highlighting issues concerning the conflict in Kashmir. In times of tensions between India and Pakistan the larger conflict receives public attention.

Most of the time, however, the fallout of the Kashmir conflict as it is debated in the public Indian discourse centres around terrorist violence which recently was most visible to the Indian public outside Kashmir. The BJP generally attempts to benefit electorally from its public positioning as an effective custodian of law and order, including the issue of terrorist acts. In contrast, the demand for abrogation of Article 370 raises the issue of national cohesion, not of law and order and, accordingly, emphasises an issue which has not had an electorally significant resonance among the Indian public after the end of the 1980s. While the issue may have a strong emotive appeal among a section of the BJP core social support base, most party supporters are more directly affected by other issues, especially as an abrogation of this particular constitutional provision only forms a distant possibility given a realistic estimate of the party's prospective parliamentary strength in the foreseeable future.

While the vast majority of party leaders would not want to forego the party's three 'core issues,' these are not considered to form issues of great public resonance even among leaders not strongly associated with the moderates' positions. In general, there is a sense of prevarication on these issues among interviewed party leaders who do not want to deny the issues' importance for the party, or sound apologetic but, at the same time, strive not to put too much emphasis on the issues as well. This is illustrated by the response of Prakash Javadekar on being questioned whether the decision to leave out the 'core issues' in coalitional arrangements could be seen as a change in BJP politics or only as a tactical withdrawal.

'See, that was the minimum agreed programme for governance by the NDA government. When the NDA was cobbled together in 1998, we made a common minimum agreed programme [...] At the time, these two or three issues were left out, and people started believing that these are the only main things for BJP. It was never that way. We have a hundred things as major issues – security, atomic bomb, poverty alleviation, economic reform. These were major points for the BJP which were accepted by NDA parties. These [three core issues] were some points, a few points. Now, take each case: As far as Uniform Civil Code is concerned, it is not BJP's demand. It is the Constitution. The Indian Constitution has provided for a Common Civil Code in its Directive Principles, in Article 44. So it is the Constitution's demand. It is the Supreme Court's judgement that this should be implemented. It is not the BJP. [...] But people don't agree, so we can't impose it on them. So, okay. Then, as far as this Article 370 is concerned, you can't just abrogate all of a sudden by the Central Government. It has to be ratified by the Jammu–Kashmir Assembly. It is such a process that it is impractical. So abrogation won't happen. So it was basically to show that there is no common treatment.'

(Interview with Prakash Javadekar, 7 March 2007, Delhi)

To be precise, the issues of law and order and terrorism are certainly highlighted by the hard liners. The issue of terrorism in particular provides an opportunity to bring together fears among large parts of the Indian electorate with the suspicions traditionally held by the Hindu nationalist movement on the loyalty of at least parts of the Muslim population of India to the Indian nation.

'Hindutva does not mean that we are against Muslims. If we say we are Hindu nationalists, this does not say that we are against Muslims, that we are opposed to Muslims. We only say we are against the terrorists. And not every Muslim is a terrorist. This is important. But, you see, every terrorist is a Muslim. The Congress started this conspiracy that they said that the BJP is against Muslims. If we would be against Muslims then we would say that India is only for the Hindus, we would dislodge all the Muslims from India. Pakistan says that it is only for the Muslims. But we have never said this. We say that those Muslims who are proud of being Indians, who call India their motherland, those Muslims are Indians. I do not actually know whether only Muslims are terrorists or others as well. Terrorists have no caste. But, by accident, in India every terrorist is a Muslim.'

(Interview with Prabhat Jha, 5 March 2007, Delhi)

The hard liners' efforts to propagate the continued validity of the three 'core issues' as part of the contest over the turn towards moderation, in many ways, can be traced back to a lack of other issues. Bereft of an opportunity to effectively challenge the moderates' dominance on the debate over the economic agenda of the party, the only other traditional hard line issues in the absence of significant threats to national cohesion and sovereignty is constituted by law and order and the 'degenerating' influence of western culture. On law and order, however, the differences between moderates and hard liners within the BJP are relatively minor. The turn towards political moderation is likely to lead to the eventual establishment of the BJP as a centre-right, instead of a right-wing political party and, as such, does not have a significant impact on the party's stance on law and order. Protecting Indian culture against western cultural influence, in turn, directly affects a part of the party's support base, especially in the metropolitan regions in India and among the younger part of the population.

While some organisations which are part of the larger Hindu nationalist movement, though not necessarily of the *Sangh Parivar*, strongly – and occasionally violently – act against the perceived degeneration of the Indian cultural ethos due to western cultural influence, the BJP has for obvious reasons found it difficult to express outright solidarity. In fact, it has on occasion opposed these moves. The following excerpt of an interview with Advani, published in the political magazine Outlook, on the party's reaction to violence against women going to pubs in Karnataka demonstrates the difficulties the BJP has when faced with radical opposition to the influence of western culture in India.

QUESTION: About the Mangalore pub attack, it has been said that your condemnation of the Sri Rama Sene came too late...

ADVANI: What do you know about it? I am shocked journalists do not know or bring out the fact that the Sri Rama Sene made itself a political party and put up 83 candidates against the BJP in Karnataka during the assembly elections. Not one candidate saved his deposit but they fought against the BJP. I do not deny that someone like Muthalik at some time may have had a link with the Sangh Parivar. But he has formed his organisation as a political party against the BJP. The other day, when they asked me about the attack at the Bangalore airport, I was inclined to say this, but I did not, as they will say he is attacking the Sri Rama Sene over the pub incident only because it put up candidates against his party during the assembly polls.

QUESTION: How did you feel about the attack?

ADVANI: I was genuinely revolted by what happened. In fact, someone said to me, please condemn this pub-going. I said, 'What do I have to do with it?' Someone may believe that prohibition is the right course. But that is irrelevant here. What is of relevance is that you just cannot go and beat up girls and women in this manner.

QUESTION: What do you think about the pink chaddi campaign?[15]

ADVANI: I think it was obnoxious.

QUESTION: What about pubs?

ADVANI: I may not approve of it, but as long as it is within the law, it is a matter of individual choice. I would never comment on going to pubs.

(Saba Naqvi. Outlook (Internet edition), 16–23 March 2009)[16]

In summary, the hard liners in the contest over the turn towards political moderation with respect to the cultural identitarian agenda are compelled to withdraw to the continued propagation of the three 'core issues,' as no other issue is either feasible for the party to follow or has any significant potential as a challenge to the turn towards moderation. Certainly, outbreaks of communal violence serve as setbacks in this respect. The anti-Muslim pogrom in Gujarat showed that the moderates' predominance within the party was still far from being completely established. Yet, communal violence does not serve as a policy alternative. The BJP can employ violence occasionally but not continuously.[17] BJP leaders, moreover, cannot openly take affirmative stances towards communal violence, even if they would do so, without facing sanctions from the institutional structure of Indian politics. Even among the most radical party leaders, affirmative responses to communal violence tend to be restricted to the expression that this particular incident of violence was a 'spontaneous' reaction by the public against grievances and, hence, could only be deplored as an over-reaction. Communal violence certainly constitutes the most potent challenge by hard liners to the turn towards moderation, but its utility in this contest in the longer term is severely restricted.

In contrast, the moderates' positioning on the cultural identitarian agenda as part of the contest over the turn towards moderation is restrained for two obvious reasons. (1) Strategically, the effective implementation of the turn towards moderation depends on the predominance of the economic over the cultural identitarian agenda. And (2) the emphasis on economic policy over cultural identity corresponds to the moderates' perception of what constitutes the best political strategy for the BJP. As such, there is hardly any rationale in emphasising the cultural identitarian agenda except in order to demonstrate the moderates' own continued allegiance to the cultural identitarian heritage within Hindu nationalist ideology.

> 'No, we have not given up our commitment for [the abrogation of] Article 370 or the Common Civil Code. And moreover, we are not apologetic. We are not, because these are not the sectarian points of view as they have been made out. Whether it is Article 370 or the Common Civil Code, we feel that ours is the right approach. People who accuse us of being sectarian, I mean, I think it is the other way around. We feel that the citizens should get equal treatment. There should not be any appeasement of any section of society. That is it. In fact, if somebody analyses it properly, if somebody analyses it honestly, if tomorrow the Common Civil Code is imposed, it will be the minorities which will get more benefit from this than the majority section. Because when we talk about the Common Civil Code, the basic emphasis is on gender equality.'
>
> (Interview with Jagdish Shettygar, 6 March 2007, Delhi)

The excerpt of the interview with Jagdish Shettygar displays the two major trends among the moderates' stances taken towards the cultural identitarian agenda: an expression of continued dedication to the ideological heritage of the Hindu nationalist movement and an attempt to highlight aspects even among the 'core issues' which are closer to the moderates' interpretation of it. The issue of the implementation of a common civil code in India obviously includes an inherent potential for its incorporation into a broadly liberal discourse, depending on the emphasis placed on either equal treatment of various social sections or the protection of minority rights. The issue, at the same time, has an inherent utility for the hard liners in the party to rouse anti-Muslim sentiments.

The emphasis on gender equality, while being acceptable to hard liners because it can be perceived to demonstrate the inferior position of Muslim vis-à-vis Hindu women in civil law cases, reformulates the issue in a way that serves to detach it to some extent from its utility to stimulate prejudices based on the cultural identitarian agenda. While this does not constitute a radical reformulation of the party's agenda, the inherent acceptability for even hard line leaders despite the different emphasis makes the issue of the common civil code valuable for the establishment of the turn towards political moderation. This partially explains Shettygar's choice of the common civil code over the abrogation of Article 370 in order to illustrate his argument that the 'core issues' are not – in his words – 'sectarian.'

The remarks by Shettygar cited above leave out the third 'core issue,' the construction of a Ram temple in place of the Babri Masjid in Ayodhya. Shettygar returned to the Ayodhya campaign later in the interview with a line of argumentation which serves to exemplify the difficulties in reconciling this particular issue to the moderates' stances. It also demonstrates, though only vaguely, a certain sense of discomfiture on talking about the Ayodhya campaign which could be perceived among other interviewees strongly associated with the moderate group in the BJP.

> '[T]ill right from the 1950s we had a committed cadre base, we had a top rung leadership. Still, we were not in a position to communicate beyond our traditional support base. It was only in the 1980s, with the Shah Bano Case and how the government behaved after it. Then again, there was this Babri Masjid, the Ayodhya movement. We did not initiate the movement. The case was growing already. But there was a Babri Masjid Action Committee that was set up by the other side. They cashed in on the sentiments of a particular section of society. And to counter that or realising the threat, we started the Ramjanmabhumi movement. Of course, it is actually the RSS and the VHP who started it, the VHP. And if you actually have analysed the history of the VHP, the VHP, let me tell you, until the 1980s, it was a most low profile organisation within the [Sangh Parivar]. It became a high profile organisation only after this movement or, I say, because of this movement. So I think for that [the increasing importance of the VHP] the sectarian Muslims, that is those who set up this Babri Masjid Action Committee, I think, they should be held responsible. So that movement was picked up [by the BJP] and that also helped us in expanding our support base. [...] And today, still, it is a bit of a fashion for our political opponents to point out that we are communal and all this. But as far as the general public is concerned, these are not the real issues.'
>
> (Interview with Jagdish Shettygar, 6 March 2007, Delhi)

Whether the remark is perceived to be correct or not, the argument that the Babri Masjid Action Committee was to blame for the rise of the VHP, coming from a BJP leader, is certainly as noteworthy as the attempt to play down the role of the BJP in the Ayodhya campaign, despite the admittance that the party benefited from it. While discussing the turn towards moderation and the contest over it within the party, however, the last two sentences of the interview excerpt are most important, as they sum up the underlying assumptions of the moderates: While the BJP may have gained a lot from the cultural identitarian agenda, and while its rivals continue to portray the party as communal, issues of cultural identity are not perceived to help the party to a significant extent to come to power again, because the electorate in general – and by implication a substantial part of the BJP support base – is not perceived to be concerned about these issues.

The contest over the turn towards political moderation, as depicted above, shows a number of key characteristics: It is largely restricted to the economic and the cultural identitarian agenda. Other policies may have an auxiliary role as far as they fit into the discourses on the two agendas, but are not in themselves major areas in which the contest in taking place. The hard liners' positioning in the contest can be characterised largely as defensive. Their unwillingness to elaborate an alternative economic agenda for the party restricts their influence on economic policy which remains dominated by the moderates and, thus, by economic liberalism instead of concepts derived from Gandhian socialism. With regard to the cultural identitarian agenda, the hard liners have by and large failed to find issues apart from a continued insistence on the three 'core issues' on which the moderates' positioning can be challenged effectively.

The moderates, in turn, have continued to emphasise economic over cultural identitarian policies. In this way, they have managed to some extent to shift the internal discourse of the party away from areas where the hard liners possess certain advantages. On the economic agenda, the moderates have largely prevailed, fortifying their predominance. At the same time, the cultural identitarian discourse of the party provides opportunities to the moderates to express their continued commitment to the party's ideological heritage, even while the latter is gradually reformulated. This reformulation is not taking place in a co-ordinated, radical way. Instead, the accent is gradually shifted within the discourse by emphasising aspects among traditionally hard line issues which more and more brings these closer to the positioning of the moderates.

The moderates' strength in the contest over the turn towards moderation stems to a significant degree from perceptions on the electoral utility of different policies held by the party leadership. This also illustrates one of the core principles of the turn towards moderation: Its origin lies in different perceptions of the best way for the party to increase its influence in Indian politics, not so much in a clash of two organised wings of the party over political power and the authority to interpret its ideological heritage. With a major part of the national BJP leadership remaining aloof from strong association with either group, the perceptions on the electoral utility of policies and political strategies within the party largely determine the outcome of the contest over the turn towards moderation. In this way, it is precisely sectional interest – i.e. the interests of the party's core support base – instead of the momentum of the discourse on nationalist ideology which decide the party's future course.

BJP policy preferences as articulated in party election manifestos

Since the party's future course is to a significant degree determined by the perception of the interests of various social sections, especially the party's core constituency, the changes which have occurred in the BJP can be expected to find their expression precisely in the preferred way in which the party reaches out to their supporters. The articulation of policy preferences in BJP election manifestos, accordingly, can be expected to demonstrate the gradual establishment of the turn towards political moderation as characterised above.

Election manifestos do not necessarily correspond to actual policies, but they constitute codifications of the evolution of a political party's internal discourse and of the relative strength of various positions in the bargaining processes which determine the party's public positioning.[18] As such, policy preferences as articulated in election manifestos can usually be expected to change more gradually than actual policies carried out while in government, but especially with regard to changes in the direction of policies and strategies of political parties provide a more accurate picture of the relative strength of the various groups supporting the respective shifts in policy preferences. Since the BJP had been in power at the national level only once, and only as part of an alliance of parties, an analysis of election manifestos also has the advantage over an analysis of actual policies of allowing a diachronically comparative analysis of policy preferences.

A quantitative analysis of election manifestos provides an opportunity to ascertain the relative importance attributed by a party's leadership to select issues vis-à-vis other issues. It does not provide a clear indication on the political effects the reference to certain issues in the manifesto may have in the overall political discourse. As an example, the inclusion of a passage in the 2004 NDA election manifesto which stated that the NDA – if re-elected – would attempt to solve the Ayodhya issue either by a consensus between the concerned parties or by a court verdict was given much more weight in the public discourse than in the manifesto compared to other issues. In the public discourse, it was interpreted as a sign that the BJP had managed to overcome resistance from its alliance partners against any inclusion of the Ayodhya issue. Having been left out of the 1999 NDA election manifesto, its inclusion in 2004 – even though it constituted a relatively small passage in the manifesto – indicated to some observers that the NDA as a whole was gradually turning away from secular nationalism.[19]

Partially, this disadvantage arising from the use of quantitative methods of analysis can be overcome by creating relatively broad categories of issues for comparison into which single issues, though possibly of high symbolic value in themselves, are submerged. The downside in this approach is that broad categories will tend to list references in one category which, if considered separately, would lead to shifts in emphasis especially regarding the distinction between 'moderate' and 'radical' issues. This is exemplified by affirmative references to the secular character of the Indian nation-state. Partially due to the demands of the Indian polity for functioning as a political party, the BJP has always included remarks on this issue in its manifestos. However, as the issue falls into the area of national identity, it is included into the broad category of cultural identitarian issues which also comprises many hard line issues. To minimise the disadvantages of using quantitative methods of analysis, select sub-categories were created which will be discussed subsequent to the more general ones.

The analysis presented below is restricted to five election manifestos between 1984 and 2004. The manifesto of 1984 was included as the first national level election manifesto of the BJP and a manifesto which was issued before the re-assertion of hard liners in the party in the late 1980s. In contrast, the 1991 election manifesto was issued at the height of the party's radical phase. The turn towards political moderation coincided with the formation of the NDA as a pre-poll alliance in 1999 and 2004. In these elections, the BJP did not issue its own election manifesto, so that in both cases, the respective NDA manifestos are included in the analysis. However, with the contest over the turn towards moderation gradually taking on a more prominent role in party affairs by the end of the second term of the NDA government, the BJP in 2004 decided to issue a separate document, the 'Vision Document,' which is treated here for analytical purposes as a separate manifesto.

The role of the NDA allies in negotiating the NDA manifestos presents certain difficulties for the analysis, since the negotiating process for these manifestos cannot be seen purely as an intra-party affair of the BJP. As most NDA allies originated from the centre-left spectrum of Indian politics, this would serve to reinforce the position of the moderates within the BJP. Conversely, the party's Vision Document in 2004, while being treated here as a manifesto, emphasises long-term aims of the party which tend to highlight cultural identitarian issues over short-term economic policies, on the one hand, and has to be regarded as a corrective measure against the perceived dilution of the BJP agenda by the formation of the NDA alliance, on the other hand. The relative importance attributed to issues in the two manifestos of 2004 is discussed separately, at first, and subsequently on aggregate.

The broad categories used for analysis comprise (1) cultural identitarian issues, (2) economic policy, (3) references to democracy and civil society, (4) references to law and order, (5) considerations of political strategy, (6) foreign policy, and (7) other issues which could not be included in any of the above categories. Category 1 comprises all references to Indian nationalism, India's national identity, issues which directly refer to Indian culture, policies aimed at promoting Indian culture or protecting it against foreign influences, and references to the cultural identitarian agenda of Hindu nationalism and its evolution. It also comprises all references to the three 'core issues,' 'Muslim appeasement,' and 'pseudo-secularism,' even when those are not directly mentioned. Category 2 evidently encompasses all references to economic and development policy as well as the underlying ideological conceptions of the economic agenda. In this, it comprises references to economic nationalism, concepts derived from 'Gandhian socialism,' and economic liberalism.

Category 3 constitutes the most heterogeneous group of issues. It includes affirmative references to the democratic system, stipulations for the reform of the democratic polity, references to the misuse of authority by the party's rivals, references to social harmony, affirmative stances towards the emancipation of formerly disadvantaged social sections, gender issues, and intra-party democracy. Category 4 comprises all references to threats to law and order or internal security including violent movements, policies aiming at maintaining or improving law and order, criminality in politics, corruption, and references to reform measures among the police and the judicial system. References to communal violence are not included here, since they are listed either in category 1 if violence is condoned or in category 3 in case communal violence is deplored.

Category 5 comprises all references to relations with rival or allied political organisations, if the relationship between the BJP and these organisations can be regarded as the most important aspect of the reference. Category 6 evidently comprises all references to foreign policy including all issues of external security and all remarks on India's position in the international order. In case a clear distinction between the categories has not been straightforward, the references were listed according to an interpretation of the most important intent of their inclusion in the manifesto. This implies a measure of subjective interpretation which is inherent in the analysis of the BJP election manifestos, so that the relative space accorded to the categories in the manifestos should be taken as approximations. The relative importance of issues was measured according to the categorisation by a word count. Figures in table 7.27 are given as percentage-wise proportions in the manifesto.

Several trends are discernable from the analysis of broad categories, though the most obvious – the trend towards enlargement of manifestos – is not shown here. The trend towards the manifestos' enlargement corresponds to the inclusion of many more issues and a significantly increased elaboration of policies and political aims in the manifestos. This is in accordance with one of the most important characteristics of the turn towards political moderation – the shift in emphasis not by downplaying certain issues associated with hard line Hindu nationalism but rather by an enlargement of issues covered in the manifesto which, in the end, diminishes the importance of 'hard line' vis-à-vis 'moderate' issues. The manifestos in this way mirror the broadening of the party's agenda since its inception. The steady enlargement of manifestos leads to situation where the Vision Document of 2004 is already encompassing two and a half times the text of the 1984 election manifesto. If the Vision Document is seen as

Table 7.27 Relative importance of issues in select BJP election manifestos, 1984–2004 (%)

	1984	1991	1999 (NDA)	2004 (BJP)	2004 (NDA)
Cultural identity	9.48	9.91	4.01	9.95	2.90
Economic policy	34.45	45.35	53.97	46.88	73.87
Democracy/civil society	15.95	16.53	17.56	18.11	10.07
Law and order	26.57	5.48	3.52	6.59	3.52
Political strategy	2.33	5.57	4.39	0.41	0.0
Foreign policy	6.08	8.99	9.05	9.72	4.48
Other issues	5.13	8.16	7.50	8.34	5.15
Total	100.0	100.0	100.0	100.0	100.0

only part of an aggregate NDA and BJP manifesto in 2004, the manifesto text in 2004 is more than five times larger than in 1984. If the NDA manifestos are not included in the analysis, since coalition compulsions may have led to an increase in issues in order to facilitate a consensus among the allied parties, there is still a strong tendency of increased inclusion and elaboration of issues in BJP manifestos.

Another trend is constituted by the relative decrease in references to law and order after 1984. This can to some extent be explained by the context in which the 1984 manifesto was issued which led to a stronger emphasis on militant secessionism at the time by the BJP. Law and order, accordingly, declined to a stable level of representation in the manifestos of approximately 5 per cent already in 1991. Another supplementary interpretation of the relative decline in law and order-related issues in the manifestos, especially between 1984 and 1991, is that law and order issues can serve as a surrogate for hard line cultural identitarian issues in times of increased dominance by moderates which would not have been needed to this extent in 1991 at the height of the radical phase in the evolution of the BJP. This would also partially explain the relatively minor rise in importance in the Vision Document vis-à-vis the two NDA manifestos, if the assumption that the Vision Document was intended as a corrective measure for the incorporation of hard line issues as part of the contest over the turn towards moderation is held to be valid.

With regard to political strategy, category 5, the obvious decline in importance after 1999 can be attributed to the establishment of the NDA as a cohesive political force during the second NDA term in government. The relatively low level of representation of these issues in 1984 can, conversely, be interpreted by the relative lack of importance of alliance formation in the national party system at the time. By and large, the manifestos tend to regard the importance of alliance formation as a relatively minor issue.

The relative importance of references to foreign policy in the manifestos mirrors the typically India-centric political discourse in the country, especially in the run-up to elections as foreign policy issues have rarely been considered decisive for electoral success in Indian politics. Interestingly, the highest proportion of references among the manifestos analysed here is found in the Vision Document of 2004, partially due to a strong emphasis on India's role and status in the international order in Hindu nationalist discourse. This signifies the Hindu nationalist perception that India had finally 'arrived' on the global stage. At the same time, it also indicates a stronger correspondence between the discourses of cultural and secular nationalisms in India: A shift in emphasis in the two nationalist discourses away from criteria for membership in the national community towards the interaction of India – whichever way its national identity is defined – with the rest of the world creates and reinforces a link between the two alternative concepts of national identity at the discursive level.

A surprisingly high relative importance across all manifestos analysed here is attributed to issues concerning democracy and civil society. This result partially contradicts arguments found in some of the literature on the party which link the party's positioning on democracy and democratic ideals mostly to the compulsions set up by constitutional and other legal stipulations the BJP is facing in order to function as a political party within the Indian polity. In order to evade legal sanctions, the party would be able to express its (at least notional) commitment to the democratic order and democratic ideals without attributing an importance to it which consistently exceeds the manifesto space allotted to issues related to cultural identity. Partially this can be explained by the political expediency of raising issues concerning the misuse of governmental authority by rival parties which falls into this category. But even in this regard, the BJP would be acting to safeguard democratic ideals, even if cannot be ruled out that it does so only selectively.

Surprisingly, the relative importance accorded to these issues decreases in the 2004 NDA manifesto, despite an ongoing debate on reforms of the Indian polity (also covered by this category), initiated by the NDA. This is partially due to the central position of economic issues in this manifesto, surpassing all other issues by far. At the same time, the relative importance of issues of democracy and civil society is highest among all manifestos in the Vision Document. Similarly to the argument proposed above on law and order issues functioning as a surrogate for hard line cultural identitarian issues, it can be argued here that affirmations of the party's commitment to democratic ideals served as a substitute for an emphasis on the economic agenda for the moderates. As the Vision Document concentrates on long-term aims as opposed to short-term measures, the influence of moderates on the negotiating process leading to the creation of the Vision Document may have led to an increased incorporation of commitments to democratic ideals instead of the moderates' typical emphasis on the economic agenda.

The most outstanding trend is constituted by the consistent prominence of economic policy in the manifestos analysed here. The economic agenda of the party is already surpassing all other issues by far in 1984, although at that time law and order issues are very prominent in the manifesto as well. It has to be noted that in the 'moderate phase' in the first half of the 1980s, represented here by the 1984 manifesto, the representation of economic policy in the manifesto is still much less pronounced than in later manifestos. The enormous increase in its representation in the manifestos between 1984 and 1991, the manifesto representing the party in the most radical phase of its evolution, can be explained by the simultaneous turn towards liberalisation and a stronger emphasis on middle class issues which went hand in hand with the emphasis on radical cultural identitarian issues during the Ayodhya campaign.

The emphasis on economic policy increases further with the creation of the first NDA election manifesto in 1999, decreases in the Vision Document, though it stays above the relative importance attributed to economic policy in 1991, and reaches a climax in the 2004 NDA manifesto where almost three quarters of the text, the largest text by far among the manifestos analysed here, are devoted to economic policy issues. As mentioned above, the Vision Document focuses on long-term aims of the party, less on day-to-day political issues and also has to be seen at least to some extent as an attempt to correct a tilt towards economic policy in the NDA manifestos. In this context, the devotion of almost half the text in the Vision Document to economic issues still serves as an indication of the predominance of the party's economic agenda, at least in the party's public positioning.

Finally, the relative importance attributed to issues of cultural identity in the manifestos remains fairly consistent: It remains below five per cent in the NDA manifestos, significantly so in the 2004 NDA manifesto, while staying marginally lower than ten per cent in BJP manifestos, without significant alterations between 1984, 1991, and the Vision Document in 2004. In effect, the relative space allotted to issues of cultural identity in the BJP manifestos is enlarged in concordance with the overall enlargement of the manifesto texts. The diminishing importance attributed to cultural identity vis-à-vis economic policy for electoral mobilisation, however, can be illustrated by comparing the relative space allotted to both categories in the manifestos, especially keeping in mind the special context of the Vision Document.

On aggregate, the ratio between cultural identitarian and economic policy issues in 2004, despite the contest over the turn towards moderation which led the party to issue the separate Vision Document remains far below the ratios in the 1984 and 1991 manifestos. As both manifestos were used for electoral mobilisation and, hence, received approval by the party leadership, the aggregate data on the manifestos of 2004 has to be taken into consideration.

The aggregate data on the two documents in 2004 by and large shows a continuation of the previous trends with a relatively high importance attributed to

Table 7.28 Ratio of cultural identitarian issues and economic policy issues in select BJP election manifestos, 1984–2004

1984	1991	1999 (NDA)	2004 (BJP)	2004 (NDA)	2004 (aggregate)
27.52%	21.85%	7.43%	21.22%	3.93%	9.29%

Table 7.29 Aggregates of the relative importance of issues in the 2004 NDA election manifesto and the 2004 BJP vision document

	Percentages
Cultural identity	5.82
Economic policy	62.69
Democracy/civil society	13.40
Law and order	4.80
Political strategy	0.17
Foreign policy	6.65
Other issues	6.47
Total	100.0

issues concerning democracy and civil society and a strong preference for mobilising support on the basis of economic policy. Issues of law and order and foreign policy, respectively, do not show any significant fluctuations with regard to previous manifestos, while issues of cultural identity are in between the two typical figures for BJP and NDA manifestos, though closer to the figures for NDA manifestos. The latter evidently is due to the relatively low importance accorded to this category in the NDA manifesto of 2004 which is significantly larger than the Vision Document.

As mentioned above, the broad categories used for analysis so far have the disadvantage of listing issues in one broad category which are not necessarily in accordance with the distinction between 'moderate' and 'radical' issues, thereby concealing nuances. As part of the analysis, the manifesto passages were also listed according to sub-categories. The figures for these sub-categories are listed below insofar as they provide additional information with regard to the distinction between 'moderate' and 'radical' issues. As the 2004 NDA manifesto, by and large, shows a slightly more pronounced continuation of the 1999 NDA manifesto, the former is left out of the analysis in order to reduce complexity. The above mentioned special context of the Vision Document in 2004 still has to be considered for analysis.

The relative weight accorded to the three sub-categories represented in BJP manifestos listed in the category of cultural identitarian issues illustrates a number of trends which are noteworthy since they serve to qualify the results of the analysis of the broader categories as described above.

The trend for the representation of key ideological issues concerning the hard line agenda in the manifestos is evident. These issues were accorded a major role in the 1991 manifesto, during the Ayodhya campaign, second only to issues of Indian (instead of Hindu) national identity and national pride. Hard line issues

Table 7.30 Relative importance of issues in select BJP election manifestos, cultural identitarian issues, 1984–2004, percentage

Category 1: cultural identity	*1984*	*1991*	*1999 (NDA)*	*2004 (BJP)*
Key ideological issues concerning the hard line agenda[1]	14.17	32.67	3.98	22.13
Affirmations of secularism, minority rights and religious/cultural diversity	25.39	29.0	34.54	34.47
National identity/national pride/Indian values not presented as Hindu values	60.44	38.33	61.48	43.40
Total	100.0	100.0	100.0	100.0

Note

1 This sub-category does not include references to the implementation of a common civil code if they are explicitly related to affirmative stances towards secularism. As the issue of Muslim Personal Law can be used to appeal to stereotypical images of Muslims among non-Muslim voters, this distinction may seem arbitrary, but it was decided that the analysis would consider only the actual meaning of text passages and not imply any possible underlying intent.

did not have high significance in 1984 (before the BJP joined the Ayodhya campaign), and were hardly (and only obliquely) referred to in the 1999 NDA manifesto, but were of significant importance in the Vision Document, though to a much lesser extent than in 1991. In the Vision Document, these issues still are represented to a much lesser extent than issues of national identity and pride and, more importantly, also take up significantly less space in the manifesto text than affirmations of secularism, religious and cultural diversity and minority rights. This serves to qualify the above mentioned argument that the Vision Document was intended to 'balance' the shift towards moderate positions and especially economic policy in the NDA manifestos: While the Vision Document certainly was originally intended to do so by the hard liners, the moderates apparently were still able to exert their predominance in the subsequent negotiation process which led to the creation of the document. This also resulted in the very strong emphasis on affirmative positions towards secularism, minority rights and religious and cultural diversity in the Vision Document, which is only marginally lower than in the 1999 NDA manifesto.

The last major trend in the representation of the various cultural identitarian issues in the manifestos is constituted by the fluctuations regarding issues of national identity and national pride: These issues played a central role in 1984 when issues of national cohesion were perceived to be highly relevant by the party. They were far less prominent in 1991 and in the Vision Document. However, issues of national identity constituted the most important part of the cultural identitarian category in the 1999 NDA manifesto, even slightly above the percentage of these issues in the 1984 manifesto. This result is all the more noteworthy since the proportion of manifesto space devoted to issues of cultural identity in 1999 was much smaller than in 1984.

Issues of national identity and national pride form a sub-category where the various strands of Hindu nationalism and secular nationalism overlap to some extent, leaving an area of concordance on which both sides can agree. As the 1999 manifesto had to be accepted by the party's secular nationalist allies, the predominance of issues of national identity and national pride within the category of

Table 7.31 Relative importance of issues in select BJP election manifestos, economic policy, 1984–2004, percentage

Category 2: economic policy	1984	1991	1999 (NDA)	2004 (BJP)
Liberalisation	4.01	16.02	11.40	7.71
Development infrastructure	29.31	10.66	39.98	38.58
Development agriculture	9.53	6.29	9.82	7.94
'Common man' issues	26.16	29.73	15.39	15.51
Economic nationalism/ *swadeshi*	7.80	32.06	11.01	7.45
Middle class issues	18.20	2.77	7.48	8.08
Total	100.0	100.0	100.0	100.0

cultural identity illustrates the common ground between the two alternative concepts of nationalism. This predominance indicates the possibilities of Hindu nationalism to enlarge its appeal within the overall nationalist spectrum of Indian politics by moderation and adaptation to the larger nationalist discourse.

The growing dominance of moderates within the BJP can also be seen in the references to economic policy in the election manifestos. This is most evident with regard to the relative space accorded to issues of economic nationalism and the *swadeshi* concept. These issues were of relatively minor importance in 1984, despite the party's commitment to Gandhian socialism at the time. In 1984, the party concentrated on expressing its obligations to middle class and 'common man' interests, instead. In 1991, however, economic nationalism was accorded the highest prominence, even above 'common man' issues. Both issues are much more visible in the discourse of the party's hard liners. While the early 1990s mark the phase in which the BJP shifted its main emphasis from economic nationalism to economic liberalism, this shift had not yet found its expression in the 1991 manifesto, even though direct references to liberalisation were represented in the manifesto text more prominently than in 1984. (In fact, the proportion of references to liberalisation is highest among the manifestos analysed here.)

References to economic nationalism were accorded significantly less space in relation to the size of the manifesto in 1999, despite the fact that a number of NDA allies were from the centre-left political spectrum. In the Vision Document, references to economic nationalism did not play a major role anymore. The continuance of the downward trend after 1999 implies that the presence of NDA allies in 1999 actually served to conceal the shift towards economic liberalism within the BJP.

While direct references to liberalisation decline significantly after 1991 and middle class interest-based issues, by and large, remain stagnant at a relatively low level, most of the space on economic policy in the manifestos after 1991 is devoted to the development of infrastructure. The emphasis on infrastructure-based development spending will certainly be justified by BJP leaders as an efficient development strategy. However, it also provides an opportunity to focus on articulating sectional interests without direct reference on these demands by specific groups. Infrastructure development especially benefits the middle classes in the Indian context. The visibly increased significance of infrastructure development also has to be seen in comparison with the, by and large, stagnant proportion of space devoted to agriculture-based development strategies which, conceivably, would benefit the BJP core constituency less directly.

For the analysis of issues within the broader categories, references to the misuse of state authority by the party's rivals were left out since they tend to be dependent to a significant degree to specific circumstances and thus do not provide clear trends. Among the issues listed in Table 7.32, polity reforms have a similar fluctuation according to the specific importance attributed to it by the BJP at various times. In 1999, for instance, the BJP had started to initiate a larger debate on polity reforms.

Table 7.32 Relative importance of issues in select BJP election manifestos, democracy and civil society issues, 1984–2004, percentage

Category 3: democracy/civil society	1984	1991	1999 (NDA)	2004 (BJP)
Affirmation democratic system	18.13	17.31	3.67	18.96
Polity reforms	48.65	19.51	35.86	19.05
Social harmony	9.71	9.19	11.31	1.31
Emancipation disadvantaged groups	4.21	35.15	28.64	19.32
Total	100.0	100.0	100.0	100.0

Expressions of the party's affirmation to the democratic political system of India take a relatively important place in BJP manifestos, but not in the 1999 NDA election manifesto. Apparently, since the commitment of the NDA allies to the democratic process is doubted to a much lesser extent by its rivals than that of the BJP, the NDA did not perceive a stronger expression of commitment to be necessary. In BJP manifestos, the issue is consistently allotted a significant part of the manifesto space, showing a greater need for the party to express its commitment. Instead, issues concerning social harmony and the emancipation of previously disadvantaged social sections were given greater prominence in absolute terms in the NDA manifesto of 1999 though, in case of the latter, not in comparison to the relative space allotted to these in the BJP manifesto of 1991.

With regard to the issue of emancipation of disadvantaged groups, the 1991 manifesto marks the advent of 'social engineering,' apart from its specific methods principally a conscious attempt by the BJP to open itself to lower caste social strata, in the political programme of the BJP. Conversely, the issue is hardly significant in the 1984 manifesto. Social harmony is consistently expressed in the manifestos until 2004, though it is not specifically accorded much prominence, with the relative space covered by the issue hovering around ten per cent. In 2004, shortly after the Gujarat pogrom, the issue hardly finds any expression in the Vision Document, both an illustration of the partial re-assertion of hard liners in the party in the wake of the large-scale communal violence and an indirect fall-out of the pogrom: According prominence to social harmony in the context of 2004 would have been perceived by large parts among the general public as an indictment of the party itself.

The relative importance attributed to various law and order-related issues in the manifestos analysed here shows a consistently low weight of the issue of criminality in politics. Although the party has raised the issue from time to time, despite having been indicted in the increasing involvement of alleged criminals in politics as well, it does not appear to be perceived as a relevant issue for election campaigns by the party leadership. In contrast, the issue of corruption is consistently accorded some importance by the party, with relative space allotted to the issue in the manifestos fluctuating between 13 and 18 per cent of the passages devoted to law and order issues.

Table 7.33 Relative importance of issues in select BJP election manifestos, law and order
issues, 1984–2004, percentage

Category 4: law and order	1984	1991	1999 (NDA)	2004 (BJP)
Political militancy/extremism (rivals)	46.56	42.57	11.13	43.32
Corruption	16.57	13.65	13.81	17.95
Criminality in politics	3.72	4.22	0.62	3.96
Total	100.0	100.0	100.0	100.0

Though a number of other issues play a role with regard to the category of law and order issues, the most important emphasis in BJP manifestos consistently is on political militancy by rival organisations and typically left-wing or Islamist extremism including terrorism and armed insurgency. The issue is consistently taking up above 40 per cent of the space dealing with law and order issues in the party's own manifestos, though it is much less significant in the 1999 NDA manifesto. The high importance the sub-category has for the BJP is another indication that law and order issues serve as an opportunity to accommodate hard line leaders without reference to hard line cultural identitarian issues. Still, as mentioned above, it also has to be taken into consideration that the differences between moderates and hard liners on these issues are relatively small, so that finding a consensus between the two groups and among the overall national leadership of the party on these issues is likely to be comparatively straightforward.

The analysis of BJP election manifestos illustrates the predominance of moderate positions within the decision-making apparatus of the party. This is notwithstanding the presence of hard line leaders in positions of influence. Rather, moderate positions have for the most part been accepted by the party as a whole, at least partially including the hard liners and those leaders not strongly associated with either group, as the most effective way of mobilising electoral support. Even in the most radical phase of the party's evolution, moderate positions remained prominent in the manifestos, especially regarding economic policy.

The manifestos also show a trend of consolidation of the moderate's influence on BJP policies. Despite the increased challenge to the turn towards moderation by hard line leaders, moderate positions have steadily increased in prominence in the manifestos. Even the Vision Document which can be considered as an attempt to rectify the policy shifts during the two terms of the NDA government by hard liners, eventually only reinforced the predominance of moderate positions as shown by the importance attributed to broadly mainstream positions within the cultural identitarian passages of the document. The results of the analysis of election manifestos support the main arguments of how the changes in the party which cumulate into the turn towards moderation are taking place.

Conclusion: the changing face of the BJP

The changing face of the BJP as it is turning towards political moderation and gradually emerging as a centre-right political party has been illustrated here in the discursive dynamics of the turn towards moderation and the contest over this political course. However, the discursive dynamics underlying the changing face of the BJP are strongly linked to factors of political economy, especially the increasing realisation within the party that its political success is directly related to its economic agenda. The latter is characterised by the articulation of sectional interests, dominated by the interests of the new middle class segments which form the party's core constituency, but to some extent balanced by the necessity to adapt pragmatically to the compulsion of selectively enlarging the party's support base.

The dependence on the economic agenda reinforces the turn towards moderation as the discourse on economic policy within the party is strongly dominated by the moderates. In turn, the contest over the turn towards moderation remains largely defensive in character. The opponents of the party's course lack viable and politically sustainable issues and strategies to challenge the moderates' dominance effectively. The moderates, at the same time, cannot affect a comprehensive paradigm shift in the party's discourse (even if they would want to) and need to articulate their positions within the larger framework of Hindu nationalist ideology. Since this ideology offers space for various interpretations, party cohesion is reinforced despite the contest over the turn towards moderation.

The gradual change of political direction, coupled with the correspondence of interests of the core constituency with the economic agenda of the party, also enables the BJP to ensure party cohesion with regard to its cadres, though the change from movement- to party-style political functioning is especially pronounced at the local level. In essence, the contest over the turn towards moderation cannot be characterised as a conflict between the local level (and national leaders with strong grassroots support) and the national level leadership dominated by the moderates. Instead, most of the party remains aloof of association with either of the two wings, the moderates and the hard liners, at both the national and the local level. The continuation of the turn towards moderation in the face of the challenge by the hard liners depends on the implicit realisation of this group of the importance of articulating sectional economic interests. By deduction, friction between the BJP and its sister organisations – the larger Hindu nationalist movement – follows the same pattern of being mostly restricted to the national leadership level.

In contrast, the only partial ability of many BJP leaders and cadres to comprehend the shift towards political moderation results in recurring sentiments of disenchantment with the party's course, especially where political success remains elusive at present. This disenchantment may lead to apathy among the cadres and friction among the leadership but so far has not endangered the party's cohesion in a way which would threaten its general course or its establishment as a viable contender for political power in India.

8 Conclusion

The BJP as a new cultural identitarian political movement

The turn towards political moderation which the BJP consciously embarked on after the end of the Ayodhya campaign has not yet led to the establishment of the party as a centre-right political force in India. Remnants of radicalism remain which under different circumstances might still have sufficient power and influence on the party's decision-making to reverse the direction of the party's future evolution. Yet, even while the party cannot be interpreted in its present state as a comprehensively moderate party, the turn towards moderation is increasingly being established and has already resulted in major changes within the party. Several key characteristics of this development are discernable.

The decision to present a more moderate face in the party's public posturing, initially, was strategic in character, a conscious attempt to reach out to social segments the party did not expect to reach (or reach for a longer period of time) by focussing on a radical interpretation of its agenda and to attempt to overcome its political isolation. The driving force behind this decision, however, was constituted by the awareness of the feasibility of electoral success by focussing on the representation of certain interests in society. As such, the turn towards moderation has to be understood as the party's adaptation to the transformation (and growth) of large segments among the Indian middle class. The middle class segments which today form the key constituency of the party's support base have emerged as a group which is distinct from the old middle classes represented earlier by the Congress, the gradually rising strata represented mostly by the 'casteist,' typically centre-left political parties in India, and the traditional support base of the BJP among the Indian small-town petty bourgeoisie.

While the BJP has not emerged as the only representative of these new middle class segments, it certainly constitutes one of the most important voices for these groups in Indian society. As a result, the party's policies and political strategies increasingly centre on articulating the economic interests of these groups which are dominated by demands for the continued disassociation of select economic sectors offering comparatively highly paid employment from the state interventionist structure of the Indian polity. Since these demands centre only on select sectors of the Indian economy, the party has, at least to some extent, been able to adapt pragmatically to the interests of other social strata, especially when it comes to the continuity of political practices still dominated by rent-seeking behaviour.

The ability of the party to adapt pragmatically to various contexts resulted in an ability to carry along its cadre base, most of the hard liners among the party's leadership and the traditional support base of the party, the latter especially since they are gradually being absorbed in the new middle class segments outlined above. The continued integration of a more radical wing within the party leads to tensions, at least from time to time, but it also forms one of the most important preconditions for the success of the turn towards moderation. In essence, a radical break of the party with hard line Hindu nationalism has never been conceivable as a politically feasible option. At the same time, a comprehensive discontinuation of the turn towards moderation, as distinct from occasional setbacks especially related to incidents of large-scale communal violence, by now does not anymore constitute a probable threat. If it is not conceivable that the BJP can be de-linked from Hindu nationalism, it is also not feasible anymore for the party to de-link itself from the aspirations and interests of the new middle class segments which form its core constituency.

While initially strategic in character, the turn towards moderation has by now acquired its own dynamic. The party's reliance on the new middle class segments carries with it an acceptance of the primacy of economic interests, not so much in terms of the ideological discourse within the party, but in actual policies. The typical vagueness of cultural identitarian ideologies on economic policy and their lack of elaboration inherently contribute to the shift towards the representation of sectional interests. The pre-eminence of nationalism facilitates the articulation of these interests under the guise of development rhetoric which strives to strengthen the Indian nation. Given the relative success of these economic policies in facilitating higher rates of economic growth and the welfare of the party's core constituency (though not necessarily redistribution or poverty alleviation), the primacy accorded to the economic agenda cannot effectively be challenged by hard line cultural identitarian leaders within the bounds of the Hindu nationalist political discourse.

The continued growth of the new middle class segments both in terms of absolute numbers and political influence and the increasing reliance of the BJP on the support of these social strata, in turn, lead to a gradual transformation of the party structure which is increasingly dominated by social sections which benefited from the party's economic agenda or aspire to emulate the success of the new middle class segments. New members can still be expected to have imbibed Hindu nationalist sentiments, and to try to carry forward the party's cultural identitarian agenda, but the primacy of the economic agenda on which the turn towards moderation rests is less likely to be challenged by them.

The cultural identitarian agenda, in turn, is for the most part not consciously reformulated. Rather, it is becoming less and less important in mobilising popular support. With the electoral utility of cultural identity issues increasingly in question, it is becoming less likely that new major policies in this regard are devised by the party. The traditional issues on which the cultural identitarian agenda rested are decreasing in their appeal to the electorate as a whole and the BJP core support base in particular. By insisting on their continued prominence, the hard liners and those resisting the turn towards moderation can disturb the shift in the party's policies but, basically, this constitutes a defensive reaction, not an alternative policy approach with any significant hope of success under the present circumstances.

The cultural identitarian discourse of the party is, instead, increasingly being shaped by the new middle class segments themselves.[1] This does not constitute a conscious redrawing of the discourse's parameters, but a gradual adaptation of Hindu nationalist propagated cultural identitarian issues to the needs of these segments. While some contents of Hindu nationalism become more and more established in the public discourse and perception of Indian national identity, and thus constrict the secular nationalist character of Indian national identity, these new middle class segments are to a greater extent concerned with projecting Indian national identity in an increasingly globalised world than with criteria for community membership. In essence, the nationalist discourse in India will focus more and more on projecting Indian nationality to the outside world than on excluding select social groups within India, since membership in the new middle class segments is mostly based on class criteria, and to a much lesser extent on community membership. This development is obviously notwithstanding the fact that existing social polarisation in India on community lines, where it is still strong, will continue to provide an opportunity for the BJP to mobilise support on communal lines.

This gradual shift in emphasis within the cultural identitarian discourse of the BJP enables the party to explore avenues of broadening support for its 'cultural nationalism' within the larger spectrum of Indian politics. The NDA experiment showed that assertions of Indian national identity, for the most part devoid of the pre-occupation with criteria for group membership, vis-à-vis the position of India in the global arena form an area of discursive space where present-day secular nationalist political parties and the BJP can reach a common ground. In this way, Hindu nationalist ideology (or cultural nationalism in general) can be expected to expand, even effecting to some degree a paradigm shift away from secular nationalism, but is also likely to lose much of its specific content in the process.

So far, the BJP has managed quite successfully to cope with the transition from its old to its new core support base, certainly to a large extent due to the fact that the party's old constituency formed one part of the original basis out of which the new middle class segments emerged and is gradually getting absorbed into the latter. In fact, the party has managed at least to some extent to create a new social coalition of relatively disparate groups under the leadership of its core constituency. However, the integration of groups which form part of this social coalition but not of its core constituency is often proving difficult for the party, more so if these groups do not to a significant extent aspire to emulate the new middle class segments. In many ways, the BJP has reached a plateau with regard to its electoral appeal. Social groups with strong linkages to other parties, especially the regional parties, remain outside the reach of its popular appeal. They may be less and less averse to co-operation with the BJP, unless these parties' social constituencies strongly include Muslim segments but, overall, the BJP has not been able to gain acceptance as a representative of these groups in its own right. The attempt to expand its appeal beyond the social coalition it represented in Uttar Pradesh actually led to a partial disintegration of the party there, severely weakening its position in national politics.

As a result, the cadre base of the party remains strongly dominated by its traditional core constituency among the long-time members and the new middle class segments among newer members, especially those who joined the party after the turn towards moderation was established. Gradually, the latter are becoming more influential in the higher positions of the party hierarchy. This reinforces the establishment of the turn towards moderation, but also results in a turn away from movement-style politics. While the BJP can always turn towards a style of campaigning typical of social movements, facilitated by its proximity to other *Sangh Parivar* organisations and its linkage at the local level with civil society associations influenced by Hindu nationalist ideology, the party is increasingly turning away from its origins as merely the political arm of the *Sangh Parivar* and emerging as a political party centred on the representation of specific interests in society.[2]

The shift from being part of a larger social movement to becoming an institutionalised political party leads to frictions within the *Sangh Parivar*. Nevertheless, these frictions should not be exaggerated. At the local level, engagement within the party and the larger movement is fluid, and the BJP – while still depending on support from the RSS and other organisations – forms a major player within the *Sangh Parivar*. Moreover, allied organisations at the local level (especially those on whom the BJP is relying most for its electoral success) often mirror the party's social structure and, specific topics aside, tend to represent similar interests. In general, the more the BJP is co-operating at the local level with organisations which are influenced by Hindu nationalist ideology but for the most part do not focus on the propagation of cultural identitarian issues – e.g. professional, caste and neighbourhood associations – the less opposition to its increasing leadership role among the larger movement the party is likely to encounter.

By and large, frictions over the shift in BJP policy preferences are restricted to conflicts among the national leaderships of the major organisations which form part of the *Sangh Parivar*. For a number of reasons, the constitution of the leadership in several key *Sangh Parivar* outfits (especially the RSS and the VHP) changes significantly slower than in the BJP. This serves to conceal changes which are already taking place at the local level. In the long term, however, these changes at the local level can be expected to exert a significant influence on the positioning of the larger movement vis-à-vis the BJP. In this regard, the RSS is much more likely to adapt to socio-economic changes in the way the BJP has been doing so in the last decades than the VHP, since its preoccupation with criteria for membership in the national community over a broadened nationalist discourse is far less pronounced. The penchant for adherence to directions issued from the leadership, party discipline, facilitates cohesion, though it can work in both ways regarding the shift in the direction of the policies preferred by the BJP.

The institutionalisation of the BJP as a major force in Indian politics goes hand in hand with a tendency to adapt to the typical style of functioning of Indian political parties. This may include an increased likelihood of party functionaries engaging in 'corrupt' and 'decadent' practices – at least in the view of the *Sangh Parivar's* custodians of ethical behaviour. The greater danger to the party's electoral prospects, however, is constituted by an increased opening to the centrifugal forces of India's state-centric party system. The RSS national leadership in one important respect functions very similar vis-à-vis the BJP than the so-called High Command in the Congress and the Politbureau for the communist parties: It helps to keep these centrifugal forces in check and protects these parties against a dispersion into often competing regional and sub-regional political parties, as happened to the centre-left spectrum of Indian politics.

The combination of a gradual loss of the party's movement character and a loss of party discipline in the wake of the institutionalisation of the BJP can be expected to increase the likelihood of disintegrating tendencies significantly. A contrary factor, enhancing cohesion, is constituted by two trends among the socio-economic development of the party's core constituency: (1) The turn towards free market orientation and the consequent demand for the dismantling of the state's interventionist structure in the economic sectors which provide much of the aspired-for employment opportunities for these social strata diminishes both the incentives and the possibilities to engage in rent allocation for electoral mobilisation, especially regarding the party's core constituency. (2) Increased mobility and the development of pan-Indian group identity among the new middle class segments, based on class criteria more than on community, is likely to increase the tendency to prefer national parties over regional ones.

In contrast, the strategic incentives for individual political leaders or groups within the leadership affecting party cohesion are likely to become more and more balanced with respect to their effects. Splitting away from the BJP may have the advantage of increasing the potential for alliance formation. The cleavage of secular versus Hindu nationalism in India has evolved in a way in which a politician severing his or her association with the BJP becomes almost immediately acceptable to secular nationalist political parties, however strong the politician's own commitment to Hindu nationalist ideology is. In contrast, the benefits of remaining attached to one of the currently two political parties which have at least a semblance of a comprehensive pan-Indian influence may outweigh the advantages of greater acceptability among secular nationalist parties. As a party with a national presence, the BJP is most likely to remain one of the major players in government formation at the centre and, at least historically, centrifugal forces have plagued its main rival, the Congress, to a much greater extent than the BJP.

Concerning its influence on Indian politics, the BJP has currently reached a plateau. Its rapid expansion in terms of electoral support in the late 1980s and early 1990s turned the party into a significant representative of middle class interests and a major political force in India. In the late 1990s, the BJP exploited the inherent potential of alliance formation to increase its seat share in parliament further. After 1999, however, the party was by and large unable to increase its appeal among the Indian electorate significantly. In the long-term, the socio-economic transformation of a large part of the Indian population, especially the growth of new middle class segments, promises a further augmentation of the party's electoral appeal, at least as long as it can overcome the current and prospective challenges to the turn towards moderation. The growth of the party's core constituency, at the same time, provides no immediate gains in terms of vote shares or seat numbers in parliament. With the new middle class segments becoming more and more influential in Indian politics, there is also a likelihood that other political parties will increasingly vie for their support. The inability of the BJP, at least so far, to emerge as a viable political alternative in several key states of India is likely to reinforce this tendency.

The prospects of the BJP emerging as a moderate, centre-right political party remain tied to the interaction of three distinct, if partially overlapping dynamics: (1) the dynamic of political pragmatism which reinforces the tendency to adapt to the institutional compulsions of Indian politics; (2) the discursive dynamic inherent in the Hindu nationalist conception of cultural identity which can – due to the relative vagueness of its underlying notions of national identity – serve as an ideological framework in which political moderation is proceeding but is equally likely to function as a major obstacle in this process; and (3) socio-economic changes and the resulting dynamic of political economy which have an immense potential of stabilising the turn towards moderation.

Following the relatively rapid succession of decisions of the BJP leadership to turn towards the promotion of, first, a radical agenda, and subsequently the initiation of the turn towards moderation, Basu argued that the evolution of the BJP followed a cyclical trend. The argument was based to a large extent on the conflicting dynamics of electoral compulsions and institutional pressures or political pragmatism, on the one hand, and the internal discourse within the party and the larger movement which had the inherent potential to periodically force the party to shift towards hard line stances, on the other (Basu 2001).[3] In contrast, the present work highlights the effects of socio-economic developments which enhanced the probability of the establishment of a path-dependent trend towards increasing moderation, despite the presence of several important obstacles which may lead to temporary setbacks. Even path-dependent processes can collapse but, being based on large-scale socio-economic developments, their stability is far less threatened by political factors than institutional and discursive dynamics.

The BJP has been depicted here as a political organisation which has an exemplary character for the evolution of a specific segment of New Cultural Identitarian Political Movements, even outside the spectrum of Hindu nationalism. In fact, the specific cultural contents of the respective ideological origins of these movements appear to be relatively insignificant as an explanatory variable for their development. While these factors define the way in which political aims are expressed in the public and internal discourse and influence the emergence of specific issues, the overall development of the respective NCIPM depends largely on other factors, most notably arising out of political economy.

The economic context under which the BJP is operating in India, and which to a significant extent explains its rise and the establishment of its turn towards political moderation, is largely characterised by sustained rent scarcity in a polity previously strongly associated with rent allocation processes. Rent scarcity in combination with institutional avenues for the meaningful participation of rising lower middle class and lower class social strata led to a process in which the previously dominant groups were gradually losing their control over rent allocation. The moderate success of Indian development policy formed the basis for the shift of middle class segments towards employment in comparatively highly paid economic sectors in which employment opportunities were removed from political contest through liberalisation policies. While rent allocation processes remain highly relevant in India for lower class groups and some segments of the middle classes, the possibility of maintaining and enhancing social status by focussing on employment in these liberalised economic sectors served to difuse social and political tensions. In essence, middle class strata were not exclusively dependent on control over the rent allocation process for maintenance of their social status and economic welfare and could, accordingly, adapt to the increasing political assertion of numerically larger competing groups.

The BJP as the most important Indian NCIPM was able to emerge as one of the main forces representing social strata shifting towards private sector employment, an amalgamation of rising and established middle and lower middle classes which form the basis for the emergence of a new middle class, in many respects distinct from the old middle class groups. In emerging as an important middle class representative, the BJP benefited from the association of the traditionally dominant secular nationalist political forces in India with rent-seeking and rent allocation. It had the advantage of a general if, at the same time, vague preference for free market economic policies, and an ideological discourse which especially because of its general vagueness remained open to pragmatic adjustments. Apart from the shift in policy preferences towards liberalisation, the BJP was able to accommodate select strata which continued to strive for increased participation in the rent allocation process, and to pragmatically switch between the articulations of diverse interests. The cultural identitarian focus of its ideology supplemented this pragmatism in economic policy in that it served as a discursive basis for the integration of diverse strata into a common political project.

The increasing dependence for political success on the representation of its core constituency's sectional interests formed the defining factor in determining the balance of power between 'radicals' and 'moderates' in that it forced those groups not strongly associated with either of the two wings to accept the increased prominence of the party's economic agenda. In this way, despite occasional setbacks and an increased contest over the turn towards moderation within the party, path-dependency in the shift from a right-wing to a centre-right wing political party was gradually established. Path-dependency does not constitute a comprehensive assurance against renewed emphasis on the party's radical agenda but, without major changes in the political and economic context the BJP is operating in, it diminishes the likelihood of significant setbacks, as opposed to occasional ones which do not affect the general trend.

Within these parameters which effectively remain based on India's political economy, discursive factors are relevant to explain the detailed evolution of the party's turn towards moderation and the contest over it. In essence, as the 'radicals' do not offer politically viable policy alternatives, their position within the discourse of the party is constricted from the outset to highlighting the traditional stances of the BJP vis-à-vis specific issues. This forces the 'moderate' group to formulate their policy approaches within the ideological framework of Hindu nationalism and in this way prevents radical reformulations of the party's ideological heritage. Apart from the fact that the 'moderates' – since they originate from the same political spectrum – cannot be expected to deviate radically from this ideological discourse anyway, the positioning of the 'radicals' actually helps to enforce party cohesion. The turn towards moderation may be slower this way, but the process of moderation is, in the end, strengthened since the party in a gradual process of moderation is more capable of carrying along sections which still possess significant influence.

The most important comparative advantage of the 'radicals' vis-à-vis the internal discursive process is constituted by their ability to employ violent means. Violence may actually help the BJP in specific circumstances to increase its electoral appeal, but it serves to limit the capacity of the party to form alliances and, hence, constricts its potential to form governments. Given the lack of external influence on Indian politics, militancy cannot form a durable policy alternative as it does in the case of some Islamist movements. In this way, campaigns targeting the predefined 'outgroup' of the Hindu nationalist movement, mostly the Muslim population of India, have a certain value for the party in increasing its popular appeal, but cannot be sustained for a longer period of time.

In essence, the discursive framework in which the turn towards moderation is taking place shows that the capacity of the BJP hard liners to challenge the general direction of party policy preferences remains limited as long as the context in which the party is operating is defined largely as outlined above. The turn towards moderation can partially be explained by a discursive process originating from a conflict over interpretations of Hindu nationalist ideology. Yet, it is not possible to dissect this discursive process from its contextual parameters which originate from the evolution of India's political economy. The latter remains the defining principle of the development of the BJP after the late 1980s.

Apart from discursive processes, other factors are of considerable importance for explaining the success of the *Bharatiya Janata Party's* turn towards moderation. These form a part of the analytical framework in which this development has to be analysed, though they remain secondary to the factors of political economy. Their presence alone – without the developments which led to the emergence of the BJP as a representative of new middle class segments specifically interested in partially dismantling the state interventionist structure of the

Indian polity concerning India's economy – remains comprehensively insufficient to explain the establishment of a path-dependent turn towards moderation, or even the emergence of the BJP as a viable political alternative in India. The most important of these secondary factors, in the case of India, are the general strategic preference of the political elite for accommodation and the lack of significant external actors which would complicate the overall situation even though their presence, at least in some cases, can also conceivably lead to a reinforcement of the process of moderation.

The analysis of the *Bharatiya Janata Party* as an exemplary model for the development of New Cultural Identitarian Political Movements illustrates the conditions under which previously radical and in their cultural identitarian orientation divisive political forces can gradually, but in a relatively stable, path-dependent way emerge as increasingly moderate, centre-right political parties. The basic framework for this development in societies where NCIPM play a significant role is provided by factors of political economy: sustained rent scarcity and at least moderately successful development policies which enable middle class segments to shift away from rent allocation processes once these become contested to significant degree by rising social strata.

This strategic shift of middle class segments from a focus on dominating rent allocation to increased emphasis on the selective dismantling of the state's interventionist capacities in the economy enables NCIPM to emerge as significant representatives of middle class interests. Increased reliance on middle class support results in the commencement of a process of dependence on sectional interests, typically economic in character. The cultural identitarian aims of the organisation are not relinquished. In fact, they continue to play an important role in that they provide a framework in which diverging sectional interests can partially be transcended, at least at the discursive level but also, especially in less centralised political systems, with regard to policy and political strategy. Instead of being relinquished, the cultural identitarian aims increasingly have to be formulated in a way which serves to buttress this role. While this does not necessarily lead to a shift away from radical interpretations of the cultural identitarian agenda, it contributes to enhanced flexibility and increasingly pragmatic adaptations to changing political contexts. The turn towards moderation and integration, however, remains largely driven by the increasing prominence accorded to economic policy and, therefore, sectional economic interests.

The predominance of factors of political economy as opposed to cultural or political and institutional factors can be shown by a comparison of the Indian case with the cases of Turkey and Algeria. In itself, the cross-cultural development of cultural identitarian movements including both Islamist and Hindu nationalist political organisations serves to illustrate the relatively low impact of specific ideological persuasions among NCIPM on their development as political forces. In terms of political economy, Turkey is much closer to India than Algeria in that rent scarcity has been sustained and economic development had been sufficient to enable middle class segments to shift towards a private sector orientation in both cases.

The major secondary factors which affected the development of the BJP in India – the strategic preference of the Indian elite for accommodation and the low level of external influence on Indian politics – however, are present in Turkey with regard to the evolution of the *Adalet ve Kalkinma Partisi* (AKP) in reverse: While Islamist political forces were represented in government in Turkey at various times in the second half of the twentieth century, real political power continued to rest with the Kemalist elite, including the Turkish military. The strategic preferences of the Turkish political elite cannot be characterised as accommodation, but rather as co-optation, with periodic intervals in which the Kemalist elite attempted to exclude Islamist political forces from being viable contenders for political power. Instead, external factors – the desire of the Turkish state to join the European Union – possessed a large impact on the evolution of the AKP. External influence protected the AKP from exclusion from the political system and enhanced the incentives for the AKP leadership to turn towards political moderation. While the secondary factors had an impact on the evolution of both political organisations, the contextual framework which enabled both the BJP and the AKP to emerge as viable contenders for political power and to establish a relatively stable turn towards moderation were set by the development of the two countries' political economies.

The case of the Algerian Islamist political spectrum, in contrast, was defined by conjuncturally dependent rent scarcity or sufficiency and a level of private sector development which remained insufficient to support a shift away from rent allocation by politically influential middle class segments. In this case, temporary rent scarcity resulted in increased radicalism, while temporary rent sufficiency enabled the Islamist political spectrum to turn towards moderation, though only by striving for co-optation. The desire for co-optation, based on temporary rent sufficiency, constitutes an obstacle for the stability of the turn towards moderation. In the case of Algeria, secondary factors play a relatively insignificant role in comparison with India and Turkey. The political economy remains strongly linked to the rentier character of the Algerian state. External factors like the presence of militant Islamist movements, the Israel–Palestine conflict, or the neighbourhood initiatives of the European Union may influence the positioning of the Islamist political spectrum in Algeria, but the latter's evolution as well as the political elite's behaviour towards it remains strongly linked with the conjunctural fluctuation of rents available for allocation.

One of the main objectives of this work was to depict the way in which political economy influences the development of political movements, even if these ostentatiously concern themselves with non-economic issues, in this case cultural identity. The analysis of the BJP has illustrated the predominance of economic factors both in the rise and the subsequent political moderation of the party, although the detailed processes of India's gradual shift away from a system of politics dominated to a significant extent by rent-seeking certainly merit much more elaborate further studies. The more this shift is becoming established, the more other factors are likely to emerge which may constrict the impact of the defining factors, as outlined above, on the evolution of the BJP and

Indian political actors in general. Additionally, the secondary factors which influence the evolution of NCIPM can only partially be analysed with reference to the BJP and the impact of sustained rent sufficiency on the development of NCIPM cannot be identified with reference to India as a case study at all.

Further comparison between various movements classified here as NCIPM and the different contexts they are operating in offers a promising area of research in order to augment our knowledge about the precise interplay of these factors as well as between these factors and those causes arising from political economy. The dynamic of this interaction determines the future evolution of political actors which already considerably impact the global order and can be expected to continue to do so in the future. For the Islamist political spectrum, various studies have already highlighted the, at times, isomorphous development of these actors across a variety of political contexts. The restriction of analyses to one culturally defined area, even large and composite areas like the Arab or the Muslim world, neglects the defining character of political economy for these developments. Studies on Islamist and Hindu nationalist movements or on cultural identitarian movements in developing societies in general can gain substantially from a perspective of cross-cultural comparison. For the time being, however, it can certainly be stated that the emergence of new middle class segments in a number of developing countries and the rise and moderation of NCIPM – in the words of Seshadri Chari cited in Chapter 7 – 'seem to be correlated.'

Notes

1 Introduction

1 On the rise and political moderation of Islamist organisations in Algeria: Ouaissa (2008).

2 The theoretical framework: the concept of new cultural identitarian political movements (NCIPM)

1 Hindu nationalism has been interpreted as a sub-type of fundamentalism by some authors (Embree 1994; Gold 1991), but is generally treated as a distinct political ideology in academic literature. There are two main clusters of arguments: (1) the large differences in religious and cultural traditions and the textual basis of these between Hinduism and the Semitic religions, and (2) the focus of Hindu nationalism on community identity, especially Indian nationality, otherwise disregarding religion almost entirely. The first argument is based primarily on the observation that Hinduism, unlike the Semitic religions, lacks a cohesive foundational scripture and a consensus on the significance and correctness with regard to the inclusion of the various scriptures of Hinduism in a comprehensive and unified textual corpus. Hinduism as a religion is, hence, perceived as lacking the very fundamentals that fundamentalism is supposed to propagate. The focus of Hindu nationalism on community identity is a common feature of many movements which are often characterised as fundamentalist in the literature. Community identity, as an example, is and has been a prominent feature of Islamist discourse, especially in South Asia, as can be seen in the importance attributed to the issue in the evolution of the Jama'at-e-Islami (JI), both in its formative years and with regard to the Pakistani section of the movement for much of its existence: Nasr (1994; 2001); Cohen (2005), Grare (2001); Pleshov (2004). Further on political Islam in Pakistan: Zaman (2004); Pirzada (2000); Ahmad (1991).

2 While the BJP cannot comprehensively be interpreted as a fascist organisation (Vanaik 1997: 317), it is occasionally interpreted to comprise fascist elements, which might gain control of the party, especially if the party would manage to come to power on its own strength. Other authors have dealt in detail with the BJP's and Hindu nationalism's origin and its early leaders' positions vis-à-vis fascism. These include among others Zavos (2000); Jha (2000); and Graham (1990). Many authors have highlighted the dangers of Hindu nationalism both as a political theory and in political practice, in some cases as part of the respective authors' concerns as political activists. This is exemplified by Noorani (2001). Scholarly concerns about the BJP also arise from the well documented Hindu nationalist involvement in communal violence in India. Several authors that have studied communal violence in India have highlighted the BJP's role in fomenting violence for political reasons. Notable publications in this regard include Brass (1997; 2003), Varshney (2002), Wilkinson (2004;

2005a; 2005b), Engineer (2004), Vanaik (1997); Shani (2007); McGuire *et al.* (1996); Kakar (1995); Akbar (1988).

3 Among the outstanding works in this regard have been the publications of the Chicago Fundamentalism Project, including Marty and Appleby (1991; 1994; 1996).

4 A noteworthy exception in this regard is the Iranian revolution of 1979, and the subsequent establishment of a fundamentalist state which is dominated to a significant extent by religious officials, instead of lay followers (Hoffman 1995: 201). Most Islamist groups, however, follow the model set by the two most influential early Islamist organisations, the Muslim Brotherhood in Egypt and the Jama'at-i-Islami in India and Pakistan, both of which included religious scholars, but chose its leadership according to political, instead of religious merit: Nasr (1994; 2001), Pleshov (2004), and Grare (2001) on the Jama'at-i-Islami and Carré and Michaud (1983), Mitchell (1969), and Lübben (2008) on the Muslim Brotherhood in Egypt. The predominance of politics over religion for the political leadership has been even more pronounced in case of the Hindu nationalist movement, even with regard to the more religiously inclined organisations within the Sangh Parivar, exemplified by the Vishwa Hindu Parishad (Katju 2003; T. Basu 1993).

5 With regard to the South Asian context, these schisms include differences between the more spiritual or mystical interpretations of the main religious doctrines in the region (Hinduism and Islam), for example certain strands of Bhakti and Sufism, and the more conventional schools of Islamic and Hindu thought. With regard to South Asian Islam, several authors have noted the increased inclination of followers of the Deobandi school to support fundamentalist organisations as compared to followers of the Barelvi school, including Metcalf (2004). Similar differences between priests belonging to different religious traditions are of importance with regard to attempts by the Vishwa Hindu Parishad and affiliated bodies to unify Hindu priesthood politically, under its leadership, and the resistance to these moves.

6 In Gandhian political ideology, moral righteousness takes a central, if not the most important role in determining the aims of political action, thus providing a moral super-structure to socio-economic development that resembles that provided by various fundamentalist movements. Gandhian approaches to modernisation show an awareness of problems arising out of modernity that is in many ways remarkably similar to fundamentalist thought, while the Gandhian insistence on religious inclusion and tolerance certainly sets the two schools of thought apart. For a detailed discussion of Gandhian political thought, especially regarding its socio-economic contents: Srinivasa (1971); Kaushik (2001).

7 In much of the Muslim world, for example, conceptions of nationality are contested between 'nationalists,' i.e. proponents of the central role of the nation-state, and the concept of an Islamic nation, the *'umma*. On this topic: Sheikh (2003); Keddie (1969). In Arab countries, pan-Arabism comprises a third alternative of nationality. These conceptions of national identity often overlap in political practice, at least to some extent (Farah 1987). A similar co-existence of alternative conceptions of nationality has played a significant role in the evolution of the Pakistani state. Here, alternative models include the conception of Pakistan as the representative and homeland of South Asian Muslims, apart from the existing nation-state of Pakistan, and Islamic solidarity (Cohen 2005; Khan 2005).

8 For a comprehensive discussion of the Indian debate on secularism: Srinivasan (2007); Bhargava (1998); Madan (1997).

9 Hindu nationalism should, in fact, be interpreted as an attempt to redefine Hindu identity above divisive elements such as sect and caste, although especially the latter remains highly relevant in political practice, if not ideological thought. For a discussion on the brahminical origins of Hindu nationalism and the role of upper castes in contemporary Hindu nationalism, especially in the *Sangh Parivar* variety: Jaffrelot (1996), Zavos (2000).

10 This is notable in the attempt to expand the concept of fundamentalism to cover areas outside the spectrum of religiously/culturally defined movements, exemplified by Schick *et al.* (2006).

11 It is interesting here to note the conceptual distinction of acts of violence by 'normal' fundamentalist groups and groups associated with Al Qaeda as made by Devji (2005). According to him, acts of violence by fundamentalist groups (and others) form part of rational politics in that they have rational motives. Al Qaeda-style acts of violence are distinct in that they do not fit into the normal patterns of political behaviour.

12 As an example, Wiktorowicz (2004) uses the theoretical approach of New Social Movements to explain the rise and evolution of Islamist movements. Due to the approach's characteristics, it is applicable without being restricted to one cultural context, but the focus on a specific area prevents the extension of the analysis to non-Islamist movements.

13 Further on Islamist political movements and democracy: Cofman Wittes (2008).

14 Chapter 3 provides an outline of this process in the Indian case.

15 On NCIPM in Algeria: Ouaissa (2008).

16 A large body of literature exists on many of the various, typically Islamist movements classified here as NCIPM, a selection of which is listed below: On the spectrum of political Islam in Turkey: Groc (2003). On political parties in Turkey in general: Schüler (1998). On earlier Islamist political parties in Turkey, especially the *Refah* Party and including a comparison with the BJP: Dutt and Girdner (2000). On the PJD in Morocco: Wegner (2004); Himeur (2008). The by and large moderate character of the economic agendas of Islamist parties with special reference to the Egyptian Muslim Brotherhood has been shown by Müller (2002). On the Al-Wasat in Egypt: Lübben (2008). On the Islamic Action Front (IAF) in Jordan: Clarke (2004). On the Islamist spectrum in Pakistan: Pleshov (2004). On the PAS in Malaysia: Farouk (2005). On the PKS in Indonesia: Kandale (2008); Fuad (2003).

17 On Hamas in the Palestinian territories: Gunning (2007).

18 Epstein and Gang (2004) have noted in their application of economic theory on the subject of fundamentalist political behaviour that rivalry among fundamentalist groups tends to increase their radicality.

19 The term license-permit-raj, the rule of licenses and permits, signifies the means and the impact of state intervention into the Indian private sector. In essence, the Indian state after independence implemented a system under which private economic activity could indirectly be controlled by local bureaucrats whose permission was necessary to engage in a broad range of economic activities. The license-permit-raj enabled politicians and bureaucrats to generate rents from free market economic activity and, at the same time, engage in preferential treatment to political supporters. On this, among others: Frankel 2005.

20 With regard to India, this process has been analysed in detail by a number of authors including Rudolph and Rudolph (1987); Frankel and Rao (1989; 1990); Kothari (1970a); Srinivas (1962); and Yadav (2000).

3 Context: politics in India

1 For a detailed analysis of the transformation in the legal framework during the early colonial period, compare, for example, Pruthi (2004). Concise overviews on British colonial policies are provided, among others, by Stein (1998) and Kulke and Rothermund (1998).

2 A large body of literature on the uprising in 1857 exists which need not be listed here comprehensively. For a detailed study: Pati (2008).

3 An overview on socio-religious reform movements in late nineteenth century India is provided by Jones (1989).

4 For studies on the transformation of the agrarian order under colonial rule among others: Rothermund (1978); Ludden (1999); Bose (1993).

5 For a comprehensive study on the Muslim League in British India cf. Malik (1997).

6 On the role of the Indian federal polity in the process of nation-building in India: Dasgupta (2001).

7 Brass (1965) has provided a detailed analysis of the role of factionalism and clientelism in the functioning of the Indian National Congress after Indian independence.

8 For an analysis of the different possible approaches to classify Indian political parties and the Indian party system: Sridharan (1997; 2002); (Hasan 2002b). Further: Schwecke (2007).

9 On the evolution of the Dravidian parties in Tamil Nadu: Subramanian (2002); Widlund (2000).

10 On Dalit political parties: Jaffrelot (2003); Pai (2002b).

11 On the land reforms in India: Varshney (1995: 28–47).

12 On Indira Gandhi and the development of the Congress party: Kochanek (2002).

13 Rutten (2003) has noted the extent to which agriculture in parts of India has moved towards capitalist modes of production as well as the spread of capitalist patterns of behaviour among the rural and semi-urban middle strata in his case study on Gujarat.

14 On the Green Revolution: Frankel (1971).

15 On the role of the Janata Party in the reorganisation of the Indian party system: Dasgupta (2002).

16 On the Khalistan movement, Sikh secessionism, and the Akali Dal: Malik (1986); A. Kumar (2004); Judge (2004).

17 The anti-Sikh violence in Delhi in 1984 has been analysed (among others) by Das (2005).

18 On the commencement of economic liberalisation in India, including the role of Rajiv Gandhi: Jenkins (1999); Sengupta (2008).

19 On the Bharatiya Kisan Union, one of the major farmer organisations in India, cf. among others Gupta (1997); Varshney (1995).

20 On OBC politics, among others: Hasan (1998); Chhibber (1999); Jaffrelot (2000).

21 On the constitutional stipulations for positive discrimination regimes and the debate on OBC reservations: Sheth (1998); Chatterji (1998); Weiner (2001). On the effects of OBC reservations: Gang *et al.* (2008).

22 On INC policies towards Muslim Personal Law, the Shah Bano Case and the reactions to these policies among others: M. Hasan (1998).

23 On corruption in India in general among others: Ghosh (1999).

24 The linkage between the decision to implement the recommendations of the Mandal Commission Report and the BJP decision to participate in the Ayodhya campaign has been studied in detail by several authors, among them Z. Hasan (1998: 121–233); Chhibber (1999: 159–76); Basu (1996).

25 On the 'social engineering' strategy of the BJP and Sangh Parivar: Jaffrelot (1996; 1998a).

26 On the decline in relevance of Mandal politics even in the Hindi heartland during the 1990s: Jaffrelot and Zérinini-Brotel (2004). The shift towards liberalisation in the early 1990s is studied in great detail by Jenkins (1999) among others.

27 The shift towards moderation by the BJP is analysed among others by Basu (2001); Jaffrelot (2005a).

28 On the interpretation of these concepts by Elsenhans: Elsenhans (1992; 1996; 1997; 2001).

29 The concepts of rentier economies, rent allocation and rent-seeking are rarely discussed among authors who focus on India. Among the exceptions: Srivastava *et al.* (2002); Chhibber (1996).

30 On the Algerian example of centralised rent allocation and the corresponding differences in the structure of the Algerian state class compared to the Indian case as outlined in this work: Ouaissa (2005).

31 Related to this: Stern (2001).
32 Fuller and Harris (2000: 25) note that organised group demands especially at the local level significantly affect bureaucratic procedures.
33 Among others, Jeffrey and Lerche (2000) have noted that elections in India, especially when studied at the local level, can largely be seen as a contest over access to the state and, accordingly, the resources controlled by it. Chandra (2004) terms Indian democracy as a 'patronage-democracy' and Indian elections as 'auctions.' Bhattacharyya (2009) depicts a similar process in his study on the 'party-society' in rural West Bengal. Further: Pai (2000b); Mitra (2001). On class- instead of caste-based clientelist politics in West Bengal: Bardhan *et al.* (2009).
34 On the local character of caste in Indian politics: Gupta (2000: 148–97).
35 The terms dominant and entrenched castes refer to concepts by Srinivas (1962) and Kothari (1970a), respectively. The former characterises the numerically large and landholding upper and intermediate castes, while the latter differs in that large size is not necessarily seen as one of the necessary prerequisites for locally powerful castes.
36 While this challenge may initially be radical, Chandra notes the tendency of initially radical opposition in India to moderate their positions and become centrist parties. In his words, this constitutes the 'centrist equilibrium of Indian politics' (Chandra 2005: 238).
37 Kumar (2004) notes that there is a lack of awareness on the effects of economic reforms on the general public, i.e. especially those social strata which do not benefit from liberalisation. This indicates a separation of economic policy into two distinct blocks, one targeting the new middle classes, the other the 'common man.' In contrast, Bardhan (2005) notes that economic reforms have become increasingly unpopular among the electorate.
38 Upadhya (2007) has shown how even in recent years the lower and lower middle classes have been excluded to a large degree from gaining employment in the Indian IT industry, despite the expansion of educational institutions to the Indian hinterland, by a corresponding shift in emphasis on the criteria for gaining employment. In summary, the more lower and lower middle class graduates have been able to gain formal educational qualifications, the more the criteria for gaining employment have tended to include 'soft skills,' including communication skills. This tendency underlines the role of the idiom of 'merit' as an instrument of exclusion.
39 Chhibber and Eldersveld (2000) note that support for economic liberalisation policies among local political elites in India is still significantly lower than in China.
40 The importance of middle class votes for the Congress and the BJP has been noted by several authors, among others: Mitra and Singh (1999).
41 The relative lack of open appeals to class-based interests in Indian politics finds its expression in the decline of class analysis in political science on India (Chibber 2006).
42 On middle class political preferences: Z. Hasan (2001); Palshikar (2001).
43 On the reconfiguration of the Indian party system: Arora (2002); Sridharan (2002).

4 Ideology and political practice of Hindu nationalism

1 On the influence of social reform movements on the evolution of Indian nationalism: Heimsath (1964).
2 Frykenberg (1993: 539) has noted the significant role of British colonialism in 'constructing' the modern conception of Hinduism. Further: Froystad (2005). According to Thapar (1989: 222) identity in India was traditionally segmented, social reform movements partially aimed at modernising Indian society by overcoming this segmentation.
3 On the development of Indian secularism both as an ideological construct and in political practice cf. among others Smith (1998); Galanter (1998); Bhargava (1995; 2007);

Chatterjee (1998); Tarkunde (1995); Madan (1997). On critical interpretations of secularism in India among others: Nandy (1995; 1998; 2003); Madan (1998). On the various criticisms of Indian secularism: Sen (1998). A concise historical analysis of secularisation in Indian society is provided by Thapar (2007).

4 Cf. Gould (2002); further Gould (2004); Sarkar (2006) on the late colonial period, Bhagavan (2008) on the period immediately after independence.

5 According to Brass (2000), fear of disorder formed one of the major incentives for the incorporation of a strong role for the state into the Indian constitution, and was widely shared among Indian politicians at the time.

6 Gooptu (1997) stresses the argument that increased urban middle class/upper caste recourse to political Hinduism resulted in a redefinition of shudra caste self-perception as martial Hindu castes which despite their role in combating Muslim political organisation remained subordinate to the upper castes due to the latter's dominance in the local politico-religious context.

7 This is exemplified by the RSS which did not have a written constitution prior to independence when it forced by the Indian state to evolve one. The RSS constitution is evidently modelled on the constitution of the Indian National Congress (Embree 1994: 625).

8 On the role of leaders with soft hindutva leanings in the INC immediately after independence: Gould (2002); Bhagavan (2008). Recent inductions of influential political leaders from the Hindu nationalist political spectrum include Shankersinh Vaghela in Gujarat and Narayan Rane in Maharashtra. Among the non-Congress secular parties this trend is exemplified by the induction of Chhagan Bhujbal into the Nationalist Congress Party (NCP) or the recent 'friendly relationship' between Kalyan Singh and the Samajwadi Party (SP) leadership.

9 A recent example for this is provided by the AIADMK's reaction to the Sethu Samudram project, which includes the broadening and deepening of shipping corridors between India and Sri Lanka, but is perceived by many Hindus to afflict Hindu religious sentiments due to the region's role in the *Ramayana*.

10 On the political thought of the leading Hindu nationalist ideologues: Kuruvachira (2006).

11 *Sarsanghchalak* (supreme organisational leader) is the title of the head of the *Rashtriya Swayamsevak Sangh*, who is elected for lifetime.

12 Excerpt from the second lecture of Deendayal Upadhyaya, introducing the concept of integral humanism, held in Bombay on 23 April 1965, as cited on the BJP homepage (www.bjp.org/philo.htm).

13 Excerpt from the second lecture of Deendayal Upadhyaya, introducing the concept of integral humanism, held in Bombay on 24 April 1965, as cited on the BJP homepage (www.bjp.org/philo.htm).

14 Lecture by Deendayal Upadhyaya, introducing the concept of integral humanism, held in Bombay on 25 April 1965, as cited on the BJP homepage (www.bjp.org/philo. htm).

15 Source: Election Commission of India. Key Highlights of General Elections, 1951, to the
First Lok Sabha. (www.eci.gov.in/SR_KeyHighLights/LS_1951/VOL_1_51_LS. PDF).

16 Further on the RSS leadership: Kanungo (2002).

17 RSS influence on educational institutions has been shown at the local level in Aligarh by Brass (2003). On the importance of education for the Hindu nationalist movement: Kumar (1996).

18 For a discussion of the RSS influence on the Bharatiya Jan Sangh: Graham (2005).

19 A relatively large body of literature exists on the VHP, a selection of which is listed below: On the VHP positioning towards modernity: Van der Veer (1994). On the problematic of conversions in India: Claerhout and Roover (2005). On the VHP

networks among Non-Resident Indians (NRI): Katju (2005a). On the VHP's support among lower caste and tribal communities aiming to escape social discrimination: Katju (2003: 127; Jaffrelot 1996: 193). On the VHP network among religious persons – sadhus, sants, mahants and acharyas: Katju 2003 (68–74). On the Gujarat pogrom, including the role of the VHP in it: Varadarajan (2002a).

20 On the Bajrang Dal's role in conducting violent campaigns among others: Katju (2005b).
21 On the BMS: Saxena (2005); Jaffrelot (2005b).
22 On the SJM: Boutron (2005).
23 For a detailed analysis of the Bharatiya Jan Sangh: Graham (1990); further Graham (2005) on the party organisation.
24 On the Swatantra Party: Erdman (1967); Sharma (1979).
25 This argument is exemplified by the excerpt of an interview with J. P. Mathur, one of the founding leaders of the BJP, conducted on 7 March 2007, provided in Chapter 5.
26 On the political and socio-economic ideology developed by Jayaprakash Narayan: Gupta 1997; Grover (1991).
27 N. Ram. 'From Nuclear Adventurism to Appeasement,' *Frontline* 15 (12), 1998.
28 For examples of the debate on the Hindu nationalist agenda on school curricula cf. Delhi Historians' Group (2001). Generally on education policy under the NDA government: Lall (2005). For a more general, highly critical study on the educational agenda of Hindu nationalism cf. Nanda (2003; 2004).
29 For an example of highly critical media reportage on these attempts: 'Sushma as "Bharat Didi",' *The Tribune* (Internet Edition), 28 February 2001, www.tribuneindia. com/2001/20010228/edit.htm#3.
30 Further on this topic: Mitra and Singh (1999).
31 On corruption scandals during the two NDA governments and their effect on BJP credibility: Singh (2005).
32 A comprehensive study of the role of violence in party competition is provided by Wilkinson (2000; 2004).
33 It has to be noted that the simultaneous BJS emphasis on moral economy and economic nationalism facilitated its alliances with the centre-left political spectrum (Bhatt 2001: 162).
34 On the predominance of liberalisation over economic nationalism in the BJP: Nayar (2000); Lakha (2007).

5 The rise of the BJP

1 Further on the 'anti-capitalist' strands of economic thought within the Hindu nationalist movement: Hansen (2005).
2 Source: Election Commission of India.
3 At the local and regional level there are sharp discrepancies regarding radical and moderate strategies for political growth in the 1980s. Shani (2005) has shown the importance of radical Hindu nationalism in his case study on the rise of Hindu nationalism as a political force in Ahmedabad.
4 BJP election manifesto for the General Elections, 1991.
5 Hasan (1993) notes the large extent of co-operation between the BJP and the *Bharatiya Kisan Union* (BKU), one of the most important representatives of farmer interests in northern India in the late 1980s and early 1990s.
6 On the Mandal Commission and previous commissions to study the issue of OBC reservation: Chatterji (1998).
7 On Congress and Janata Dal politics vis-à-vis the Ayodhya campaign: Parikh (1993).
8 'Advani Regrets Babri Masjid Demolition,' *The Hindu*, 2 June 2005.
9 Rao, Dasu Kesava. 'An Ally's Dilemma,' *Frontline*, 19 (10), 2002.

10　Sukumar Muralidharan. 'Time of Economic Troubles,' *Frontline* 18 (18), 1–14 September 2001.

11　On defections in Indian politics: Kashyap (2003); Spiess and Pehl (2003).

12　V. Venkatesan. 'Who Is In, Who Is Out,' *Frontline* 17 (19), 16–29 September 2000.

13　Venkitesh Ramakrishnan. 'What Price Victory?,' *Frontline* 25 (16), 2–15 August 2008.

14　V. Venkatesan. 'Parties and Funds,' *Frontline* 18 (7), 31 March–13 April 2001.

15　'Now, 'Kargil Coffin' Haunts Govt.,' *The Hindu*, 12 December 2001.

16　'Cash for Questions. 11 MPs Caught on Camera. No One Will Be Spared: Speaker,' *The Tribune*, 13 December 2005.

17　On Article 356 of the Indian constitution cf. Suryaprasad (2001).

18　V. Venkatesan. 'Probes and Questions,' *Frontline* 18 (7), 31 March–13 April 2001.

19　'"India Shining" Advertisement Series Challenged,' *The Hindu*, 14 February 2004.

20　An alternative explanation of the processes often summarised in India under the term anti-incumbency is provided by Chhibber and Nooruddin (2008) where 'anti-incumbency' is explained as being based on the (lack of) fiscal space available to Indian state governments for allocating funds to policy initiatives and, accordingly, not to the maintenance and expansion of the administrative apparatus which would be more indicative of rent allocation.

21　V. Venkatesan. 'Govindacharya's Leave,' *Frontline* 19 (2), 19 January–1 February 2002.

22　Satyendra Sharma is a former president of the BJP local unit in Aligarh city.

23　Mathur (2003) notes that stereotypical images of Muslims as a (hostile) out-group are wide-spread especially among the Indian middle classes, and not restricted to supporters of Hindu nationalism.

24　On the pogrom in Gujarat in 2002: Wilkinson (2005a).

25　'VHP Bid to Hold Meet in Ayodhya Foiled,' *The Hindu*, 18 October 2003; 'Praise for Mulayam Govt.,' *The Hindu*, 19 October 2003.

26　'Govt. Will Act Tough: PM,' *The Hindu*, 2 March 2002.

27　'It's a Black Mark, Says PM,' *The Hindu*, 3 March 2002.

28　Anjali Mody. 'Ahmedabad Quiet, Toll 431,' *The Hindu*, 4 March 2002.

29　'Modi Need Not Quit: Advani,' *The Hindu*, 12 March 2002.

30　Neena Vyas. 'Allies Raise Storm over "Asti Yatra", to Meet Today,' *The Hindu*, 22 March 2002.

31　'Violence Must End: PM,' *The Hindu*, 25 March 2002.

32　'Bill on POTO Passed,' *The Hindu*, 27 March 2002.

33　'Vajpayee Puts Modi on Notice,' *The Hindu*, 28 March 2002.

34　Manas Dasgupta. 'Gujarat Incidents a Blot: PM,' *The Hindu*, 5 April 2002.

35　Neena Vyas. 'BJP to Modi: Don't Quit But Dissolve Assembly,' *The Hindu*, 13 April 2002.

36　Neena Vyas. 'No Need to Be Apologetic: Advani,' *The Hindu*, 14 April 2002.

37　'"I Am More than a Match for You",' *The Hindu*, 15 April 2002.

38　V. Venkatesan. 'Reclaiming Hindutva,' *Frontline*, 19 (9), 2002.

39　'Report of Concerned Citizens Indicts Modi Govt for Riots,' *Times of India* 21 November 2002.

40　Venkitesh Ramakrishnan. 'Battles Within,' *Frontline* 21 (21), 9–22 October 2004.

41　V. Venkatesan. 'The Blame Game in Mumbai,' *Frontline* 21 (14), 3–16 July 2004. Further: Jaffrelot (2005c).

42　B. Muralidhar Reddy. 'A Conscious Effort,' *Frontline* 22 (13), 18 June–1 July 2005.

43　V. Venkatesan. 'Image and Reality,' *Frontline* 22 (13), 18 June–1 July 2005.

44　'Advani's Secretary Sudheendra Kulkarni Quits,' *Indian Express*, 4 July 2005.

45　Venkitesh Ramakrishnan. 'Resistance and Surrender,' *Frontline* 22 (20), 27 September–7 October 2005.

46　The Sethusamudram controversy arose out of an infrastructure development project aiming to enlarge navigable shipping corridors between India and Sri Lanka which was alleged by Hindu nationalists to threaten the existence of islands between the two countries which are revered by Hindus due to their alleged mentioning in the Ramayana.

47 'Muslims Must Have First Claim on Resources,' *Indian Express*, 9 December 2006.

6 The BJP at the regional and at the local level: Uttar Pradesh and Aligarh

1 A comprehensive analysis of politics in Uttar Pradesh is provided by Hasan (1998).
2 Pai (1993: 9) has noted the predominance of agrarian/rural over industrial/urban interests in UP and the corresponding influence on politics by mostly agrarian castes.
3 On the enormous expansion of employment in the Indian administration and the problems arising out of this: Debroy (2009). On the mass transfers within the Indian administration: Banik (2001).
4 Cf. Purnima S. Tripathi. 'Waiting to Strike,' *Frontline* 20 (17), 16–29 August 2003.
5 In the 2009 elections to the *Lok Sabha* the Congress won a surprisingly high number of seats with an equally surprisingly high vote percentage. While this may be interpreted as a sign of Congress recovery, it may just as well have been due to a negative vote against the Congress' rivals in the state. It is certainly not yet possible to predict whether the Congress can revive itself in UP, especially as the party neither has a significant organisation at the local level nor has managed to emerge as the clear first preference of any distinct support base.
6 The BSP is currently classified as a national party by the Election Commission, the SP has so far failed to achieve this status.
7 On the rise and subsequent political moderation of the BJP in Uttar Pradesh: Zérinini-Brotel (1998).
8 Source: Election Commission of India.
9 Source: Election Commission of India.
10 Venkitesh Ramakrishnan. 'Consolidation in Uttar Pradesh,' *Frontline* 16 (22), 23 October–5 November 1999.
11 The following narrative of events until the end of 2002 is based on Schwecke (2003), unless marked otherwise.
12 The term *doab* signifies the region between the confluence of two rivers. In Uttar Pradesh, the term is generally used to signify the region between Yamuna and Ganga.
13 On the demography of Aligarh city in terms of caste and religious community cf. Brass (2003: 43–56).
14 Interview with Vivek Bansal, at the time Congress MLA from Aligarh, 30 January 2007.
15 'Har baar sampradaayiktaa hii haavii rahii cunaav men,' *Dainik Jagran* (Aligarh edition), 8 March 2007.
16 Interview with S. D. Gupta, Faculty of Economics, Shri Varshney College, Aligarh, on the evolution of the local BJP unit (Aligarh, 20 February 2007).
17 On the partial shift of Brahmin votes towards the BSP in the 2007 assembly elections in UP: Verma (2007). While a noticeable shift took place in this election, the BSP in UP never came close to emerge as the principal representative of Brahmins in the state and most Brahmins appear to have preferred the BJP even in 2007. More generally on the BSP attempts to expand its support base: Jaffrelot (1998b).
18 'Don't Get Humiliated, Join Me. Uma to BJP Men,' *The Indian Express*, 7 April 2006.

7 The changing face of the BJP

1 Interview with Radha Sharma, 25 February 2006, Aligarh. All interviews with members of the local BJP unit in Aligarh except for the interviews with Krishna

Kumar Navman, Dr. Shivkumar Sharma and Satyendra Sharma were conducted by the author in Hindi and later translated by the author into English.

2 Prakash Javadekar was the BJP national spokesperson at the time of the interview.

3 Chhibber (1997) notes that the BJP relies substantially on middle class support which, in addition, is not perceived by him to be based on a greater emphasis on religion (or culture.) Middle class preference for the BJP was especially large in the late 1990s, although the party still maintained a similar level of middle class support in the 2004 general elections than the Congress (Fernandes 2006: 181).

4 Vivek Thakur was a national level youth wing leader of the BJP, former vice-president of the BJP youth wing Bihar at time of the interview.

5 Interview with Satyendra Sharma, former president of the local unit of the BJP in Aligarh city, 30 March 2006.

6 Ashutosh Varshney was the mayor of Aligarh city at the time of the interview.

7 Results of a survey conducted in co-operation with the Department of Sociology and Social Work, AMU, among 450 households in three pre-selected localities in Aligarh city.

8 Krishna Kumar Navman is a former MLA.

9 Prof Krishan Sahab Saxena was a local BJP and RSS activist, in Aligarh at the time of the interview.

10 At the same time, it has to be noted that among some hard line Hindu nationalists a perception of betrayal by defectors might not have been present if the defection was rhetorically tied to the turn towards moderation of the BJP.

11 Savitri Varshney, was the mayor of Aligarh at the time of the interview.

12 Satyendra Sharma is former president of the local BJP unit in Aligarh.

13 The interview with Vinay Katiyar was conducted by the author in Hindi and later translated by the author into English.

14 The necessity to formulate economic policy within the bounds of Hindu nationalist ideology and the inherent flexibility of the party in utilising strategies derived from economic nationalism and moral economy when reaching out to social sections apart from the new middle classes also explains why, despite all its commitment, the NDA government failed to move forward on economic reform in a radical way, as stated by Mayer (2007).

15 The Pink Chaddi Campaign in early 2009 involved a protest against the attacks, especially on couples celebrating Valentine's Day, by sending underwear (chaddi) to the headquarters of the Sri Rama Sene which had carried out the attacks.

16 Saba Naqvi. 'It's Good that the Overconfidence in the Party Has Gone' (Interview with L. K. Advani), *Outlook* (Internet edition), 16–23 March 2009. www.outlookin-dia.com/article.aspx?240010 (last accessed, 19 March 2009.)

17 Tambiah (2005: 2) interprets communal violence in India as 'politics by other means.' Certainly, the political character of communal violence in India has to be emphasised. As with all policies and political strategies, however, the utility of violence for political and electoral success is restricted to specific political contexts.

18 For a plea to take party manifestos in India seriously: Yogendra Yadav. 'Why Manifestos Matter,' *The Hindu*, 9 April 2009.

19 P. M. Damodaran. 'Ayodhya Still Core Issue for BJP,' *The Milli Gazette*, 1–15 May 2004.

8 Conclusion: the BJP as a new cultural identitarian political movement

1 Chopra (2006) notes striking similarities in Dalit and Hindu nationalist online discourses, with the former apparently imitating the latter at least partially. In this way, the reach of Hindu nationalism as an alternative concept of identity, driven nowadays by the new middle classes, can expand, although it is becoming increasingly vague itself in the process.

2 Already in 1998, Parvathi noted that BJP membership at the time was much more numerous than membership in the RSS which, in his argumentation, facilitates a gradual de-linkage of the two organisations, since the BJP does not anymore rely on RSS support to the same extent as previously (Parvathi 1998).
3 On the institutional impetus for the moderation of the BJP: Ruparelia (2006).

Bibliography

Abootalebi, Ali Reza (2000) *Islam and Democracy. State–Society Relations in Developing Countries, 1980–94*, New York: Garland Publishing.

Adeney, Katharine and Saez, Lawrence (ed.) (2005) *Coalition Politics and Hindu Nationalism*, London: RoutledgeCurzon.

Ades, Alberto and Di Tella, Rafael (2005) 'Rents, Competition, and Corruption,' in Ajit Mishra (ed.) *The Economics of Corruption*, New Delhi: Oxford University Press, 270–90.

Ahmad, Imtiaz and Reifeld, Helmut (ed.) (2001) *Middle Class Values in India and Western Europe*, New Delhi: Social Science Press.

Ahmad, Mumtaz (1991) 'Islamic Fundamentalism in South Asia. The Jamaat-i-Islami and the Tablighi Jamaat of South Asia,' in Martin E. Marty and R. Scott Appleby (ed.) *Fundamentalisms Observed*, Chicago: Chicago University Press, 457–530.

Akbar, Mobashar Jawed (1988) *Riot after Riot. Reports on Caste and Communal Violence in India*, New Delhi: Penguin.

Albrecht, Holger (ed.) (2008) *Politischer Islam im Vorderen Orient. Zwischen Sozialbewegung, Opposition und Widerstand*, Baden-Baden: Nomos.

Alter, Joseph S. (1994) 'Somatic Nationalism. Indian Wrestling and Militant Hinduism,' *Modern Asian Studies* 28 (3), 557–88.

Andersen, Walter K. and Damle, Shridhar D. (2005) 'RSS: Ideology, Organization, and Training,' in Christophe Jaffrelot (ed.) *The Sangh Parivar. A Reader*, New Delhi: Oxford University Press, 23–55.

Arora, Balveer (2002) 'Political Parties and the Party System. The Emergence of New Coalitions,' in Zoya Hasan (ed.) *Parties and Party Politics in India*, Oxford: Oxford University Press, 504–32.

Askandar, Kamarulzaman (ed.) (2005) *Understanding and Managing Militant Movements in Southeast Asia*, Penang: Southeast Asian Conflict Studies Network.

Banerjee, Sikata (2000) *Warriors in Politics. Hindu Nationalism, Violence, and the Shiv Sena in India*, Boulder, Colo.: Westview.

Banerjee, Sumanta (2007) 'Thirty Years after the Emergency,' *Economic and Political Weekly*, 4 August, 3193–5.

Banik, Dan (2001) 'The Transfer Raj. Indian Civil Servants on the Move,' *European Journal of Development Research* 13 (1), 106–35.

Bardhan, Pranab K. (2005) 'Nature of Opposition to Economic Reforms in India,' *Economic and Political Weekly* 40 (48), 4995–8.

Bardhan, Pranab; Mitra, Sandeep; Mookherjee, Dilip; and Sarkar, Abhirup (2009) 'Local Democracy and Clientelism. Implications for Political Stability in Rural West Bengal,' *Economic and Political Weekly* 44 (9), 46–58.

Basu, Amrita (1996) 'Mass Movement or Elite Conspiracy? The Puzzle of Hindu Nationalism,' in David E. Ludden, *Making India Hindu. Religion, Community, and the Politics of Democracy in India*, Delhi: Oxford University Press, 55–80.

Basu, Amrita (2001) 'The Dialectics of Hindu Nationalism,' in Atul Kohli (ed.) *The Success of India's Democracy*, Cambridge: Cambridge University Press, 163–90.

Basu, Tapan (1993) *Khaki Shorts, Saffron Flags*, Hyderabad: Orient Longman.

Berglund, Henrik (2006) *The Saffronisation of Civil Society. A Study of Hindu Nationalism and Organisational Life in Varanasi, Uttar Pradesh (EASAS Conference Papers)*, Online. Available at: www.sasnet.lu.se/EASASpapers/34HenrikBerglund.pdf (accessed 1 July 2009).

Berman, Paul (2003) *Terror and Liberalism*, New York: Norton.

Bhagavan, Manu (2008) 'The Hindutva Underground. Hindu Nationalism and the Indian National Congress in Late Colonial and Early Post-Colonial India,' *Economic and Political Weekly* 43 (37), 39–48.

Bhargava, Rajeev (1995) 'The Secular Imperative,' *India International Centre Quarterly* 22 (1), 3–16.

Bhargava, Rajeev (ed.) (1998) *Secularism and its Critics*, New Delhi: Oxford University Press.

Bhargava, Rajeev (2007) 'The Distinctiveness of Indian Secularism,' in T. N. Srinivasan (ed.) *The Future of Indian Secularism*, New Delhi: Oxford University Press, 20–53.

Bhatt, Chetan (2001) *Hindu Nationalism. Origins, Ideologies and Modern Myths*, New York: Berg.

Bhatt, Chetan (2004) 'Democracy and Hindu Nationalism,' *Democratization* 11 (4), 133–54.

Bhattacharyya, Dwaipayan (2009) 'Of Control and Factions. The Changing "Party-Society" in Rural West Bengal,' *Economic and Political Weekly* 44 (9), 59–69.

Boeckh, Andreas and Pawelka, Peter (ed.) (1997) *Staat, Markt und Rente in der internationalen Politik*, Opladen: Westdeutscher Verlag.

Bose, Sugata (1993) *Peasant Labour and Colonial Capital. Rural Bengal since 1770 (The New Cambridge History of India Vol. 3, 2)*, Cambridge: Cambridge University Press.

Boutron, Isabelle (2005) 'The Swadeshi Jagaran Manch. An Economic Arm of the Hindu Nationalist Movement,' in Christophe Jaffrelot (ed.) *The Sangh Parivar. A Reader*, New Delhi: Oxford University Press, 393–410.

Brass, Paul R. (1965) *Factional Politics in an Indian State. The Congress Party in Uttar Pradesh*, Berkeley: University of California Press.

Brass, Paul R. (1997) *Theft of an Idol. Text and Context in the Representation of Collective Violence*, Calcutta: Seagull.

Brass, Paul R. (2000) 'The Strong State and the Fear of Disorder,' in Francine R. Frankel, Zoya Hasan, Rajeev Bhargava and Balveer Arora (ed.) *Transforming India. Social and Political Dynamics of Democracy*, New Delhi: Oxford University Press, 60–88.

Brass, Paul R. (2003) *The Production of Hindu–Muslim Violence in Contemporary India*, New Delhi: Oxford University Press.

Brosius, Christiane (2005) *Empowering Visions. The Politics of Representation in Hindu Nationalism*, London: Anthem.

Carré, Olivier and Michaud, Gérard (1983) *Les frères musulmans. Egypte et Syrie (1928–82)*, Paris: Gallimard.

Chandra, Kanchan (2004) 'Elections as Auctions,' *Seminar* 539. Online. Available at: www.india-seminar.com/semframe.html (accessed 1 July 2009).

Chandra, Kanchan (2005) 'Ethnic Parties and Democratic Stability,' *Perspectives on Politics* 3 (2), 235–52.

Chatterjee, Partha (1998) 'Secularism and Tolerance,' in Rajeev Bhargava (ed.) *Secularism and Its Critics*, New Delhi: Oxford University Press, 345–79.

Chatterji, P. C. (1998) 'Reservation. Theory and Practice,' in T. V. Sathyamurthi (ed.) *Region, Religion, Caste, Gender and Culture in Contemporary India (Social Change and Political Discourse in India. Structures of Power, Movements of Resistance Vol. 3)*, Delhi: Oxford University Press, 293–313.

Chhibber, Pradeep and Eldersveld, Samuel (2000) 'Local Elites and Popular Support for Economic Reform in China and India,' *Comparative Political Studies* 33 (3), 350–73.

Chhibber, Pradeep K. (1996) 'State Policy, Rent Seeking, and the Electoral Success of a Religious Party in Algeria,' *Journal of Politics* 58 (1), 126–48.

Chhibber, Pradeep K. (1997) 'Who Voted for the Bharatiya Janata Party?' *British Journal of Political Science* 27 (4), 631–9.

Chhibber, Pradeep K. (1999) *Democracy without Associations. Transformation of the Party System and Social Cleavages in India*, New Delhi: Vistaar.

Chhibber, Pradeep K. and Nooruddin, Irfan (2008) 'Unstable Politics. Fiscal Space and Electoral Volatility in the Indian States,' *Comparative Political Studies* 41 (8), 1069–91.

Chibber, Vivek (2006) 'On the Decline of Class Analysis in South Asian Studies,' *Critical Asian Studies* 38 (4), 357–87.

Chopra, Rohit (2006) 'Global Primordialities. Virtual Identity Politics in Online Hindutva and Online Dalit Discourse,' *New Media and Society* 8 (2), 187–206.

Claerhout, Sarah and Roover, Jakob de (2005) 'The Question of Conversion in India,' *Economic and Political Weekly* 40 (28), 3048–55.

Clarke, Janine (2004) 'Social Movement Theory and Patron-Clientelism. Islamic Social Institutions and the Middle Class in Egypt, Jordan, and Yemen,' *Comparative Political Studies* 37 (8), 941–68.

Cofman Wittes, Tamara (2008) 'Islamist Parties. Three Kinds of Movements,' *Journal of Democracy* 19 (3), 7–12.

Cohen, Stephen Philip (2005) *The Idea of Pakistan*, New Delhi: Oxford University Press.

Das, Veena (2005) 'Privileging the Local. The 1984 Riots,' in Stephen I. Wilkinson (ed.) *Religious Politics and Communal Violence*, New Delhi: Oxford University Press, 91–100.

Dasgupta, Jyotirindra (2001) 'India's Federal Design and Multicultural National Construction,' in Atul Kohli (ed.) *The Success of India's Democracy*, Cambridge: Cambridge University Press, 49–77.

Dasgupta, Jyotirindra (2002) 'The Janata Phase. Reorganization and Redistribution in Indian Politics,' in Zoya Hasan (ed.) *Parties and Party Politics in India*, Oxford: Oxford University Press, 370–96.

Debroy, Bibek (2009) 'Dismantling the Steel Frame' *Seminar* 594. Online. Available at: www.india-seminar.com/2009/594/594_bibek_debroy.htm (accessed 1 July 2009).

Delhi Historians' Group (2001) *Communalisation of Education. The History Textbooks Controversy*, New Delhi: Jawaharlal Nehru University News.

Desai, Meghnad (1994) *The Economic Policy of the BJP*, Melbourne, Vic.: National Centre for South Asian Studies.

Desai, Radhika (2004) *Slouching towards Ayodhya. Three Essays*, New Delhi: Three Essays.

Devji, Faisal (2005) *Landscapes of the Jihad. Militancy, Morality, Modernity*, Ithaca, N.Y.: Cornell University Press.

Dirks, Nicholas (2001) *Castes of Mind. Colonialism and the Making of Modern India*, Princeton: Princeton University Press.

Dutt, Nitish and Girdner, Eddie J. (2000) 'Challenging the Rise of Nationalist-Religious Parties in India and Turkey,' *Contemporary South Asia* 9 (1), 7–24.

Eckert, Julia M. (2003) *The Charisma of Direct Action. Power, Politics, and the Shiv Sena*, Oxford: Oxford University Press.

Eckert, Julia M. (2004) *Partizipation und die Politik der Gewalt. Hindunationalismus und Demokratie in Indien*, Baden-Baden: Nomos.

Edwardes, Michael (1967) *British India, 1772–1947. A Survey of the Nature and Effects of Alien Rule*, London: Sidgwick & Jackson.

Elsenhans, Hartmut (1992) *Equality and Development*, Dhaka: Centre for Social Studies.

Elsenhans, Hartmut (1994) 'Fundamentalismus in der Dritten Welt als Herausforderung an das internationale System des 21. Jahrhunderts. Kultursoziologie oder Politökonomie als Therapie,' *Comparativ* 4 (6), 9–20.

Elsenhans, Hartmut (1996) *State, Class and Development*, London: Sangam.

Elsenhans, Hartmut (1997) 'Politökonomie der Rente als Herausforderung des Kapitalismus in seiner Genese und seiner möglichen Transformation,' in Andreas Boeckh and Peter Pawelka (ed.) *Staat, Markt und Rente in der internationalen Politik*, Opladen: Westdeutscher Verlag, 64–93.

Elsenhans, Hartmut (2001) *Das internationale System zwischen Zivilgesellschaft und Rente*, Berlin: Lit.

Elsenhans, Hartmut (2009) *Kapitalismus kontrovers. Zerklüftung im nicht so sehr kapitalistischen Weltsystem (WeltTrends Papiere 9)*, Potsdam: Universitätsverlag Potsdam.

Embree, Ainsli T. (1994) 'The Function of the Rashtriya Swayamsevak Sangh. To Define the Hindu Nation,' in Martin E. Marty and R. Scott Appleby (ed.) *Accounting for Fundamentalism. The Dynamic Character of Movements*, Chicago: University of Chicago Press, 617–52.

Engineer, Ashgar Ali (2004) *Communal Riots after Independence. A Comprehensive Account*, Delhi: Shipra.

Epstein, Gil S. and Gang, Ira N. (2004) *Understanding the Development of Fundamentalism (IZA Discussion Paper No. 1227)*. Online. Available at: http://ssrn.com/abstract=571722 (accessed 1 July 2009).

Erdman, Howard L. (1967) *The Swatantra Party and Indian Conservatism*, London: Cambridge University Press.

Farah, Taufiq (ed.) (1987) *Pan-Arabism and Arab Nationalism. The Continuing Debate*, Boulder, Colo.: Westview.

Farouk, Azeem Fazwan Ahmed (2005) 'Intra-ethnic party competition in plural society, the case of United Malays National Organization (UMNO) and Parti Islam Se-Malaysia (PAS) in Malaysia,' in Askandar, Kamarulzaman (ed.) *Understanding and Managing Militant Movements in Southeast Asia*, Penang: Southeast Asian Conflict Studies Network.

Fernandes, Leela (2000) 'Restructuring the New Middle Class in Liberalizing India,' *Comparative Studies of South Asia, Africa and the Middle East* 20 (1–2), 88–102.

Fernandes, Leela (2006) *India's New Middle Class. Democratic Politics in an Era of Economic Reform*, Minneapolis: University of Minnesota Press.

Frankel, Francine R. (1971) *India's Green Revolution. Economic Gains and Political Costs*, Princeton: Princeton University Press.

Frankel, Francine R. (2005) *India's Political Economy, 1947–2004. The Gradual Revolution*, New Delhi: Oxford University Press.

Frankel, Francine R. and Rao, M. S. A. (ed.) (1989) *Dominance and State Power in Modern India. Decline of a Social Order (Vol. 1)*, Delhi: Oxford University Press.

Frankel, Francine R. and Rao, M. S. A. (ed.) (1990) *Dominance and State Power in Modern India. Decline of a Social Order (Vol. 2)*, Delhi: Oxford University Press.

Frankel, Francine R.; Hasan, Zoya; Bhargava, Rajeev; and Arora, Balveer (ed.) (2000) *Transforming India. Social and Political Dynamics of Democracy*, New Delhi: Oxford University Press.

French-Davis, Ricardo (2000) *Reforming the Reforms in Latin America. Macroeconomics, Trade, Finance*, Basingstoke: Macmillan.

Froystad, Kathinka (2005) *Blended Boundaries. Caste, Class, and Shifting Faces of 'Hinduness' in a North Indian City*, New Delhi: Oxford University Press.

Frykenberg, Robert Eric (1993) 'Constructions of Hinduism at the Nexus of History and Religion,' *Journal of Interdisciplinary History* 23 (3), 523–50.

Fuad, Muhammad (2003) 'Limits to Radicalism in Indonesia,' *Seminar* 527. Online. Available at: www.india-seminar.com/2003/527/527%20muhammad%20fuad.htm (accessed 1 July 2009).

Fuller, C. J. and Bénéi, Veronique (ed.) (2000) *The Everyday State and Society in Modern India*, New Delhi: Social Science Press.

Fuller, C. J. and Harris, John (2000) 'For an Anthropology of the Modern Indian State,' in C. J. Fuller and Veronique Bénéi (ed.) *The Everyday State and Society in Modern India*, New Delhi: Social Science Press, 1–30.

Galanter, Marc (1998) 'Secularism, East and West,' in Rajeev Bhargava (ed.) *Secularism and its Critics*, New Delhi: Oxford University Press, 234–67.

Gang, Ira N.; Sen, Kunal; and Yun, Myeong-Su (2008) *Was the Mandal Commission Right? Living Standard Differences between Backward Classes and Other Social Groups in India (CEDI Working Paper 08–12)*, London: Centre for Economic Development and Institutions.

Garver, John W. (2002) 'The China–India–US Triangle. Strategic Relations in the Post-Cold War Era,' *NBR Analysis* 13 (5).

Ghosh, Partha S. (1999) 'Corruption in India. A Holistic Analysis,' in D. D. Khanna and Gert W. Kueck (ed.) *Principles, Power and Politics*, Delhi: Macmillan, 57–91.

Gold, D. (1991) 'Organized Hinduism. From Vedic Truth to Hindu Nation,' in Martin E. Marty and R. Scott Appleby (ed.) *Fundamentalism Observed*, Chicago: Chicago University Press, 531–93.

Gooptu, Nandini (1997) 'The Urban Poor and Militant Hinduism in Early Twentieth Century Uttar Pradesh,' *Modern Asian Studies* 31 (4), 879–918.

Gould, William (2002) 'Congress Radicals and Hindu Militancy. Sampurnanand and Purushottam Das Tandon in the Politics of the United Provinces, 1930–1947,' *Modern Asian Studies* 36 (3), 619–55.

Gould, William (2004) *Hindu Nationalism and the Language of Politics in Late Colonial India*, Cambridge: Cambridge University Press.

Graham, Bruce D. (1990) *Hindu Nationalism and Indian Politics. The Origin and Development of the Bharatiya Jana Sangh*, Cambridge: Cambridge University Press.

Graham, Bruce D. (2005) 'The Leadership and Organization of the Jana Sangh, 1951 to 1967,' in Christophe Jaffrelot (ed.) *The Sangh Parivar. A Reader*, New Delhi: Oxford University Press, 225–67.

Grare, Frédéric (2001) *Political Islam in the Indian Subcontinent. The Jamaat-i-Islami*, New Delhi: Manohar.

Groc, Gérard (2003) 'Islam et democratie en Turquie. Une nouvelle dimension,' *Revue des deux mondes* (4) 2003, 116–31.

Grover, Verinder (ed.) (1991) *Jayaprakash Narayan (Political Thinkers of Modern India Vol. 8)*, New Delhi: Deep & Deep.

Gunning, Jeroen (2007) *Hamas in Politics. Democracy, Religion, Violence*, London: Hurst.

Gupta, Dipankar (1982) *Nativism in a Metropolis. The Shiv Sena in Bombay*, New Delhi: Manohar.

Gupta, Dipankar (1997) *Rivalry and Brotherhood. Politics in the Life of Farmers in Northern India*, Delhi: Oxford University Press.

Gupta, Dipankar (2000) *Interrogating Caste. Understanding Hierarchy and Difference in Indian Society*, New Delhi: Penguin.

Gupta, Niti Das (1997) *The Social and Political Theory of Jayaprakash Narayan*, New Delhi: South Asian Pub.

Hansen, Thomas Blom (2002) *Violence in Urban India. Identity Politics, 'Mumbai,' and the Postcolonial City*, Delhi: Permanent Black.

Hansen, Thomas Blom (2004) 'Politics as Permanent Performance. The Production of Political Authority in the Locality,' in John Zavos, Andrew Wyatt and Vernon Hewitt (ed.) *The Politics of Cultural Mobilization in India*, New Delhi: Oxford University Press.

Hansen, Thomas Blom (2005) 'The Ethics of Hindutva and the Spirit of Capitalism,' in Jaffrelot, Christophe (ed.) *The Sangh Parivar. A Reader*, New Delhi: Oxford University Press, 371–92.

Hasan, Mushirul (1998) 'The Changing Position of Muslims and the Political Future of Secularism in India,' in T. V. Sathyamurthi (ed.) *Region, Religion, Caste, Gender and Culture in Contemporary India (Social Change and Political Discourse in India. Structures of Power, Movements of Resistance Vol. 3)*, Delhi: Oxford University Press, 200–28.

Hasan, Zoya (1993) 'Shifting Ground. Hindutva Politics and the Farmers' Movement in Uttar Pradesh,' *Journal of Peasant Studies* 21 (3–4), 165–94.

Hasan, Zoya (1998) *Quest for Power. Oppositional Movements and Post-Congress Politics in Uttar Pradesh*, Delhi: Oxford University Press.

Hasan, Zoya (2001) 'Changing Political Orientations of the Middle Classes in India,' in Imtiaz Ahmad and Helmut Reifeld (ed.) *Middle Class Values in India and Western Europe*, New Delhi: Social Science Press, 152–70.

Hasan, Zoya (ed.) (2002a) *Parties and Party Politics in India*, Oxford: Oxford University Press.

Hasan, Zoya (2002b) 'Introduction: Conflict Pluralism and the Competitive Party System in India,' in Zoya Hasan (ed.) *Parties and Party Politics in India*, Oxford: Oxford University Press, 1–36.

Heath, Oliver (2002) 'Anatomy of BJP's Rise to Power. Social, Regional, and Political Expansion in 1990s,' in Zoya Hasan (ed.) *Parties and Party Politics in India*, Oxford: Oxford University Press, 232–56.

Heimsath, Charles H. (1964) *Indian Nationalism and Hindu Social Reform*, Princeton: Princeton University Press.

Heuzé, Gérard (2000) 'Populism, Religion, and Nation in Contemporary India. The Evolution of the Shiv Sena in Maharashtra,' *Comparative Studies of South Asia, Africa and the Middle East* 20 (1), 3–43.

Himeur, Chihab Mohammed (2008) *Le paradox de l'islamisation et de la secularisation dans le Maroc contemporain. Essay sur le Parti de la Justice et du Developpement*, Paris: L'Harmattan.

Hoffman, Valerie J. (1995) 'Muslim Fundamentalists. Psychosocial Profiles,' in Martin E. Marty and R. Scott Appleby (ed.) *Fundamentalisms Comprehended*, Chicago: Chicago University Press, 199–230.

Huntington, Samuel P. (1993) 'The Clash of Civilizations?,' *Foreign Affairs* 72 (3), 22–49.

Jaffrelot, Christophe (1996) *The Hindu Nationalist Movement and Indian Politics, 1925 to the 1990s. Strategies of Identity-Building, Implantation and Mobilisation (with Special Reference to Central India)*, London: Hurst.

Jaffrelot, Christophe (1998a) 'The Sangh Parivar between Sanskritization and Social Engineering,' in Christophe Jaffrelot and Thomas Blom Hansen (ed.) *The BJP and the Compulsions of Politics in India*, Oxford: Oxford University Press, 22–71.

Jaffrelot, Christophe (1998b) 'The Bahujan Samaj Party in North India. No Longer Just a Dalit Party?,' *Comparative Studies of South Asia, Africa and the Middle East* 18 (1), 35–51.

Jaffrelot, Christophe (2000) 'The Rise of the Other Backward Classes in the Hindi Belt,' *Journal of Asian Studies* 59 (1), 86–108.

Jaffrelot, Christophe (2003) *India's Silent Revolution. The Rise of the Lower Castes in North India*, London: Hurst.

Jaffrelot, Christophe (2005a) 'The BJP at the Centre. A Central or a Centrist Party?,' in Christophe Jaffrelot (ed.) *The Sangh Parivar. A Reader*, New Delhi: Oxford University Press, 268–317.

Jaffrelot, Christophe (2005b) 'Work and Workers in the Ideology and Strategies of the BMS,' in Christophe Jaffrelot (ed.) *The Sangh Parivar. A Reader*, New Delhi: Oxford University Press, 355–70.

Jaffrelot, Christophe (2005c) 'The BJP and the 2004 General Election. Dimensions, Causes and Implications of an Unexpected Defeat,' in Katharine Adeney and Lawrence Sáez (ed.) *Coalition Politics and Hindu Nationalism*, London: RoutledgeCurzon, 237–53.

Jaffrelot, Christophe (ed.) (2005d) *The Sangh Parivar. A Reader*, New Delhi: Oxford University Press.

Jaffrelot, Christophe and Hansen, Thomas Blom (ed.) (1998) *The BJP and the Compulsions of Politics in India*, Oxford: Oxford University Press.

Jaffrelot, Christophe and Zérinini-Brotel, Jasmine (2004) 'Post-"Mandal" Politics in Uttar Pradesh and Madhya Pradesh,' in Rob Jenkins (ed.) *Regional Reflections. Comparing Politics across India's States*, New Delhi: Oxford University Press, 139–74.

Jayal, Niraja Gopal (ed.) (2001) *Democracy in India*, New Delhi: Oxford University Press.

Jeffrey, Craig and Lerche, Jens (2000) 'Stating the Difference. State, Discourse, and Class Reproduction in Uttar Pradesh, India,' *Development and Change* 31 (4), 857–78.

Jenkins, Rob (1999) *Democratic Politics and Economic Reform in India*, Cambridge: Cambridge University Press.

Jenkins, Rob (ed.) (2004) *Regional Reflections. Comparing Politics across India's States*, New Delhi: Oxford University Press.

Jha, Prem Shanker (2000) *The Fascist Impulse in Developing Countries. Two Case Studies*, New Delhi: Ms.

Jones, Kenneth W. (1989) *Socio-Religious Reform Movements in British India. (The New Cambridge History of India Vol. 3, 1)*, Cambridge: Cambridge University Press.

Joshi, Sanjay (2001) *Fractured Modernity. Making of a Middle Class in Colonial North India*, Delhi: Oxford University Press.

Judge, Paramjit S. (2004) 'Politics of Sikh Identity and its Fundamentalist Assertion,' *Economic and Political Weekly* 39 (35), 3947–54.

Kakar, Sudhir (1995) *The Colours of Violence*, New York: Viking.

Kandale, Frauke-Katrin (2008) *Der Islam in Indonesien nach 1998 am Beispiel der Partai Keadilan Sejahtera*, Berlin: Regiospectra Verlag.

Kanungo, Pralay (2002) *RSS's Tryst with Politics. From Hedgewar to Sudarshan*, New Delhi: Manohar.

Kashyap, Subhash C. (2003) *Anti-Defection Law and Parliamentary Privileges*, Delhi: Universal Law Pub.

Katju, Manjari (2003) *Vishva Hindu Parishad and Indian Politics*, Hyderabad: Orient Longman.

Katju, Manjari (2005a) 'The Vishva Hindu Parishad Abroad,' in Christophe Jaffrelot (ed.) *The Sangh Parivar. A Reader*, New Delhi: Oxford University Press, 429–35.

Katju, Manjari (2005b) 'The Bajrang Dal and Durga Vahini,' in Christophe Jaffrelot (ed.) *The Sangh Parivar. A Reader*, New Delhi: Oxford University Press, 335–41.

Kaushik, Asha (2001) *Politics, Symbols, and Political Theory. Rethinking Gandhi*. Jaipur: Rawat Pub.

Keddie, Nikki R. (1969) 'Pan-Islam as Proto-Nationalism,' *Journal of Modern History* 41 (1), 17–28.

Keddie, Nikki R. (1998) 'The New Religious Politics. When, Where, and Why Do "Fundamentalisms" Appear?' *Comparative Studies in Society and History* 40 (4), 696–723.

Khan, Hamid (2005) *Constitutional and Political History of Pakistan*, Oxford: Oxford University Press.

Khanna, D. D. and Kueck, Gert W. (ed.) (1999) *Principles, Power and Politics*, Delhi: Macmillan.

Kochanek, Stanley A. (2002) 'Mrs. Gandhi's Pyramid. The New Congress,' in Zoya Hasan (ed.) *Parties and Party Politics in India*, Oxford: Oxford University Press, 76–106.

Kohli, Atul (1990) *Democracy and Discontent. India's Growing Governability Crisis*, Cambridge: Cambridge University Press.

Kohli, Atul (ed.) (2001) *The Success of India's Democracy*, Cambridge: Cambridge University Press.

Kothari, Rajni (1964) 'The Congress System in India,' *Asian Survey* 4 (12), December 1964, 1161–73.

Kothari, Rajni (1970a) 'Introduction: Caste in Indian Politics,' in Rajni Kothari (ed.) *Caste in Indian Politics*, Hyderabad: Orient Longman, 3–26.

Kothari, Rajni (ed.) (1970b) *Caste in Indian Politics*, Hyderabad: Orient Longman.

Kulke, Hermann and Rothermund, Dietmar (1998) *Geschichte Indiens. Von der Induskultur bis heute*, 2nd edn, München: C. H. Beck.

Kumar, Ashutosh (2004) 'Electoral Politics in Punjab. Study of Akali Dal,' *Economic and Political Weekly* 39 (14–15), 1515–20.

Kumar, Krishna (1996) 'Hindu Revivalism and Education in North–Central India,' in Martin E. Marty and R. Scott Appleby (ed.) *Fundamentalisms and Society. Reclaiming the Sciences, the Family, and Education*, Chicago: Chicago University Press, 536–57.

Kumar, Sanjay (2004) 'Impact of Economic Reforms on Indian Electorate,' *Economic and Political Weekly* 39 (16), 1621–32.

Kuruvachira, J. (2006) *Hindu Nationalists of Modern India. A Critical Study of the Intellectual Genealogy of Hindutva*, Jaipur: Rawat.

Lakha, Salim (2007) 'From Swadeshi to Globalization. The Bharatiya Janata Party's Shifting Economic Agenda,' in John MacGuire and Ian Copland (ed.) *Hindu Nationalism and Governance*, New Delhi: Oxford University Press, 106–30.

Lall, Marie (2005) 'Indian Education Policy under the NDA Government,' in Katharine Adeney and Lawrence Saez (ed.) *Coalition Politics and Hindu Nationalism*, London: RoutledgeCurzon, 153–70.

Lapidus, Ira M. (1997) 'Islamic Revival and Modernity. The Contemporary Movements and the Historical Paradigms,' *Journal of the Economic and Social History of the Orient* 39 (4), 444–60.

Lele, Jayant (1995) 'Saffronisation of Shiv Sena. Political Economy of City, State, and Nation,' *Economic and Political Weekly* 30 (25), 1520–28.

Lübben, Ivesa (2008) 'Die ägyptische Muslimbruderschaft. Islamische Reformbewegung oder politische Partei?,' in *Moderate Islamisten als Reformakteure?*, Bonn: Bundeszentrale für Politische Bildung, 101–14.

Ludden, David E. (ed.) (1996) *Making India Hindu. Religion, Community, and the Politics of Democracy in India*, Delhi: Oxford University Press.

Ludden, David (1999) *An Agrarian History of South Asia (The New Cambridge History of India Vol. 4, 4)*, Cambridge: Cambridge University Press.

MacGuire, John and Copland, Ian (ed.) (2007) *Hindu Nationalism and Governance*, New Delhi: Oxford University Press.

Madan, T. N. (1997) *Modern Myths, Locked Minds*, New Delhi: Oxford University Press.

Madan, T. N. (1998) 'Secularism in its Place,' in Rajeev Bhargava (ed.) *Secularism and its Critics*, New Delhi: Oxford University Press, 297–320.

Malik, Nadeem Shafiq (1997) *The All India Muslim League, 1906–1947*, Islamabad: National Book Foundation.

Malik, Yogendra K. (1986) 'The Akali Party and Sikh Militancy. Move for Greater Autonomy or Sikh Secessionism in Punjab,' *Asian Survey* 26 (3), 345–62.

Malik, Yogendra K. and Singh, V. B. (1994) *Hindu Nationalists in India. The Rise of the Bharatiya Janata Party*, New Delhi: Vistaar.

Manor, James (2005) 'In Part, a Myth. The BJP's Organisational Strength,' in Katharine Adeney and Lawrence Saez (ed.) *Coalition Politics and Hindu Nationalism*, London: RoutledgeCurzon, 55–74.

Marty, Martin E. and Appleby, R. Scott (ed.) (1991) *Fundamentalism Observed*, Chicago: Chicago University Press.

Marty, Martin E. and Appleby, R. Scott. (ed.) (1994) *Accounting for Fundamentalism. The Dynamic Character of Movements*, Chicago: University of Chicago Press.

Marty, Martin E. and Appleby, R. Scott (ed.) (1995) *Fundamentalisms Comprehended*, Chicago: Chicago University Press.

Marty, Martin E. and Appleby, R. Scott (ed.) (1996) *Fundamentalisms and Society. Reclaiming the Sciences, the Family, and Education*, Chicago: Chicago University Press.

Mathur, Shubh (2003) 'Mapping the Enemy. Images of Islam,' *Economic and Political Weekly* 38 (37), 3875–8.

Mayer, Peter (2007) 'The Hindu Rate of Reform. Privatization under the BJP – Still Waiting for that Bada Kadam,' in John MacGuire and Ian Copland (ed.) *Hindu Nationalism and Governance*, New Delhi: Oxford University Press, 131–59.

McGuire, John; Reeves, Peter; and Brasted, Howard (ed.) (1996) *Politics of Violence. From Ayodhya to Behrampada*, New Delhi: Sage.

Metcalf, Barbara D. (2004) *Islamic Contestations. Essays on Muslims in India and Pakistan*, New Delhi: Oxford University Press.

Mishra, Ajit (ed.) (2005) *The Economics of Corruption*, New Delhi: Oxford University Press.

Mitchell, Richard P. (1969) *The Society of the Muslim Brothers*, London: Oxford University Press.

Mitra, Subrata K. (1996) 'Subnational Movements in South Asia. Identity, Collective Action and Political Protest,' in Subrata K. Mitra and R. Alison Lewis (ed.) *Subnational Movements in South Asia*, Boulder, Colo.: Westview, 14–42.

Mitra, Subrata K. (2001) 'Ballot Box and Local Power,' in Niraja Gopal Jayal (ed.) *Democracy in India*, New Delhi: Oxford University Press.

Mitra, Subrata K. and Lewis, R. Alison (ed.) (1996) *Subnational Movements in South Asia*, Boulder, Col.: Westview.

Mitra, Subrata K. and Singh, V. B. (1999) *Democracy and Social Change in India*, New Delhi: Sage.

Müller, Herta (2002) *Marktwirtschaft und Islam. Ökonomische Entwicklungskonzepte in der islamischen Welt unter besonderer Berücksichtigung Algeriens und Ägyptens*, Baden-Baden: Nomos.

Nanda, Meera (2003) *Postmodernism and Religious Fundamentalism. A Scientific Rebuttal to Hindu Science*, Pondicherry: Navayana.

Nanda, Meera (2004) *Prophets Facing Backwards. Postmodernism, Science, and Hindu Nationalism*, Delhi: Permanent Black.

Nandy, Ashis (1985) 'An Anti-Secularist Manifesto,' reprinted in *India International Centre Quarterly* (1995) 22 (1), 35–64.

Nandy, Ashis (1998) 'The Politics of Secularism and the Recovery of Religious Toleration,' in Rajeev Bhargava (ed.) *Secularism and Its Critics*, New Delhi: Oxford University Press, 321–44.

Nandy, Ashis (2003) *The Romance of the State and the Fate of Dissent in the Tropics*, New Delhi: Oxford University Press.

Nasr, Seyyed Vai Reza (1994) *The Vanguard of the Islamic Revolution. The Jama'at-i-Islami of Pakistan*, London: I. B. Tauris.

Nasr, Seyyed Vali Reza (2001) *Islamic Leviathan. Islam and the Making of State Power*, Oxford: Oxford University Press.

Nasr, Seyyed Vali Reza (2005) 'The Rise of "Muslim Democracy",' *Journal of Democracy* 16 (2), 13–27.

Navlakha, Gautam (1998) 'Invoking Union. Kashmir and Official Nationalism of "Bharat",' in T. V. Sathyamurthi (ed.) *Region, Religion, Caste, Gender and Culture in Contemporary India (Social Change and Political Discourse in India. Structures of Power, Movements of Resistance Vol. 3)*, Delhi: Oxford University Press, 64–106.

Nayar, Baldev Raj (2000) 'The Limits of Economic Nationalism in India. Economic Reforms under the BJP-Led Government, 1998–1999,' *Asian Survey* 40 (5), 792–815.

Noorani, A. G. (2001) *The RSS and the BJP. A Division of Labour*, New Delhi: Left-Word.

Ouaissa, Rachid (2005) *Staatsklasse als Entscheidungsakteur in den Ländern der Dritten Welt. Struktur, Entwicklung und Aufbau der Staatsklasse am Beispiel Algerien*, Münster: Lit.

Ouaissa, Rachid (2008) 'Aufstieg und Mäßigung des politischen Islam in Algerien,' in Holger Albrecht (ed.) *Politischer Islam im Vorderen Orient. Zwischen Sozialbewegung, Opposition und Widerstand*, Baden-Baden: Nomos, 143–64.

Pai, Sudha (1993) *Uttar Pradesh. Agrarian Change and Electoral Politics*, Delhi: Shipra.

Pai, Sudha (2000a) *State Politics, New Dimensions. Party System, Liberalisation and Politics of Identity*, Delhi: Shipra.

Pai, Sudha (2000b) 'New Social and Political Movements of Dalits. A Study of Meerut District,' *Contributions to Indian Sociology* 34 (2), 189–220.

Pai, Sudha (2002a) 'Electoral Identity Politics in Uttar Pradesh. Hung Assembly Again,' *Economic and Political Weekly* 37 (14), 6 April 2002, 1334–41.

Pai, Sudha (2002b) *Dalit Assertion and the Unfinished Democratic Revolution. The Bahujan Samaj Party in Uttar Pradesh*, New Delhi: Sage.

Palshikar, Suhas (2001) 'Politics of India's Middle Classes,' in Imtiaz Ahmad and Helmut Reifeld (ed.) *Middle Class Values in India and Western Europe*, New Delhi: Social Science Press, 171–93.

Parikh, Manju (1993) 'The Debacle at Ayodhya. Why Militant Hinduism Met with a Weak Response,' *Asian Survey* 33 (7), 673–84.

Parvathy, A. A. (1998) 'RSS and BJP,' *Mainstream*, 14 February 1998, 7–8.

Pati, Biswamoy (ed.) (2008) *The 1857 Rebellion*, New Delhi: Oxford University Press.

Pirzada, Sayyid A. S. (2000) *The Politics of the Jamiat Ulema-i-Islam Pakistan, 1971–1977*, Oxford: Oxford University Press.

Pleshov, Oleg V. (2004) *Islamism and Travails of Democracy in Pakistan*, Delhi: Greenwich Millenium Press.

Pruthi, R. K. (2004) *Rule of the British East India Company. A Study of the State and the Law*, New Delhi: A. P. H. Publications.

Riesebrodt, Martin (1990) *Fundamentalismus als patriarchalische Protestbewegung. Amerikanische Protestanten (1910–28) und iranische Schiiten (1961–79) im Vergleich*, Tübingen: Mohr.

Riesebrodt, Martin (2000) *Die Rückkehr der Religionen. Fundamentalismus und der 'Kampf der Kulturen'*, München: C. H. Beck.

Rothermund, Dietmar (1978) *Government, Landlord, and Peasant in India. Agrarian Relations under British Rule, 1865–1935*, Wiesbaden: Steiner.

Rudolph, Lloyd I. and Rudolph, Susanne Hoeber (1969) *The Modernity of Tradition. Political Development in India*, Bombay: Orient Longmans.

Rudolph, Lloyd I. and Rudolph, Susanne Hoeber (1987) *In Pursuit of Lakshmi. The Political Economy of the Indian State*, Chicago: University of Chicago Press.

Ruparelia, Sanjay (2006) 'Rethinking Institutional Theories of Political Moderation. The Case of Hindu Nationalism in India, 1996–2004,' *Comparative Politics* 38 (3), 317–36.

Rutten, Mario (2003) *Rural Capitalists in Asia. A Comparative Analysis on India, Indonesia, and Malaysia*, London: RoutledgeCurzon.

Said, Edward W. (2001) 'The Clash of Ignorance,' *The Nation*, 4 October 2001.

Sarkar, Jayabrata (2006) 'Power, Hegemony and Politics. Leadership Struggles in Congress in the 1930s,' *Modern Asian Studies* 40 (2), 333–70.

Sarkar, Sumit (2001) 'Indian Democracy. The Historical Inheritance,' in Atul Kohli (ed.) *The Success of India's Democracy*, Cambridge: Cambridge University Press, 23–46.

Sathyamurthi, T. V. (ed.) (1998) *Region, Religion, Caste, Gender and Culture in Contemporary India (Social Change and Political Discourse in India. Structures of Power, Movements of Resistance Vol. 3)*, Delhi: Oxford University Press.

Saxena, Kiran (2005) 'The Hindu Trade Union Movement in India. The Bharatiya Mazdoor Sangh,' in Christophe Jaffrelot (ed.) *The Sangh Parivar. A Reader*, New Delhi: Oxford University Press, 342–54.

Schick, Carol; Jaffe, JoAnn; and Watkinson, Ailsa M. (ed.) (2006) *Contesting Fundamentalisms*, Delhi: Aakar.

Schüler, Harald (1998) *Die türkischen Parteien und ihre Mitglieder*, Hamburg: Deutsches Orient-Institut.

Schwecke, Sebastian (2003) 'The Rationality of Politics in Uttar Pradesh. Towards a Re-evaluation of the Concept of Factionalism,' Heidelberg Papers in South Asian and Comparative Politics. Online. Available at: www.sai.uni-heidelberg.de/abt/SAPOL/HPSACP.htm.

Schwecke, Sebastian (2007) 'An Introduction to the Indian Party System,' in Klaus Voll and Doreen Beierlein (ed.) *Rising India. Europe's Partner? Foreign and Security Policies, Politics, Economics, Human Rights and Social Issues, Media, Civil Society and Intercultural Dimensions*, Berlin: Weißensee, 474–82.

Schwecke, Sebastian (2009) 'The Limitations of "Mere" Performance. The BJP and the Failure of its Yatras,' in Lidia Guzy and Uwe Skoda (ed.) *Power Plays. Politics, Rituals and Performances in South Asia*, Berlin: Weißensee, 57–78.

Sen, Amartya (1998) 'Secularism and its Discontents,' in Rajeev Bhargava (ed.) *Secularism and its Critics*, New Delhi: Oxford University Press, 454–85.

Sen, Amartya (2006) *Identity and Violence. The Illusion of Destiny*, New York: Norton.

Sengupta, Mitu (2008) 'How the State Changed Its Mind. Power, Politics and the Origins of India's Market Reforms,' *Economic and Political Weekly* 43 (21), 35–42.

Shah, Ghanshyam (1998) 'The BJP's Riddle in Gujarat. Caste, Factionalism and Hindutva,' in Christophe Jaffrelot and Thomas Blom Hansen (ed.) *The BJP and the Compulsions of Indian Politics*, New Delhi: Oxford University Press, 243–66.

Shah, Ghanshyam (2002) 'Contestation and Negotiations. Hindutva Sentiments and Temporal Interests in Gujarat Elections,' *Economic and Political Weekly* 37 (48), 4838–43.

Shani, Ornit (2005) 'The Rise of Hindu Nationalism in India. The Case Study of Ahmedabad in the 1980s,' *Modern Asian Studies* 39 (4), 861–96.

Shani, Ornit (2007) *Communalism, Caste, and Hindu Nationalism. The Violence in Gujarat*, Cambridge: Cambridge University Press.

Sharma, P. D. (1979) 'A Diagnostic Appraisal of the Swatantra Party in Indian Politics 1959-74,' *The Indian Journal of Politics* 13 (3) 1979, 51–9.

Sheikh, S. Naveed (2003) *The New Politics of Islam. Pan-Islamic Foreign Policy in a World of States*, London: RoutledgeCurzon.

Sheth, D. L. (1998) 'Changing Terms of Élite Discourse. The Case of Reservation for "Other Backward Classes",' in T. V. Sathyamurthi (ed.) *Region, Religion, Caste, Gender and Culture in Contemporary India (Social Change and Political Discourse in India. Structures of Power, Movements of Resistance Vol. 3)*, Delhi: Oxford University Press, 314–33.

Singh, Gurhapal (2005) 'Managing the Anti-Corruption Rhetoric. The National Democratic Alliance, Transparency and Corruption,' in Katharine Adeney and Lawrence Saez (ed.) *Coalition Politics and Hindu Nationalism*, London: RoutledgeCurzon, 136–52.

Singh, Prakash (2006) *The Naxalite Movement in India*, New Delhi: Rupa.

Smith, D. E. (1998) 'India as a Secular State,' in Rajeev Bhargava (ed.) *Secularism and its Critics*, New Delhi: Oxford University Press, 177–233.

Soros, George (1998) *The Crisis of Global Capitalism (Open Society Endangered)*, New York: Public Affairs.

Spiess, Clemens and Pehl, Malte (2003) 'Floor Crossing and Nascent Democracies – a Neglected Aspect of Electoral Systems? The Current South African Debate in the Light of the Indian Experience,' in Forschungsstelle für Völkerrecht und Ausländisches Öffentliches Recht, Hamburger Gesellschaft für Völkerrecht und Auswärtige Politik,

Verfassung und Recht in Übersee. Vierteljahresschrift für Fragen der Verfassungs- und Rechtsentwicklung der Staaten Afrikas, Asiens und Lateinamerikas, Baden-Baden: Nomos, 195–224.

Sridharan, E. (1997) *Duverger's Law, Its Reformulation and the Evolution of the Indian Party System (IRIS-India Working Paper No. 35)*, College Park: IRIS.

Sridharan, E. (2002) 'The Fragmentation of the Indian Party System, 1952–1999. Seven Competing Explanations,' in Zoya Hasan (ed.) *Parties and Party Politics in India*, New Delhi: Oxford University Press, 475–503.

Srinivas, M. N. (1962) *Caste in Modern India and other Essays*, New York: Asia.

Srinivasa, Inguva. 1971. *Gandhi and Development Theory. An Inquiry into the Economic Philosophy of Mahatma Gandhi* vis-à-vis *Modern, Western Theory of Economic Development*, Machilipatnam: I. S. Publishers.

Srinivasan, T. N. (ed.) (2007) *The Future of Indian Secularism*, New Delhi: Oxford University Press.

Srivastava, Manoj; Corbridge, Stuart; Veron, Rene; and Williams, Glynn (2002) 'Making Sense of the Local State. Rent-Seeking, Vernacular Society and the Employment Assurance Scheme in Eastern India,' *Contemporary South Asia* 11 (3), November 2002, 267–99.

Stein, Burton (1998) *A History of India*, New Delhi: Oxford University Press.

Stern, Robert W. (2001) *Democracy and Dictatorship in South Asia. Dominant Classes and Political Outcomes in India, Pakistan, and Bangladesh*, Westport, Conn.: Praeger.

Subramanian, Narendra (2002) 'Bringing Society Back in. Ethnicity, Populism, and Pluralism in South India,' in Zoya Hasan (ed.) *Parties and Party Politics in India*, Oxford: Oxford University Press, 397–428.

Suryaprasad, K. (2001) *Article 356 of the Constitution of India. Promise and Performance*, New Delhi: Kanishka.

Swami, Praveen (1999) *The Kargil War*, New Delhi: LeftWord.

Tambiah, Stanley J. (1998) 'The Crisis of Secularism in India,' in Rajeev Bhargava (ed.) *Secularism and its Critics*, New Delhi: Oxford University Press, 418–53.

Tambiah, Stanley J. (2005) 'Urban Riots and Cricket in South Asia. A Postscript to "Levelling Crowds",' *Modern Asian Studies* 39 (4), 897–927.

Tarkunde, V. M. (1995) 'Secularism and the Indian Constitution,' *India International Centre Quarterly* 22 (1), 143–52.

Tétreault, Mary Ann (2003) 'New Odysseys in Global Political Economy. Fundamentalist Contention and Economic Conflict,' in Mary Ann Tétreault, Robert A. Denmark, Kenneth P. Thomas, and Kurt Burch (ed.) *Rethinking Global Political Economy. Emerging Issues, Unfolding Odysseys*, London: Routledge, 3–20.

Tétreault, Mary Ann; Denmark, Robert A.; Thomas, Kenneth P.; and Burch, Kurt (ed.) (2003) *Rethinking Global Political Economy. Emerging Issues, Unfolding Odysseys*, London: Routledge.

Thapar, Romila (1989) 'Imagined Religious Communities? Ancient History and the Modern Search for a Hindu Identity,' *Modern Asian Studies* 23 (2), 209–31.

Thapar, Romila (2007) 'Is Secularism Alien to Indian Civilization?' in T. N. Srinivasan (ed.) *The Future of Indian Secularism*, New Delhi: Oxford University Press, 83–108.

Upadhya, Carol (2007) 'Employment, Exclusion and "Merit" in the Indian IT Industry,' *Economic and Political Weekly*, 19 May 2007, 1863–8.

van der Veer, Peter (1994) 'Hindu Nationalism and the Discourse of Modernity. The Vishva Hindu Parishad,' in Martin E. Marty and R. Scott Appleby (ed.) *Accounting for Fundamentalism. The Dynamic Character of Movements*, Chicago: Chicago University Press, 653–68.

Vanaik, Achin (1997) *The Furies of Indian Communalism. Religion, Modernity, and Secularization*, London: Verso.

Varadarajan, Siddharth (2002a) 'Chronicle of a Tragedy Foretold,' in Siddharth Varadarajan (ed.) *Gujarat. The Making of a Tragedy*, New Delhi: Penguin, 1–44.

Varadarajan, Siddharth (2002b) *Gujarat. The Making of a Tragedy*, New Delhi: Penguin.

Varshney, Ashutosh (1995) *Democracy, Development, and the Countryside. Urban–Rural Struggles in India*, Cambridge: Cambridge University Press.

Varshney, Ashutosh (2000) 'Is India Becoming More Democratic?' *Journal of Asian Studies* 59 (1), 3–25.

Varshney, Ashutosh (2002) *Ethnic Conflict and Civic Life. Hindus and Muslims in India*, New Delhi: Oxford University Press.

Verma, A. K. (2007) 'Mayawati's Sandwich Coalition,' *Economic and Political Weekly* 42 (22), 2039–43.

Voll, Klaus and Beierlein, Doreen (ed.) (2007) *Rising India. Europe's Partner? Foreign and Security Policies, Politics, Economics, Human Rights and Social Issues, Media, Civil Society and Intercultural Dimensions*, Berlin: Weißensee.

Wegner, Eva (2004) *The Contribution of Inclusivist Approaches towards the Islamist Opposition to Regime Stability in Arab States. The Case of the Moroccan Parti de la Justice et du Developpement*, Badia Fiesolana: Robert Schuman Centre for Advanced Studies. Online. Available at: www.iue.it/RSCAS/WP-Texts/04_42.pdf (accessed 1 July 2009).

Weiner, Myron (2001) 'The Struggle for Equality. Caste in Indian Politics,' in Atul Kohli (ed.) *The Success of India's Democracy*, Princeton: Princeton University Press, 193–225.

Wiarda, Howard J. and Mott, Margaret MacLeish (2001) *Catholic Roots and Democratic Flowers. Political Systems in Spain and Portugal*, Westport, Conn.: Praeger.

Widlund, Ingrid (2000) *Paths to Power and Patterns of Influence. The Dravidian Parties in South Indian Politics*, Stockholm: Elanders Gotab.

Wiktorowicz, Quintan (ed.) (2004) *Islamic Activism. A Social Movement Theory Approach*, Bloomington: Indiana University Press.

Wilkinson, Steven I. (2000) 'India, Consociational Theory, and Ethnic Violence,' *Asian Survey* 40 (5), 767–91.

Wilkinson, Steven I. (2004) *Votes and Violence. Electoral Competition and Ethnic Violence in India*, Cambridge: Cambridge University Press.

Wilkinson, Steven I. (2005a) 'Commentary: Putting Gujarat in Perspective,' in Steven I. Wilkinson (ed.) *Religious Politics and Communal Violence*, New Delhi: Oxford University Press, 391–404.

Wilkinson, Steven I. (2005b) 'Communal Riots in India,' *Economic and Political Weekly* 40 (44/45).

Wilkinson, Steven I. (ed.) (2005d) *Religious Politics and Communal Violence*, New Delhi: Oxford University Press.

Yadav, Yogendra (2000) 'Understanding the Second Democratic Upsurge. Trends of Bahujan Participation in Electoral Politics in the 1990s,' in Francine R. Frankel, Zoya Hasan, Rajeev Bhargava and Balveer Arora (eds), *Transforming India: Social and Political Dynamics of Democracy*, Delhi: Oxford University Press, 120–45.

Zaman, Muhammad Qasim (2004) *The Ulama in Contemporary Islam. Custodians of Change*, Oxford: Oxford University Press.

Zavos, John (2000) *The Emergence of Hindu Nationalism in India*, Cambridge, Mass.: Oxford University Press.

Zavos, John; Wyatt, Andrew; and Hewitt, Vernon (ed.) (2004) *The Politics of Cultural Mobilization in India*, New Delhi: Oxford University Press.

Zérinini-Brotel, Jasmine (1998) 'The BJP in Uttar Pradesh. From Hindutva to Consensual Politics?,' in Thomas Blom Hansen and Christophe Jaffrelot (ed.) *The BJP and the Compulsions of Politics in India*, Delhi: Oxford University Press, 72–100.

Index

Note: Page numbers in *italics* denote tables, those in **bold** denote figures or illustrations.

For Product Safety Concerns and Information please contact our EU
representative GPSR@taylorandfrancis.com
Taylor & Francis Verlag GmbH, Kaufingerstraße 24, 80331 München, Germany